KEEPING THE PEOPLE
WHO KEEP YOU IN BUSINESS

KEEPING THE PEOPLE WHO KEEP YOU IN BUSINESS

24 WAYS TO HANG ON TO YOUR MOST VALUABLE TALENT

LEIGH BRANHAM

American Management Association

New York · Atlanta · Boston · Chicago · Kansas City · San Francisco · Washington, D. C.
Brussels · Mexico City · Tokyo · Toronto

Special discounts on bulk quantities of AMACOM books are
available to corporations, professional associations, and other
organizations. For details, contact Special Sales Department,
AMACOM, a division of American Management Association,
1601 Broadway, New York, NY 10019.
Tel.: 212-903-8316. Fax: 212-903-8083.
Web site: www.amacombooks.org

This publication is designed to provide accurate and authoritative
information in regard to the subject matter covered. It is sold with the
understanding that the publisher is not engaged in rendering legal,
accounting, or other professional service. If legal advice or other expert
assistance is required, the services of a competent professional person
should be sought.

Library of Congress Cataloging-in-Publication Data

Branham, Leigh
    Keeping the people who keep you in business : 24 ways to hang on to your most
    valuable talent / Leigh Branham.
       p.   cm.
    Includes bibliographical references and index.
    ISBN 0-8144-0597-5
    1. Employee retention.   2. Labor turnover.   I. Title.

  HF5549.5.R58   B72   2000
  658.3—dc21   00–044793

Printing number

10 9 8 7 6 5

This book is dedicated to
Cheryl, Christopher, and **Spencer**
In appreciation for their love, patience,
encouragement, and support.

Contents

The Second Key—Select the Right People in the First Place   63

The Third Key—Get Them Off to a Great Start   137

Preface

Twenty-five years ago, I made a difficult decision, one that more people than ever before are making—I quit my job. But it was about more than just quitting a job. It was about finding the right fit. The right fit for me was to become a career counselor and job search coach, which involved making a radical career change.

Since then, mostly as a result of my fifteen years as a career transition consultant to more than a thousand displaced managers and other workers, my interest in what makes for a good fit between the individual and the organization has intensified. I have conducted hundreds of "exit interviews" with my clients, helping them understand what went wrong and how they got into the wrong jobs in the first place. The most gratifying part of the work is seeing clients become clearer about the kind of job, manager, and organizational fit they want, then go out and find or create it.

For three years I had the opportunity to consult with a large corporation in the design and implementation of an employee career development system that helped managers and their people come together and find ways to create the best fit within the organization. The company was successful in retaining countless employees it might otherwise have lost because it was committed to taking action.

In 1995, I wrote an article about how local businesses can compete for talent in a tight labor market by putting more time and energy into keeping the good people they already have. As a result, I was invited to speak to the Labor Deficit Task Force of a local chamber of commerce. In preparing for this talk, I began devouring every book, article, and news item I could find on the subject of employee retention, and I haven't stopped since. This book is the product (though not the end) of that research, and of whatever wisdom I have acquired as a coach and as a manager in my own business career.

In the 1990s the United States experienced an acceleration of economic, lifestyle, and demographic changes that transformed the traditional employment contract between the individual and the organization. The word "loyalty" has been redefined for all workers. So it is a challenging time to be a manager of people. The booming economy has created a seller's job market such as the country has never seen before. A recent issue of *Fortune* even ran an article bearing the title "The Joy of Quitting."

So the pressure is on you, the manager, to keep your most valued and productive people from quitting. How have you responded to that pressure? Some have responded by saying, "Retention is the responsibility of human resources," or "My hands are tied as long as the company can't pay enough or provide the right benefits." The feelings behind those responses are understandable. The human resources department does play a role. Pay and benefits are major factors. But if there is one thing I have learned in my experience and research, it is that good management is what keeps the most and the best. The best managers work hard at all the four phases of retention by which this book is organized—attracting, selecting, integrating, and coaching.

Taking primary ownership of keeping your key people, then, is your first step to success. The next step is to make a commitment, as many company leaders have done across the United States—to make keeping good people a strategic priority, to find out what is making them start thinking about leaving in the first place, to ask your people what it will take for you to keep them, to show them you know they have other lives, to let them know how much you value them, and to be creative and caring in responding to their needs. It is really about caring, commitment, creativity, and common sense—what I call the four C's of "keepology." Business leaders with common sense now know that talent retention is what drives customer retention and that customer retention sustains profitability. And that is what's most exciting. But make no mistake—it is work, and it does take time.

Here's hoping you enjoy that work and that this book, by presenting the leading edge of common-sense talent retention practices, helps you and your company create many long-term "good fits" in the days ahead.

Leigh Branham
Lake Quivira, Kansas
March 2000

Acknowledgments

For their encouragement, I am grateful to Bob Compton, John Cox, Lorrie Eigles, Bill Holland, Bill McDonald, and all my colleagues at Right Management Consultants who, over the past four years, never stopped asking, "How's the book coming?"

For their material assistance, I owe a special thanks to Fran Dennison, Patti Hanson, Bobbie Hoff, Jari Holland-Buck, Pola Firestone, Vince Sabia, Martha Seymour, Gordon Smith, Karl Sweigart, Kathy Voska, Karen G. Worth, and Don Wehe.

For their many suggestions and ideas for improvement, which helped shape the direction and the focus of the book, I wish to thank the many managers and human resource professionals who have attended our retention management seminars.

For his initial and continuing inspiration, I must also acknowledge the influence of my mentor, and mentor to many, Richard Nelson Bolles.

For her belief in the vision of this book, I thank my acquisitions editor at AMACOM Books, Adrienne Hickey.

And for all the above, my deepest thanks go to my wife, Cheryl.

INTRODUCTION

Why You Are Fighting the War for Talent

If you recruit, hire, train, and manage people, you are engaged in fighting the war for talent every day. In fact, you may be feeling "battle fatigue."

You are tired—tired of the resignations on short notice, tired of new hires leaving after only a few days on the job, tired of spending so much of your time and money on recruitment and on getting new hires up to speed, tired of the disruptions in customer service created when a key person quits, tired of asking your other workers to pick up the slack, and tired of the way it feels to be "fired" by one of your employees. In fact, you may be thinking about quitting yourself.

American companies and managers like you will continue to fight the war for talent for at least the next twenty years. Why? Here are some facts:

- By the year 2008, there will be 161 million jobs, but only 154 million people to fill those jobs—a shortfall of 7 million (see Figure I-1).[1]

Let's just deal with the present—what is the situation today?

- Each month, more than 13 percent of workers quit to take other positions. That's more than one in seven workers, compared to one in ten in 1995.[2]
- The average public company loses half its employees every four years.[3]
- Fifty-five percent of U.S. employees think often of quitting or plan to quit within a year.[4]
- The average time required to fill job openings has increased from forty-one to fifty-one days.[5]

Figure I-1. Projected job growth to projected workforce growth ratio.

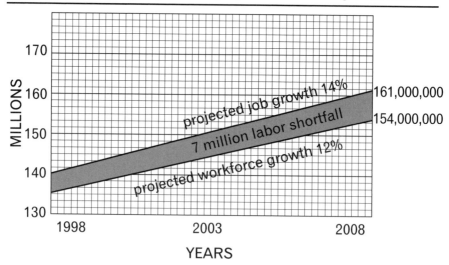

- Companies are typically spending $10,000 to $50,000 to replace and retrain after the loss of a departing employee, when only the tangible costs are added up.
- More than half of organizations report increasing turnover, and only 9 percent rate their retention efforts as highly successful.[6]

The situation has been created by a set of unprecedented business conditions. These include:

- The widespread employee anxiety, insecurity, and cynicism caused by waves of downsizing, reorganizations, and constant change.
- The erosion of the old "employment contract" that offered good employees a reasonable expectation of long-term employment, and the mutual loyalty and commitment that went with it.
- The continuing focus by company executives on achieving short-term economic returns instead of on building longer-term value based on investment in human assets. This has created unprecedented pressure on managers to reduce costs, do more with less, and get more out of fewer people.
- The disappearance of rungs on career ladders where jobs have been eliminated, further diminishing workers' hopes of internal advancement.
- The general decline in interest among workers in seeking traditional full-time employment, along with increasing options for self-em-

ployment and "free agent" contracting. In the year 2000, these "nontraditional" workers accounted for 50 percent of the professional workforce.

- A limited and diminishing pool of qualified available candidates to replace valuable employees when they do leave.

So how are companies responding to these conditions and facts?

While 75 percent of senior executives say that employee retention is a major concern, only 15 percent have made it a strategic priority in their companies.[7]

Instead of investing their time and money in innovative new retention strategies, many companies have adopted a "replacement mentality," and are spending more money than ever on recruitment, even as their turnover rates continue to increase dramatically. As Dr. John Sullivan, chief talent officer of Agilent Technologies, put it, that is like a doctor deciding to increase the speed of a transfusion when the patient starts bleeding faster.

How about you and your company? Try this quick quiz to gauge your own readiness to retain the right people:

Circle "Yes," "No," or "?" (Don't Know) for each of the following questions:

Yes	No	?	1. I know how much it costs me every time I lose an employee and have to hire and train a replacement.
Yes	No	?	2. I know why people leave my organization.
Yes	No	?	3. I know why people stay in my organization.
Yes	No	?	4. My turnover rate is below the industry/area average.
Yes	No	?	5. I am spending more time on retention than on recruiting.
Yes	No	?	6. Pay and rewards are linked to performance.
Yes	No	?	7. My organization trains managers to select, orient, coach, recognize, and retain good people and rewards us for doing these things well.
Yes	No	?	8. Our employees would say, if asked, that they are viewed as investments to be maximized instead of costs to be reduced.
Yes	No	?	9. My organization is a "preferred employer" in the community.
Yes	No	?	10. My organization is doing what it takes to retain valued employees.

Five or more "No's" or "Don't Know's" indicates that both you and your organization have considerable room for improvement in retaining your most valuable talent.

The continuing acceleration of the pace of change and the increasing demands on all managers have created a world where it is more difficult that ever to stop and "sharpen the saw." There is less and less time, it seems, to think about how the job has changed before we start interviewing, to orient new hires properly, manage employees' expectations, set performance goals, give feedback on employees' performance, recognize them when they perform well, discipline them when they don't, and know how to motivate different employees differently.

Still, a growing number of companies, big and small, are figuring out how to win the war for talent. They are thriving despite the obstacles because they have committed themselves to doing whatever it takes to keep their most valuable people. Why? Because they know that these are the people who keep them in business. They realize that if these people stay longer, they will get better at what they do and build stronger relationships with their most valued customers. This leads to long-term success in the marketplace.

In a service economy where a premium is placed on knowledge and direct service, the winners of the war for talent will also be the winners of the war for customers, market share, profits, and long-term value. The guidelines recommended in this book are based on the practices these companies are using, and their success stories are sprinkled throughout.

This book has three main objectives:

1. To help you gain a better understanding of the factors within your control or influence that can improve employee retention in your organization
2. To give you new ideas based on the successful practices of other companies
3. To help you develop an action plan for retaining your most highly valued talent

You will have the opportunity to review twenty-four practices that can help you meet these objectives. At the end of our discussion of each practice, you can rate how well you and your organization are already doing on that practice. You will consider using those you have not yet tried, and you will, I hope, gain a new perspective on some retention practices you may have underutilized in the past. At the end of the book, you will find a Selective Retention Action Plan that will help you identify your key people and learn specific steps you can take immediately to help keep them on board.

I do have one request. As your efforts to keep the right people begin to bear fruit, please send me your success stories as well (quiv4@aol.com) so that I may pass them on as I continue to train and speak to others on this topic.

Truths about Turnover

Truth #1: Turnover Happens

Turnover, like poverty, will always be with us. Achieving zero percent turnover is neither realistic nor desirable. People move on for a variety of unpreventable reasons—more money, better benefits, the appearance of greener pastures, partner relocation, the desire to be a full-time parent, to retire, to return to college, and so on. There may be nothing you can do about it.

As long as the job market is healthy, the pull of the headhunters' calls or a better job found on the internet will be hard for you and your company to overcome. Spending your energies trying equally hard to keep everyone is probably not a realistic solution. The wiser route for most companies is to focus on keeping those you can least afford to lose.

This begins with tracking "avoidable turnover rate" and defections that occur among targeted employees that you most want to keep and then finding out how the loss of such key people can be prevented in the future (see Retention Practice #4).

Truth #2: Some Turnover Is Desirable

Zero turnover is not desirable for a couple of reasons. First, if all employees stay and the organization grows steadily, most employees will be at or near the top of their pay ranges, and salary expenses will be extremely high. Second, new employees bring new ideas, approaches, abilities, and attitudes and keep the organization from becoming stagnant. Consequently, some amount of turnover is generally considered healthy.

As we know, sometimes the wrong people do stay, while the right people leave. As one manager put it, "Some quit and leave . . . others quit and stay." This, of course, begs the question, "Who are the right and the wrong people?"

The right people are the ones we want to keep, but they don't have to be "water-walkers." They are our steady performers as well. The wrong ones are usually those who are irresolvably incompetent, mismatched, disillusioned, plateaued, or burned-out. In some of these cases the company will need to initiate the turnover, often to the relief of the affected individual and their coworkers.

Truth #3: Turnover Is Costly

Do you know what turnover is costing your organization? Most managers have little idea. Two-thirds of 1,290 managers were unable to quantify the cost of turnover when asked in a recent poll.[1]

The cost of hiring and training a new employee can vary greatly—from only a few thousand dollars for hourly employees to between $75,000 and $100,000 for top executives. Estimates of turnover costs range from 25 percent to almost 200 percent of annual employee compensation.[2] These kinds of costs are tough to incur even when the turnover is desired.

We also know that turnover equates to reduced profits. The food service industry, for example, failed to produce profit growth parallel with increasing sales over recent years partly because restaurants did not do a good enough job of managing employee retention. Operators with annual turnover rates in the 250 percent range had average operating profits of 8.7 percent. Those in the 200 percent range had profits of 10.1 percent, while those with turnover rates of 150 percent had profits of 10.8 percent.[3]

We all know that turnover is costly; just how costly depends on what you consider to be turnover costs. To reach the most meaningful figure, your organization should focus on what it costs to replace the most critical, difficult-to-replace, top-performing people, because these are the ones you can least afford to lose. When figuring costs, consider both direct and indirect costs of hiring and replacing the departing employee. The table that follows will help you calculate the direct and indirect turnover costs that you incur during the time after an employee quits, including the time it takes you to hire a replacement and to get that new hire up to the level of effectiveness of the departed employee.

To get a better handle on what turnover may be costing you, go back and determine the direct costs involved in previous turnovers, and try to estimate the indirect costs. Of course, many of the costliest items are those that are the most difficult to estimate, such as revenue lost because of poor customer service while you are looking for a replacement. Try your best to estimate such costs, and fill in your direct costs below for the most recent employee you lost and had to replace. When you have totaled both direct and indirect costs for at least one individual, you will have started to get a handle on your true costs of turnover.

TURNOVER COSTS	ACTUAL or ESTIMATED COSTS
Direct Costs	
■ Recruitment Advertising	$_____
■ Agency/Search Fees	$_____
■ Internal Referral Bonus	$_____
■ Applicant Expenses	$_____
■ Relocation Expenses	$_____
■ Selection Testing	$_____
■ Medical Exam	$_____
■ Drug Screening	$_____
■ Background Check	$_____
■ Recruiter's Expenses	$_____
Indirect Costs:	
■ Employment Office Overhead	$_____
■ Staff Salary and Benefits for Processing Time	$_____
■ Management Time	$_____
■ Direct Supervisor's Time	$_____
■ Orientation Time	$_____
■ Training Time/Resources	$_____
■ Lost Opportunity Cost (Estimated)	$_____
■ Learning Curve Productivity Loss (Estimated)	$_____
■ Customer Service Disruption/Defections/Lost Business (Estimated)	$_____
TOTAL	$_____

Other inestimable costs include emotional costs, loss of morale, burnout and absenteeism among remaining employees, and loss of experience, continuity, and "corporate memory."

Truth #4: More Money Is Not THE Answer

As Peter Block wrote in his book, *Stewardship*, "Anyone who says they work just for the money has given up the hope that anything more is possible. . . . Our organizations do not have the money to really make sure someone will stay, and they usually do not pay so little that someone has to leave."[4]

This is good news. If money is not the "silver bullet" for reducing turnover, then you can save yourself the dollars you would have otherwise spent fighting wage wars and matching offers. This is not to say that money isn't important, because it is.

Talented workers want to feel they are being paid salaries or wages comparable to those other companies pay for similar work in the industry. They also care about being paid salaries or wages comparable to those being paid to others in similar positions who are making comparable contributions. When employees feel their pay is fair and comparable to that being paid by other employers, and when they have interesting and meaningful work, done in acceptable working conditions, supported by good management practices, the prospect of making a little more money in another organization where these softer factors are unknown is usually not enough to pull those employees away.

Still, an alarming 89 percent of managers truly believe that employee retention is largely about money.[5] "The only way to fight turnover is with dollars," a restaurant manager once told me. Many managers would prefer to believe that money is the answer, because it is easier to throw money at the problem than to take the time to grapple with the intangible, soft, seemingly uncontrollable and time-consuming issues of motivation and retention.

According to a recent survey, there are seventeen factors that have been found to contribute most to employee commitment, and money ranked tenth on the list.[6] Most surveys of this type have reported similar findings.

When it comes to pay, the most talented people seem to want something more—something most companies don't give—the assurance that the better they perform, the more they can earn. Linking pay to performance is a powerful, yet vastly underutilized, motivational tool. Only about 35 percent of U.S. workers truly believe that their performance has a significant impact on their pay increases.[7]

Truth #5: You, the Manager, Are in the Best Position to Fix the Problem

As a manager, you cannot coerce your employees into staying. The decision to go or stay is the employee's, unless, of course, you have decided to terminate the employee. And, as already acknowledged, some turnover is unavoidable.

There are other factors beyond your control as well—the economy, the supply of and demand for workers in the various positions you need to fill or refill, and your company's competitive position, market strategy, culture, management style, compensation/benefits structure, and human resources policies. You may feel that these are the very factors that make it hard for you to keep your most valued employees. The temptation is to become preoccupied with all the things that are wrong with your organization. It may seem as if you are swimming upstream in this struggle, but the danger in complaining or giving up is that you will become a powerless victim just when you should be taking action.

When it comes to keeping people, "managers trump companies," as the Gallup research on great managers shows.[8] In other words, what *you* do matters most in whether your people stay or go. One study showed that 50 percent of the typical worker's job satisfaction was determined by the relationship he or she had with the immediate supervisor.[9]

This is why managers of people, not human resources departments, must take primary ownership of employee retention. Many companies are floundering today in their attempts to improve employee retention because the primary responsibility and initiative has been placed with human resources instead of line managers.

So what can you do? If you manage other managers, you can start tracking how well they select and retain the right people. You can hold them accountable for specific results in these areas and reward them accordingly. You can partner with human resources in starting a retention task force. You can influence senior managers to make a needed change in company policy. You can ask each of your people to come talk with you before deciding to resign. Most of all, you can directly implement twenty-one of the twenty-four retention practices that follow.

Remember, you, the manager, are the front-line soldier in your company's fight to win the war for talent.

Truth #6: Reducing Turnover Takes Commitment

Most companies and most managers aren't committed to reducing unwanted turnover. They know the price they would have to pay—mostly the time they would have to invest in coaching, developing, motivating, and listening to their people.

Ultimately, it comes down to this question: Which is more expensive, the cost of doing the things necessary to retain your most valuable people, or the cost of losing and replacing those people? In recent years, more and more managers and companies have decided that the cost of losing and replacing their best people is the greater cost because they know that customer defections follow employee defections.

The companies that achieve dramatic reductions in turnover are often the ones at which the top executive or owner makes the commitment to do something about it. When the CEO is committed, the organization usually falls in line.

When senior management is not committed, however, and organizational practices, policies, and culture actually undermine employee retention, then a committed manager is at a distinct disadvantage. Though this can be a discouraging situation for a manager concerned about losing good people, he or she can still have an impact on the factors that most contribute to employee commitment. As we know, some units of an organization have much lower turnover rates than others, mainly because of the influence of one great and caring manager.

If your CEO is not committed enough to retaining the right people as a long-term business strategy, it may be only because he or she has not yet realized the cost implications and long-term business consequences of continuing turnover. Perhaps you and other managers in your organization can form a retention task force, do turnover cost analysis, research why key people are leaving in your areas, and make a report with recommendations to senior management. If you run the numbers, most CEOs, and CFOs, of course, will pay attention to them.

Why Good Performers Leave

Think for a moment about the jobs you've held and why you left them. Also consider any good performers who have left your current or previous employers. In how many of these situations did the reason for leaving originate from dissatisfaction with the job or work environment? Your reasons will probably fit into one of the following six most frequent underlying reasons that good performers leave:

1. *They see no link between their pay and their performance.* In exit interviews, departing employees most often say they left for "a better opportunity," which is usually taken to mean "more money." Actually, it often does mean they received a salary offer greater than what they were previously making, but there are usually deeper motivations involved.

Many top performers get calls from recruiters enticing them to pursue more lucrative positions with other companies. Yet they often decline to pursue these opportunities. Why? Because they are satisfied where they are.

The top performers who do pursue these invitations are usually dissatisfied in one or more key areas—growth prospects, lack of challenge, or a poor relationship with the boss. We refer to these as "push factors" because they push the employee in the direction of leaving the company. The recruiter's call, on the other hand, is a "pull factor" that stimulates the employee to take action.

One of the key "push factors" is the employee's inability to see any link between performance and pay. It is demotivating to most top performers when they work harder and smarter and get better results than their peers, yet receive the same percentage pay increase or bonus. Yet when the opposite situation exists—when employees know they will be rewarded monetarily in proportion to greater results—they become motivated, ener-gized, and less likely to leave. If, as the research shows, 65 percent of U.S. employees see little if any relationship between pay and performance, there is a ripe opportunity for senior management and compensation specialists to team up and change things for the better (see Retention Practice #2).

2. *They don't perceive growth or advancement opportunities.* The key word here is "perceive." If an employee perceives no growth or advancement opportunities, even when they exist, then for all practical purposes, they do not exist.

In a common scenario, an employee announces his resignation to his manager, who responds, "I'm surprised and disappointed. I had plans for you." This often happens because neither the employee nor the manager has taken the time to schedule a meeting where career options and oppor-tunities can be discussed.

Hidden opportunities can be found in companies of all sizes, especially when they are growing. But when employees become dissatisfied, they all too often start looking outside in "knee-jerk" fashion before checking out the inside possibilities. Moving internally has the advantage of generally being easier to bring about, but the options available in the red-hot job market may be just too tempting. Managers are at fault for failing to ask employees about their career goals, tell them about whatever plans they may have for them, and maintain an ongoing career dialogue.

On top of this, as is still the practice in many large companies, succes-sion planning goes on at the higher levels of the company, and those plans are kept top secret. Why not share these plans with the "high potentials" to encourage them and allow them to visualize the opportunities that oth-ers see in their futures?

3. *They don't see their work as important, or their contributions are not recog-nized and valued by others.* Remember the old story about the two stone ma-sons who are asked what they are doing? One replies, "I'm carving stone," while the other says, "I'm building a cathedral." Which one do you think is more likely to stay on the job? The cathedral builder, of course.

The point is that every employee must be made to feel that he or she is "building a cathedral." All workers need to believe that their work is centrally important to the success of the enterprise, whether the job is res-taurant server, housekeeper, data processor, or factory worker. This means that the employee's manager needs to convey, with strong belief, exactly how that worker's job is central to the company's mission.

The manager must also be willing to back up his statement of belief by offering variable rewards of some kind based on the employee's actual performance. Managers must also learn not to be stingy with praise, for this is a major factor in reinforcing the belief that the job is vital. If you are willing to invest the time to walk around catching employees doing something right, then your people will begin to believe their jobs must be important.

4. *They don't get to use their natural talents.* Many people take jobs out of economic necessity without giving much thought to whether the job will make use of their natural abilities. Likewise, many companies hire workers out of economic necessity, because they need a body in that position now more than they need the right person in that position. After a while, both employer and employee grow weary of the mismatch between talents and tasks. Eventually, one or the other initiates a reassignment or termination, creating another costly turnover.

It isn't easy to accurately assess an applicant's natural abilities, but the art and science of employee selection has advanced to the point where it can be taught, as we shall see in Retention Practices #6 and 7.

5. *They have unclear or unrealistic expectations.* New graduates often expect immediate challenge and rapid advancement. When it doesn't happen, they either "quit on the job" or quit altogether. Manual laborers sometimes quit because they realize after a few days on the job how dirty or greasy the work is. Office workers quit because they are assigned to a cubicle instead of the office they expected.

What's not happening in these examples? Employees are not being given a realistic preview of the job and the working conditions, often because those doing the hiring are afraid the applicant might not take the job if she were.

Employers have expectations as well—that the worker will show up on time, use good judgment, have the necessary abilities, get along with coworkers, and so on. Some of these expectations may be reasonable and some may not, but when they are not discussed openly there is a very real danger that the unwritten contract will collapse, and another turnover will result.

Sometimes, when employees resign to accept a job with another employer, they come to realize that their expectations about the new job were unrealistic. We call this the "greener pastures" syndrome. When they find that the new job is not what they expected, they sometimes even call the former employer, wanting to know if they can have their old job back.

6. *They will no longer tolerate abusive managers or toxic environments.* The job market has been too good recently for most workers to feel they have to stay in an environment where they must tolerate abusive treatment or unreasonable stress. In their book *Corporate Abuse*, Marti Smye and Lesley Wright present three types of abuse:

a. Systemic abuse, as when a company is not "walking the talk" and reneges on commitments

b. Structural abuse, generally caused by outside market pressures, where employees may feel "trapped in a bubble of fear and stress"
c. Deliberate abuse by individual managers, where the manager berates and negates employees instead of motivating them

An all-too-familiar type of abusive culture is what Smye and Wright call a "Culture of Sacrifice," characterized by:

- Excessive demands for personal sacrifices
- Continual crisis
- Demands on employees to be available at all hours
- Employees subject to unreasonable deadlines
- "Pony Express" management ("ride 'em 'til they drop")

Cultures of Sacrifice tend to yield the following results:

- Employee burnout, stress, depression, and turnover
- Absenteeism, accidents, and costly mistakes
- No energy for idea creation and risk taking
- Poor quality of life and family conflict
- Retention of passive, dependent employees[1]

Waves of downsizings and the proliferation of toxic and abusive companies have killed loyalty. It's no wonder that more younger workers than ever aspire to the dream of self-employment rather than their parents' dream of working for a large corporation.

Who *Are* the People Who Keep You in Business?

Put simply, the people who are keeping you in business are the ones you value the most, the ones you can least afford to lose, the indispensable ones, the hardest to replace, the ones who cost the most to replace, and the ones who are most critical to the success of your company's business strategy.

However you describe them, the time and energy you have available to spend doing the things it takes to keep them is limited. Too often managers spend way too much time dealing with their "problem" employees and nonperformers instead of proactively managing and working to retain their best and most valued employees. The price they pay for their perceived indifference is the resignation of key people at the worst possible times.

Ask yourself this question: Who are the employees you most want to keep?

Possible answers are:

- The most loyal workers
- Top producers
- The most experienced workers
- Good people managers
- Women and minority workers
- Those who best fit the culture
- Hard-to-find technical specialists
- Those who can best manage conflict
- Those who might go to work for a competitor
- Those who could take customers and revenues with them
- Those who could take secrets or valuable knowledge with them

In most situations, the two most important factors to consider are the cost and difficulty of finding a replacement and, of course, the value of the employee's contribution. From a performance standpoint, employees tend to fall into the following four categories:

1. *Star Performers (the top 10 percent or so).* These are your "most valuable players," the "water walkers," the high achievers who consistently exceed your expectations and those of your customers. You count on them to lead the charge toward the attainment of company objectives. Many of your present and future leaders will come from this group. As long as their needs are aligned with those of the organization, and they fit into your culture, you need to do everything in your power to keep them on your team.

One caution: When star performers become prima donnas instead of team players, they can become "problem" or "high-maintenance" employees. At some point, you may question whether they are worth the trouble. Or, you may decide that their contributions do make them worth the trouble.

2. *High Performers (about 20–30 percent).* Because they may not get as much attention and recognition for their consistently high-quality performance as the top performers do, this group is probably more easily recruited by your competition. They are key to your success because they usually meet and often exceed expectations. When matched with assignments that are an optimal fit for their best talents, high performers can become stars. Much of your "selective retention" activity must be focused on this valuable group.

3. *Steady Performers (the majority of employees, about 40–50 percent).* Though they may not achieve at the levels of the first two groups, these "solid citizens" are usually competent, reliable, and loyal. They may not be leaders, but they may be excellent followers. They usually get to work on time and are often willing to work overtime if they can be compensated for it. They may not want to work sixty-hour weeks; they usually want a balanced life with time for friends, family, and leisure interests. They may not be interested in climbing the corporate ladder, but many would like to believe that longevity with one organization is still possible.

Steady performers will respond to employers who create "worker-friendly" policies and management practices that recognize that employees have lives outside of work. They also want to work in organizations whose managers notice their contributions, not just their hours worked. When matched with a challenge that fully engages their "motivated abilities," they can become high performers. The largest segment of your workforce, this group should not be taken for granted.

4. *Poor/Marginal Performers (as much as 15–20 percent)*. These are the functionally ineffective workers—those who were mishired or misassigned into the wrong jobs, or those with bad attitudes, a poor work ethic, or a "victim mentality" that causes them to resist necessary change and to feel entitled to rewards they have not earned.

Though they are a minority of your workforce, poor and marginal performers account for the majority of errors, absenteeisms, accidents, and thefts.

These are the people you are paying to lower the quality of your product or service, to create customer discontent, and to increase your costs.

Selective retention is a process to be used by management to minimize the loss of those in the first three groups and to move those in the last group into other jobs where they can be more successful. In fact, one of the greatest causes of low morale among the top three performer groups is the continued retention of nonperformers. Sometimes the right job for these people is in a better-fitting job within another part of the organization. And, of course, often that right job is outside the organization.

Questions to consider:

- How might a manager passively encourage turnover among stars or high-performing employees?
- How do you know whether to develop, transfer, or terminate a non-performing employee?

Right People = Right Fit

Another consideration in selecting and keeping the right people is, of course, the types of people who are right for your organization from a values perspective. The most talented people fall into four main categories, according to an article by Charles Fishman in *Fast Company* magazine, in terms of the kinds of recruitment messages that prospective employers send out:

- *Message #1: "Go with a Winner."* Attracts those who want rapid advancement with a high-performing company.
- *Message #2: "Big Risk, Big Reward."* Attracts those who are willing to take a risk for the possibility of a big payoff.
- *Message #3: "Save the World."* Attracts those who mainly want a company with an inspiring mission or exciting challenge.
- *Message #4: "Lifestyles."* Attracts those who want better lifestyle benefits, a desirable location, or more flexibility.[1]

While these categories may be simplistic, they serve as a reminder that the right people for your organization need to fit your culture, business mission, and compensation strategy. Or, if your compensation strategy is not designed to attract and keep the right people, you may need to redesign it.

What Is Your "Employment Brand"?

What we are really saying here is that in a market-driven employment marketplace where the compensation for talent is fierce, smart companies will need to apply traditional marketing principles to achieve the status of "Employer of Choice."

Employment branding has been described as "the process of placing an image of being "a great place to work" in the minds of the targeted candidate pool. It is a concept borrowed from the business side of the enterprise. Product branding is designed to develop a lasting image in the minds of the consumers, so that they can automatically start to associate quality with any product or service offered by the owner of the brand. An employment brand does the same in that it creates an image that makes people want to work in the organization because it is a well-managed company where workers are continually learning and growing.[2]

Examples of companies with distinctive employment brands include: Southwest Airlines (employees have fun, so customers can have fun), SAS Institute (workforce friendly to the nth degree), Disney (great customer service training), Cisco Systems (leading-edge and fast-growing), and General Electric (long-term success built on progressive management practices), to name only a few. You can probably think of certain companies in your own community who continue to attract the right kinds of employees because of their distinctive employment brands.

Has your company established a "brand image" in the minds of those it is trying to recruit? Your employment brand image is really what people say about your company when they gather with their friends at weekend barbecues and describe what it's like to work there. Are they saying what you want them to say? If not, then you and others in management will need to build a new brand from the inside out. It does no good to advertise yourself as a great place to work if recruits buy that message, then come to find out that the reality is not what was promised.

As you reflect on the "best-fit" prospects you need to recruit, consider which of the twenty-four retention practices will serve you best in building the employment brand image that you hope to establish in their minds and in the minds of your current employees. Also, consider this: By building the right kinds of retention practices into the unit you manage, you can create an attractive employment brand image for your department within the larger organization.

Keys to Keeping the Right People

There is no one key or "silver bullet" answer to keeping the right people, unless it is the Golden Rule, or, better yet, what has been called the Platinum Rule—"treat others as they would like to be treated."

Keeping the right people involves doing many small things that also serve to enhance performance, motivation, and job satisfaction. You might call these practices and ideas "the leading edge of common sense."

Some of these practices you may already be doing, and some you may need to be reminded about. There may even be a few you have not considered. Take comfort in the fact that you will not have to equally apply all twenty-four of these practices in your company or department in order to have a positive impact. You will need to focus on the employees you most want to keep, however, and commit yourself to consistently applying those practices that will work best to retain them.

The retention practices I have studied seemed to fall naturally into four areas that more or less parallel the phases of an employee's life cycle in the organization:

The First Key: *Be a company people want to work for*. The organization's leaders must build a culture that models, encourages, and rewards commitment and attracts prospective employees by creating a reputation as an "employer of choice" in the community.

The Second Key: *Select the right people in the first place*. The hiring managers, in coordination with the human resources department (if there is one), must clearly define the talent needed, recruit from the right sources, screen, assess, and interview candidates effectively, and make the hires that will allow the organization to implement its business strategies successfully.

The Third Key: *Get them off to a great start.* The organization and its managers must integrate new employees in such a way that they are made to feel welcomed, valued, prepared, and challenged.

The Fourth Key: *Coach and reward to sustain commitment.* The manager and the organization both have roles to play in maintaining employee commitment, but it is the direct manager who must be alert to constantly manage the "performance agreement," recognize results, and facilitate employees' career growth and advancement.

Retention Practices Pre-Checklist

In this section we present a checklist of twenty-four retention practices organized according to the four main keys. As you scan the list, place a check in the box if you believe you as a manager generally engage in that practice or take that action.

Be a company people want to work for.

☐ 1. Adopt a "give-and-get-back" philosophy.

☐ 2. Measure what counts and pay for it.

☐ 3. Inspire commitment to a clear vision and definite objectives.

Select the right people in the first place.

☐ 4. Understand why some leave and why others stay.

☐ 5. Redesign the job itself to make it more rewarding.

☐ 6. Define the results you expect and the talent you need.

☐ 7. Ask the questions that require proof of talent.

☐ 8. Use multiple interviewers and reference checking.

☐ 9. Give a realistic job preview.

☐ 10. Reward employee referrals of successful new hires.

☐ 11. Hire and promote managers who have the talent to manage people.

☐ 12. Hire from within when possible.

☐ 13. Creatively expand your talent pool.

Get them off to a great start.

☐ 14. Give new hires the "red-carpet treatment."

☐ 15. Communicate how their work is vital to the organization's success.

☐ 16. Get commitment to a performance agreement.

☐ 17. Challenge early and often.

☐ 18. Train for autonomy and initiative.

Coach and reward to sustain commitment.

☐ 19. Proactively manage the performance agreement.

☐ 20. Recognize results.

☐ 21. Train managers in career coaching and expect them to do it.

☐ 22. Give employees the tools to take charge of their careers.

☐ 23. Know when to keep and when to let go.

☐ 24. Have more fun!

Generally, the more you checked, the better. You might be a little unsure about exactly what each practice involves, as some are more self-evident than others. As you read further, you will gain a better understanding of each practice, and you will have the opportunity to evaluate your organization's performance, and your own, on each of the twenty-four practices. Remember—you and your organization will need to focus on the ones that will work best to keep the people who will most help you achieve your particular business objectives.

THE FIRST KEY

Be a Company That People Want to Work For

Cultures of Abuse vs. Cultures of Commitment

There are certain companies in every community that have built reputations as companies where people want to work. They have become "employers of choice"—an enviable status in today's war-for-talent economy. Some, like Hewlett-Packard, have built this reputation over many years. Others, like the SAS Institute of Cary, North Carolina, have built such a reputation in just the past few years.

Both these companies have something in common besides excellent products—they treat their employees like family and with respect, with an attitude and philosophy of nurturing and caring. What is even more interesting is that both companies have become extremely successful industry leaders, and both have built that success by investing time and money in their people.

Companies have always given lip service to the idea that "people are our most important asset." In one survey of executives a few years ago, nine out of ten told researchers that people were their company's most important asset. Yet those same executives ranked "people performance" sixth in a list of seven key issues in determining the success of their businesses.[1] Many of these same executives are now waking up to the reality that in order to compete in the war for talent, they must finally start "walking the talk."

One notable example of an executive who woke up to the need for a new management style is Mort Meyerson, chairman and CEO of Dallas-based Perot Systems. In 1996 he wrote an article for *Fast Company* maga-zine, "Everything I Thought I Knew about Leadership Is Wrong," in which he confessed that he had spent years at EDS bullying his people into eighty-hour workweeks, emphasizing profit-and-loss "to the exclusion of other values" and creating a culture of "destructive contention."[2]

Meyerson realized, after leaving EDS for Perot Systems, that continu-ing the same kinds of management practices in his new company would mean risking "becoming a company where the best people in the industry wouldn't want to work." Through a series of culture change initiatives, management retraining, 360-degree evaluations, greater employee owner-ship, and heightened sensitivity to employee lifestyle needs, he trans-formed Perot Systems into an organization that can compete in the war for talent.

Still, there are thousands of companies that have not adapted to the new realities. Their leaders continue to see their people as factors of pro-duction, like fuel to be burned. When they see their employees coming, they see costs—salaries, benefits, and overhead, instead of investments.

They have put their employees into a situation where they have to work at a pace that is not sustainable. They seem to have accepted high turnover as a cost of doing business. These "cultures of sacrifice" seem to be saying to their people, "Go ahead—burn yourself out, and then you can leave." As one employee joked, "My company's version of flextime is 'work any eighteen hours you want.' "

It is no joke. The percentage of U.S. employees who report that they have experienced job-related burnout rose from 39 percent in 1993 to 53 percent in 1998.[3] In 1998, absenteeism rates, an early warning sign of turn-over, hit a seven-year high, up a whopping 25 percent from 1997![4] The reason cited: Burnout and work-family conflicts have increased the num-ber of unscheduled absences. This trend equates to higher rates of absen-teeism, increased health care costs, lower productivity and morale, and, of course, higher turnover rates.

Many employers still have a hard time accepting that so-called soft issues really matter to employees. Yet the "war for talent" is making it harder for employers to ignore these issues. In a recent study of 3,000 workers, 56 percent of employees said their companies failed to show con-cern for them, 45 percent said their companies failed to treat them fairly, and 41 percent said their employers failed to trust them. Partly as a result, only 24 percent of employees said they were "truly loyal" to their employ-ers and plan to stay for at least two years.[5]

Employers who create feelings like these end up being chronically short on talent but often remain oblivious to the fact that they themselves have created the situation.

Companies that truly regard their employees as assets in which to invest still seem to be in the minority. Those that do, like USAA, Starbucks, Men's Wearhouse, MBNA, Chick-Fil-A, Amgen, Nordstrom, and Motorola, to name a few, have some of the lowest turnover rates in their industries. By their actions, they say to their people, "We want to create an environment that attracts people, that makes them want to stay."

In his book *The Loyalty Effect*, Frederick Reichheld profiles companies that have worked to maintain a high degree of employee loyalty over the years as their primary strategy to maximize profits. These "loyalty leaders," as he describes them, "see people as assets rather than expenses, and they expect those assets to pay returns over a period of many years. . . . They view asset defections as unacceptable, value-destroying failure, and they work constantly to eradicate them."[6]

The author gives several examples of how the economics of loyalty leadership pays high dividends, among them:

- A. G. Edwards. This St. Louis–based brokerage found that four-year customer retention rates declined from 75 percent for customers who kept the same broker, to 61 percent for customers who had worked for two different brokers, all the way down to 53 percent for those who had three or more brokers.
- An auto service chain found that the top third of its stores in retention rates were also the top third in productivity, with 22 percent higher sales per employee. "Stores with 'low' turnover (100 percent on average) had profit margins more than 50 percent higher than stores with high employee turnover (averaging 150 percent)."

Reichheld laments the current state of affairs, where "U.S. corporations now lose half their customers in five years, half their employees in four years and half their investors in less than one. . . . Experience has shown us that disloyalty at current rates stunts corporate performance by 25 to 50 percent."

Loyalty leaders, on the other hand, such as Lexus, State Farm, and Chick-Fil-A, are committed to "creating so much value for customers that there will be plenty left over for employees and investors." Given enough time and patience, the strategy works like this:

- Phase 1: Provide superior value proposition to most profitable, and potentially, most loyal, customers . . . which leads to . . . .
- Phase 2: Business growth attracts and keeps the best employees, who take pride in delivering superior value to customers . . . which leads to . . . .
- Phase 3: Long-term employees get to know long-term customers

better, learning how to deliver still more value and reinforcing mutual loyalty . . . which leads to . . . .

- Phase 4: "Value proposition" is further enriched by cost reductions and quality improvements of longer-term employees, allowing the company to fund superior compensation and better tools and training . . . which leads to . . . .
- Phase 5: Spiraling productivity, coupled with increased efficiency in dealing with loyal customers, generates the kind of cost advantage that is very difficult for competitors to match . . . which leads to . . .
- Phase 6: Sustainable cost advantage and loyal customers who generate the kind of profits that are appealing to investors . . . which leads to . . . .
- Phase 7: Loyal investors behave like partners, stabilizing the system, lowering the cost of capital, and ensuring that cash is put back into the business to further enhance the company's value-creating potential.

Does your company's culture look more like a "culture of commitment" or more like a toxic or abusive culture that is indifferent to employee burnout and turnover? Use the following checklist to help you answer this question:

A Culture of Commitment:

————————— Views employees as partners.

————————— Recognizes the human needs of all employees.

————————— Invests in people as the primary source of competitive advantage.

————————— Communicates clear corporate mission, vision, strategy, goals, and objectives.

————————— Commits to long-term strategy and the people needed to carry it out.

————————— Reward system and management styles support the mission and strategy.

————————— Focuses on "managing the performance contract," not controlling the people.

————————— Puts a premium on employee involvement in new ideas and innovation.

————————— Focuses on results, not on who gets credit.

————————— Trusts employees enough to delegate.

————————— Tolerates "intelligent error" and experimentation.

Which results in:

_____ High-performing, confident, innovative, committed work-force

_____ Achievement of company mission and lasting competitive advantage

Cultures of commitment become "employers of choice" largely because their senior leadership teams create environments where three key retention management practices are put into place (Retention Practices #1–3). While these three practices are largely under the control of your company's senior leaders, this does not mean you cannot implement them yourself on a smaller scale within your own team, or that you cannot influence your senior leaders to start implementing them companywide.

RETENTION PRACTICE #1

Adopt a "Give-and-Get-Back" Philosophy

> Workers always give to the organization or firm in direct proportion to what they perceive themselves receiving from it.
> —Jack Hawley, *Reawakening the Spirit in Work*

Who comes first—customers or employees? Many companies that espouse the belief that the customer always come first actually abuse their employees in the name of customer service, thereby creating employees who take out their frustrations on those very customers.

Progressive companies have begun to recognize that the reverse is also true. By treating employees as number one, they are creating employees who will more happily and responsively serve the needs of customers. They have made the decision that they will give to employees in order to get something in return. This is a controversial philosophy in this age of entitlement, when employees already seem to feel unduly entitled as it is. Yet, it's difficult to argue with success.

It has been demonstrated that companies that institute practices designed to keep the workforce loyal have greater customer loyalty as well. One study reported that companies with employee turnover of 10 percent or less achieve customer retention rates 10 percent higher than those of companies with employee turnover of 15 percent or more.[1]

Who's Doing It

■ *Wilton Conner*, owner of a highly successful printing company that bears his name, has become an employer-of-choice in Charlotte, North Carolina, because Mr. Conner cared enough about his people (and his company's long-range profitability) to adopt the following "family-friendly" services:

- On-site laundry
- Free meals in the company cafeteria
- Handyman services at employees' homes provided by company janitor at reduced rates
- Nurse educators to explain health benefits
- Free English classes for non-English-speaking employees
- Van pools to help all employees get to work

These kinds of services send an important message to employees—that they are important enough to invest in, that the company cares about their welfare, that the company knows they have lives outside work and wants to make their lives easier so that they will have more energy and focus when they are at work. Employees have responded by working to help Wilton Conner create an unprecedented record of revenue growth and quality.

- The *Maids* franchise owner in Johnson County, Kansas, Alice Errett, goes to great lengths to keep good housecleaning workers. Here a few of her retention initiatives:

- Putting a full-service kitchen in the office so that workers can fix breakfast or dinner for themselves or their families
- Setting up a bilingual library of periodicals and books for her employees to read, providing all workplace written materials in both Spanish and English
- Becoming an expert in daycare and sick-child referrals, car loans, home loans, and even bail-bond resources
- Training employees in household budget management
- Providing team-building and interpersonal skills training classes to help workers get along with one another
- Paying for her employees' flu shots and vitamins
- Subsidizing a full-size county bus that picks up fifteen to twenty workers at two locations in another county and drops them off at work
- Offering a $5 bonus to team members' paychecks for each day a cleaning team gets no complaints

"I will do everything in my power to make it possible for the people who work for me to be healthy and be here," says Errett.[2]

- *SAS Institute*, of Cary, North Carolina, the software development company that ranked third on the list of *Fortune* magazine's 1999 list of "The 100 Best Companies to Work for in America," is a prime example of how a giving philosophy can yield a high return-on-investment.

SAS's strategy was to do everything it could to become an employer of choice. Here is a partial list of the benefits it provides:

- The best on-site childcare center in the state
- Workout clothes laundered daily
- Billiards, ping pong, volleyball
- Golf, tennis, tai chi, and dance classes
- Cafeteria with piano music
- Art on every wall
- Health clinic
- No limit on sick days
- Elder care coordinator
- Financial planning for college and retirement
- M&M candies distributed every Wednesday afternoon
- Company gates that don't open until 7 A.M. and close promptly at 6 P.M.

Some may call this "tree huggery." Others may react by saying that creating this sort of "employee utopia" is either unnecessary for retaining key people or beyond their company's financial means. But for SAS these practices represent an investment in attracting just the right kind of employees for implementing its business strategy. And the strategy is working.

Despite the fact that SAS offers its employees no stock options (practically unheard of in the software industry) and pays salaries that are no better than competitive, the company has achieved a 3.7 percent turnover rate, way below the 20 percent industry average. Given that SAS has 5,000 employees, that's 850 it is not losing compared to the competition.

On the basis of these numbers, the company's CEO, Jim Goodnight, says the company has calculated, using an average salary of $50,000, that it is saving $67.5 million per year, which allows it to spend an extra $12,500 per employee on benefits. The company's new benefits committee meets monthly to consider new benefits, which must meet three key criteria—do they fit the culture, do they affect a significant number of employees, and are they cost accountable?[3]

- The Kansas City–based Hereford House restaurant also understands the economics of giving before getting. Because it knows that its more experienced servers will average $1 more per tab than inexperienced servers, it provides better benefits, insurance, and tuition contributions (up to $1,200 per year) to servers who stay at least a year.

- Steve Wynn, CEO of Mirage Resorts, has made his company one of the most innovative and successful in the hospitality industry by demonstrating his belief that high employee morale will pay off in better customer service. To back it up, he spent more per square foot to build the employee cafeteria that he did on the hotel's coffee shop, and he decorated the back corridors that employees use in the same bright and cheery colors as the guest corridors.

Benefits provided by companies in *Fortune*'s annual list of the "100 Best Companies to Work for in America" include:

- Providing on-site dry cleaning, shoe repair, and beautician services (MBNA, Wilmington, Delaware)
- Providing $2,500 grants to support education of children adopted by employees (MBNA, Wilmington, Delaware)
- Allocating $50,000 per employee for training (Edward Jones, St. Louis)
- Giving grants of $3,000 a year per child for college tuition (Finova Group, Phoenix)
- Indexing health insurance premiums to income: The more you make, the more you pay (TDIndustries, Dallas)
- Encouraging managers, when responding to flextime requests, to "do what is right and human" (Edward Jones, St. Louis)
- Driving employees who work late into the night home by a free limo service (Goldman Sachs, New York)
- Offering free bagels and fruit every Tuesday and Thursday, plus free ice cream in the summer (CDW Computer Centers, Vernon Hills, Illinois)
- Allowing all employees to pick their own titles (Scitor, Sunnyvale, California)
- Giving employees laptops for telecommuting and keys to company buildings so that they can set their own hours (Great Plains, Fargo, North Dakota)
- Allowing employees to take twelve weeks at full pay to care for a sick spouse, child, or parent (AFLAC, Columbus, Georgia)
- Offering free prescription drugs made by the company, including Viagra and Prozac (Pfizer, New York, and Eli Lilly, Indianapolis)
- Giving new fathers and adoptive parents six-week paid leaves (Republic Bancorp, Owosso, Michigan)
- Offering "wheels on loan" if an employee's car is in the shop, "you've got it maid" discounts on maid service, and "gourmet to go" ready-to-eat meals (Valassis Communications, Livonia, Michigan)
- Providing on-site car rentals and shuttles to airport (Amgen, Thousand Oaks, California)
- Allowing 95 percent of employees to have flexible work hours and providing nap room with futons and dock space for kayaking commuters (WRQ, Seattle)

- Covering laser eye surgery (Merck, Whitehouse Station, New Jersey)
- Offering "wellness dollars" to employees who practice ten healthy behaviors (First Tennessee Bank, Memphis)
- Giving every employee a business card and a $650 ergonomic chair; allowing employees to include one nontraditional household member, including a sibling, in-law, domestic partner, or live-in nanny, in their employer-subsidized healthcare coverage (American Century, Kansas City)
- Kicking in $250 of support if an employee's child plays on a sports team (Qualcomm, San Diego)
- Providing employees with their own gardening plots on company land (Rodale, Emmaus, Pennsylvania)
- Making vacation days available on half an hour's notice (Capitol One, Falls Church, Virginia)
- Providing employees with limo service on their wedding day, plus $500 and a week of vacation (MBNA, Wilmington, Delaware)
- Reimbursing tuition costs 100 percent up to $9,600 per year (Bureau of National Affairs, Washington, D.C.)
- Providing $2,000 toward a down payment when employees buy a house in the working-class area where the company was founded sixty-one years ago (Third Federal S&L, Cleveland)
- Providing a room at the Four Seasons Hotel at no cost (Four Seasons Hotel, Toronto, Ontario)
- Granting thirty paid days off per year, along with free haircuts and manicures, two on-site gyms, an indoor lap swimming pool open all the time, and use of company jet for emergencies (JM Family Enterprises, Deerfield Beach, Florida)
- Picking up the entire health insurance premium for employees (Wegmans Food Markets, Rochester, New York)
- Offering eighteen days off in the first year of employment (VHA, Irving, Texas)
- Providing concierge services and free on-site massage (Finova Group, Phoenix)
- Sponsoring daily half-hour meditation sessions (Griffin Hospital, Derby, Connecticut)
- Creating "a city within a company"—full-service gym with personal trainers, indoor basketball court, hair salon, two restaurants, and a car wash (BMC Software, Houston)
- Having everyone, including the CEO, work in a cubicle and having no assigned parking spaces (Intel, Santa Clara, California)
- Permitting 90 percent of workers to use flextime and 30 percent to telecommute (American Management Services, Fairfax, Virginia)
- Hosting "reboot-your-mind" parties every Friday afternoon (National Instruments, Austin, Texas)

- Sponsoring an on-site clinic with seven primary-care doctors and five dentists to provide free medical and dental care for all employees and retirees and their family members (American Cast Iron Pipe, Birmingham, Alabama)
- Granting ten paid days for personal business and a week off at Christmas (Dell Computer, Round Rock, Texas)
- Allowing employees to take a break in meditation rooms or to play table tennis, pinball, or trashcan basketball; "the only dress code is that you must" (Sun Microsystems, Palo Alto, California)
- Eliminating employee premiums for health insurance (WRQ, Seattle)
- Providing free Starbucks coffee, an ultra-relaxed dress code, and generous time-off provisions (Janus, Denver)
- Creating an "e-doc" network of doctors who respond to e-mail advice seekers (Acxiom, Conway, Arkansas)
- Having an employee stock ownership plan (ESOP) to which the company contributes 15 percent of annual employee pay (W. L. Gore & Associates, Newark, Delaware)
- Offering employees free first-Friday lunches and installing a driving range behind the plant (Kingston Technology, Fountain Valley, California)
- Permitting unlimited accumulation of unused vacation time (Qualcomm, San Diego)
- Offering health club reimbursement if the employee goes three times a week (Synovus Financial, Columbus, Georgia)
- Offering two-week paid leave for new fathers (REI, Kent, Washington)
- Providing an extra paid week off between Christmas and New Year's (Lucas Digital, San Raphael, California)
- Offering six-week paid sabbaticals every four years (AutoDesk, San Raphael, California)
- Giving infant car seats to new parents (Valassis Communication, Livonia, Michigan)
- Allowing employees to use vacation condos with paid airfare (Fenwick & West, Palo Alto, California)
- Offering three weeks' vacation in first year (Capital One, Falls Church, Virginia)
- Scheduling free on-site health screenings, flu shots, and mammograms (J. D. Edwards, Denver)
- Having no assigned parking spaces, no titles on doors, and no dress code (BMC Software, Houston)
- Giving expectant mothers in their thirty-third week free parking near their offices (Bureau of National Affairs, Washington, D.C.)

- Offering full benefits, plus stock options and a pound of coffee, to any employee who works twenty hours a week (Starbucks, Seattle)
- Allowing sick days and personal days to be taken "as needed" (Genentech, South San Francisco)
- Offering free breakfast every day (Computer Associates, Islandia, New York)
- Allowing employees use of the company airplane in case of a family crisis (BE&K, Birmingham)
- Providing 100 percent tuition reimbursement with no cap (Johnson & Johnson, New Brunswick, New Jersey)
- Having a 401K plan that matches 8 percent of pay (AlliedSignal, Morristown, New Jersey)
- Offering health coverage to employees who work as few as seventeen hours per week (Federal Express, Memphis)
- Providing interest-free loans of up to $3,000 to employees who wish to buy a personal computer (Harley-Davidson, Milwaukee)
- Giving lifetime medical and dental care to each employee and his or her spouse if the employee stays with the company until retirement (ACIPCO, Birmingham)
- Giving window offices to employees at lower and middle levels while managers use interior offices (Quantum, Milpitas, California)
- Reimbursing childcare fees when parents travel on business (Union Pacific Resources, Fort Worth)
- Closing doors on Fourth of July and New Year's so that all employees can spend the day with their families (Nordstrom, Seattle)
- Giving parents four hours' paid time off per year to attend teacher conferences (Granite Rock, Watsonville, California)

You are competing with companies like these in the war for talent.

The shares of public companies on *Fortune*'s list rose 37 percent annualized over the previous three years, compared to 25 percent for S&P 500 companies, providing further proof that companies who give to their employees get returns in performance. But the real story here is that these companies are trying to help employees balance their personal and business lives and make their working lives more livable. Flexibility is an important theme, as the following breakdown of benefits shows:

Benefit	Number Offering
Flexible schedules	70
Job sharing	72
Telecommuting	87
Compressed workweek	89
Reduced summer hours	45

Telecommuting continues to grow in popularity as a tool for attracting and keeping a workforce that wants flexibility. "It's absolutely the number one way to retain employees," says Deborah Tuchlowski, manager of the telework program at Arthur Andersen in St. Charles, Illinois. "It's not a perk, it's a business strategy." Many other companies, Merrill Lynch, US West, and Cisco Systems among them, have reported reductions in turnover and in recruiting fees thanks to their decisions to allow telecommuting. "We have key technical people throughout the company who we wouldn't have been able to hire without a telecommuting policy," says John Hotchkiss, Cisco's human resources manager. Arthur Andersen has found that employees who work at home are 25 percent more productive.[4]

Popularity of Vacation Time on the Increase

In a 1999 survey, employees ranked paid vacation as the fourth most important benefit after medical insurance, pensions, and matched retirement savings plans. Those results show a dramatic change since 1995, when vacation ranked tenth among the top twenty-three benefits. In fact, employer understanding of employees' need for time off with their families ranked number one among the top ten things managers can do to increase workforce commitment.

Providing more vacation time is a viable strategy for small companies that have to compete with big companies, which can usually outspend them in compensation. Many companies have reduced the tenure required for more lengthy vacations. Other companies are doing away with sick leave days and giving an equal number of "discretionary days" instead. Allowing employees to carry over unused vacation time into the following year and offering cash payments for unused days are proving to be attractive retention tools, which are now used by 63 percent of companies.

According to Aon Consulting, providing more paid vacation may be one of the most effective strategies available for attracting and keeping front-line customer service workers.[5]

While turnover data were not available on all the top 100 companies, many in the Fortune year 2000 survey reported employee turnover statistics much lower than their industry averages. SAS led the way, with a voluntary turnover rate of 4 percent, compared to the software industry average of 17 percent. Enron's turnover rate was 4 percent, compared to 12 percent for the energy industry. Plante & Moran maintained a 6 percent rate compared to 25 percent for professional staff in the accounting industry. Synovus reported a turnover rate of 20 percent, compared to 49 percent at other banks. Pfizer's 1 percent rate among manufacturing workers was considerably less than the 10 percent of pharmaceutical manufacturing workers in general, and Lucas Digital's 5 percent for computer graphics workers contrasted with the 15 percent turnover rate among its competitors.

Two companies on the year 2000 list—Pella and USAA—have never had layoffs in their long histories. Three companies on the list—Southwest Airlines, Harley-Davidson, and Federal Express—have adopted official no-layoff policies. These companies aren't just being charitable. The policy itself acts as a retention tool, making employees much more likely to dig in and commit, even in tough times.

How New Benefits Are Born—Paying Attention to Employee Needs

You may think the *Fortune* list is a comprehensive one, but every year dozens of companies come up with new ideas for employee services and benefits because they have simply decided to pay attention to what employees need and want.

Quick Solutions has won local fame among the business community of Columbus, Ohio, by finding a unique way of giving and getting back. For consultants who stay with his company for at least three years, CEO Mike Quick pays for a monthly professional housecleaning service.

Some companies are now trying to win their employees' hearts through their stomachs, offering free gourmet food and take-home meals. Google, an on-line search firm, treats its seventy employees to free meals such as Moroccan-style Chilean sea bass, chicken breast stuffed with mushrooms and asparagus, and quinoa and corn chowder. At Target's Minneapolis headquarters, chefs prepare cookie dough that employees can decorate for the holidays and take home. Software firm Autodesk, in San Raphael, California, provides employees with meals they can take home at the end of the day. Ceridian Employer Services surveyed employers and found that more of them (36 percent) offer free food and beverages than offer telecommuting as a workplace perk.

What services and benefits do your people want or need to help bring balance to their lives or make their working lives easier?

PRACTICAL TIP: To find out what your people need . . . just ask!

Example: A Hyatt hotel restaurant manager simply asked his kitchen staff what would make their jobs easier. Their request—new knives and a new blender—was easy to honor. The manager has continued asking this question on a regular basis and, in most cases, has been able to give his people what they requested. The result is greater staff morale and a higher retention rate among kitchen staff.

Can you think of a service needed by employees in your company that you would like to provide? Have you asked your people lately? Has your company conducted an employee survey to find out what new benefits and services your workers would value most? With so many other companies doing innovative things in this area, perhaps yours should too, just to remain competitive.

Speaking of Giving and Getting Back—Don't Forget Training!

Fortune's "100 Best Companies to Work for in 2000" provided an average of forty-seven hours of training to each employee in 1998, a full day more than two years before. The number one company on the list, The Container Store, provided 135 hours of training to its employees in 1999. Instead of treating training as a frill, many companies are making major investments in employee education by starting corporate universities, building multi-million-dollar facilities, and offering generous tuition-reimbursement programs.

Marriott International keeps around 65 percent of its workforce annually, when most in the hotel industry only do half as well, through a comprehensive cross-training program that prepares workers at all levels for advancement. Trainees frequently move from hourly jobs into management ranks and take everything from coaching and mentoring to breakfast preparation.

These companies understand that there are several good reasons to invest in training: to give people the skills they need to achieve business objectives, to ensure that the company and its people keep pace with the rate of change, to teach basic competencies that many employees should have been taught in school, and, of course, to attract employees who will go only where they can stay current in their field.

There are three key reasons that retention-focused companies and their managers should invest in training for their employees:

1. It sends the message that they are valuable enough to invest in.
2. It contributes directly to the creation of long-term customer value.
3. Companies generally retain more of the people they train.

In fact, the percentage of employees who say they will change jobs within a year is lower among those who receive job-related training

(14 percent) than among those who don't (24 percent), according to Talent Alliance.[6]

Who's Doing It

■ The Men's Wearhouse built a 35,000 square-foot training center at its headquarters in Fremont, California. In one year it sent 600 "clothing consultants" through "Suits High and Selling Accessories University." New employees spend about four days in one of about thirty sessions held yearly at a cost to the company of $1 million. The company, which has invested far more in training than have most of its competitors, also has a significantly lower turnover than most of them.

■ Edward D. Jones immerses new brokers in seventeen weeks of classes and study sessions at a cost of $50,000–$70,000 per head. "We consider training an investment rather than an expense," explains Dan Timm, a principal of the firm. "If we don't prepare our people well, we have not served the firm."[7]

■ Computer Associates enrolls newly hired computer science graduates in a three-and-a-half-month course in the company's software technology, and training for all employees continues at the rate of 120 hours per year.

■ Taco, Inc., a heating and cooling equipment manufacturer in Cranston, Rhode Island, created a Learning Center after investing $15 million in plant and equipment costs over a five-year period. The company made this offer to their employees: It would provide employees with the opportunity to learn the necessary new skills, the employees would take advantage of that opportunity, and the company would not eliminate any jobs as it introduced more sophisticated technology. The courses included instruction on everything from how to operate the sophisticated equipment, to English as a second language, to math skills, to how to use a dictionary, to how to handle a checking account. The company even taught a mandatory course on what the different departments do so that everybody in the plant was exposed to some training in marketing, sales, human resources, and quality control. In the first year, about 450 of the company's 470 employees took courses, most of which were optional and taught on company time.

Since the creation of the Learning Center, Taco's annual employee turnover rate has shrunk to less than 1 percent, and revenues have grown 15–20 percent annually. The company's president, John H. White, believes the Learning Center was an integral part of the company's turnaround, because employees will give more in their jobs "the more they feel you're trying to help them. The payback is incredible."[8] The lesson here is that training is more effective the more it reflects a genuine concern for the employee as well as for the company.

Turnover is a major problem for all organizations, because there is a direct correlation between the rate of turnover and the quality of customer service. Turnover can be an especially serious problem for a small or medium-size business such as Taco, Inc., because a handful of people are likely to carry broad responsibilities and have strong personal relationships with key customers. Investing in training for these valued employees helps create a bond between employee and employer that encourages workers to stay.

What Kinds of Training Do Your People Need?

The best kind of training is that which helps your people do their jobs better and bring more value to the company. The best place to start is with the company's business strategies and operational concerns; you need to ask, "What skills do my people need to best meet these strategies and address these concerns?" In other words, employee training should be driven by business objectives, not by the training programs themselves.

The American Society for Training and Development (ASTD) has identified the skills companies will most desire in the workers of the future. They include learning, reading, writing, computation, and communication skills, personal management skills, adaptability, teamwork, and influencing others.

Emerging retention-focused trends in training include:

- Use of "financial literacy" or "open book management," which is designed to teach employees the financial workings of the company so that they can become more fully-empowered business partners (this is often used to supplement employee-ownership, as at Springfield Remanufacturing Company, in Springfield, Missouri, and Robbie Manufacturing, in Kansas City).

Robbie's CEO, Irv Robinson, shows his employees everything from profit-and-loss statements to sales projections to statements explaining the reasons for management decisions and how their jobs fit into the big picture. The company has launched Robbie University, a program designed to teach all 125 employees more about the ins and outs of the business.

- Having CEOs conduct new employee orientations or teach management development classes and more powerfully communicating the company's values and passing on keys to success (Jack Welch, chairman of General Electric, is the best-known example).

- "Level-to-level" training in which managers learn a competency, then teach it to their direct reports only after they have modeled the skill on the job (Bill Brandt, American Woodmark Corporation).

To start expanding training in your own company, look first at your business objectives and the results expected from key employees. Consider having your employees complete a training needs survey, or, more simply, ask them what kinds of training would help them the most in doing their jobs and better serving their customers.

To maximize retention among high performers, consider on-the-job cross-training or rotations in different functional areas to increase employees' long-term value and versatility. Also, make sure the managers of your most critical people are trained in the interactive/people skills—interviewing, coaching, delegating, empowering, motivating—they will need to put these ideas to good use. For additional assistance, contact your local chapter of the American Society for Training & Development (ASTD).

Finally, seek to avoid the two most common factors that sabotage company training efforts—trainers who ignore organizational business realities and managers who fail to support and reinforce the training.

Giving Means More Than Just Training and Benefits

As a manager, you may not be able to decide what benefits and training to give your people, but you do hold the keys to giving what matters most—simply caring about your people as people, showing your appreciation, and treating them with respect. In fact, there is a danger in giving as much attention as I have already to training and benefits: It may cause some managers to forget that the most important thing the company can give to an employee is good management. Managers who abuse and belittle their people account for thousands of turnovers each day.

In his book *Brutal Bosses and Their Prey,* Harvey Hornstein presents the strategies that abusive managers use to cope with their own pressures and then pass them on to their subordinates. He describes several different types of abusive managers—Dehumanizers (who transform subordinates into faceless victims), Blamers (who treat workers like wayward children), and Rationalizers (who justify abuse by focusing on some greater corporate good). Other types of abusive managers are just plain malicious—Conquerors (who are obsessed with demonstrating their personal power), Performers (who try to make their own work seem more important by denigrating that of others), and Manipulators (who tend to "waffle, dancing to and fro on the periphery of an idea, until the matter's success or failure becomes clear").[9]

Many managers don't even know when they are abusive, and sometimes simple lack of sensitivity is enough to drive an employee away. One employee reported that he quit the company where he and his parents had worked for decades because of one act by his former employer "that showed such a profound lack of concern that he could not brush it off."[10] His boss ordered him to fly to a monthly budget meeting in a distant city even though his pregnant wife was three days overdue. By the time he got a phone call telling him that his wife was to undergo a Caesarean section, it was too late to catch a plane home.

Much abuse and insensitivity comes from selecting the wrong people for managerial positions in the first place (see Retention Practice #11). But most managers can learn to become less abusive and more caring, especially when their organizations stop tolerating such behavior. As they come to understand that this kind of behavior is causing the loss of key talent during a severe talent shortage and that the survival of their businesses is being threatened, top executives of many companies are no longer tolerating abusive managerial behavior. They are taking corrective action, which may be one or more of the following actions:

- Immediate corrective feedback
- Negative performance review
- Withholding of bonus or salary increase
- Transfer or reassignment to a nonmanagerial position
- 360-degree feedback with developmental coaching
- Referral to a psychologist in the Employee Assistance Program

If you manage an abusive or dysfunctional manager, consider taking these actions immediately. If you think your own abusive behavior may have resulted in the loss of one or more valued employees, seek feedback to confirm how you are coming across so that you can begin to take corrective action on your own or seek help from your company.

Twelve Easy Ways You Can Give and Get Back Every Day

It doesn't cost much to gain the trust, respect, and loyalty of your people. These intangibles will come back to you if you will just start giving in small, consistent, and tangible ways:

1. Smile, make eye contact, and say "good morning" to every person you supervise. Continue to acknowledge each person throughout the day.

2. Stop every now and then to ask them sincerely, "How are you doing?"
3. When they speak, really listen, and don't interrupt.
4. Ask, don't tell; say please and thank you (just like your mother taught you).
5. Be generous with praise at every opportunity.
6. Correct people only in private, not in front of coworkers.
7. Respect, even celebrate, those on your team who are different; they bring a diversity of perspective, background, and strength that all teams need.
8. When you say you will do something, do it. Honor your commitments to your staff.
9. Give honest and constructive feedback, and tell the truth about what's happening in the organization.
10. Trust people to do the job well without your constant monitoring.
11. When one of your staff members faces a personal crisis, serious illness, or emergency, do everything in your power to help the person through it.
12. Act as if you are there to serve your employees, not the other way around.

Now it's time for you to give your organization and yourself as a manager a grade on Retention Practice #1: "Adopt A 'Give-and-Get-Back' Philosophy."

How good a job is your organization doing in this area?

Circle one: (A) Excellent   (B) Very good   (C) Good   (D) Fair   (F) Poor

How good a job are you as a manager doing on this practice?

Circle one: (A) Excellent   (B) Very good   (C) Good   (D) Fair   (F) Poor

How important do you believe this practice is to your organization's strategy to attract and retain the talent necessary to meet its business objectives?

Circle one: (A) Critical (B) Very important (C) Somewhat important
        (D) Not important

What can the organization do to improve on this practice?

What can you as a manager do to improve on this practice?

RETENTION PRACTICE #2

Measure What Counts and Pay for It

Small wonder that when I ask groups to raise their hands if they feel they are paid for performance, 90 percent of them miss out on this chance for exercise.

—Peter Block, *Stewardship*

What role does money play in keeping the right people? We know that what people earn in their jobs has a unique importance to them. Because it represents what their employers believe they are worth, it affects their self-esteem. Pay, for better or worse, places people in a socioeconomic niche. It determines what they can and cannot buy and provide for their families. All these factors make employee compensation an emotional issue.

Yet, interestingly enough, in survey after survey, pay ranks behind factors such as using one's talents, meeting a challenge, having a good manager, pursuing meaningful work, and having opportunity for advancement as a motivator of both performance and commitment. Of course, we cannot hope to retain the right people without first paying them equitably on the basis of what others in the same organization are making and paying them competitively measured against what other companies in the same industry are paying for similar work. Once we have done that, the softer factors we have cited begin to take on more importance. It should be noted that pay does seem to motivate some employees more than others, such as the "high-risk, high-reward" types, and it can be an effective driver of short-term achievement.

Retention-focused companies, in their attempts to build "cultures of commitment" based on partnership and empowerment, seem to be looking to new pay practices, not so much to drive performance, but to:

- Send employees a strong message about what results are valued.
- Recognize and reinforce important contributions so that employees feel valued.
- Provide a sense of "emotional ownership" and increased commitment that comes from giving employees "a piece of the action."
- Maintain or cut fixed payroll costs and allocate variable pay to the employees they most want to attract and keep.

In 2000, about two-thirds of large and medium-size companies offered some kind of variable pay, such as profit sharing or bonus awards, to their employees, compared to fewer than 50 percent in 1990.

"Who Says We Pay for Performance?"

For years companies said they paid for performance when they really did not. Many companies justly earned the cynicism of their employees by force-ranking them to determine which of the lucky few would be subjectively judged by their supervisors as worthy of receiving a 3 percent or 4 percent yearly "merit pay" increase.

Only about a third of U.S. workers and about half of all managers say they see any connection between their performance and the pay increases they receive. This means that most companies and their managers are getting little or no reinforcement value out of what could be their most powerful retention tool—the true linkage of pay with performance.

In a recent survey, 2,000 managers were asked the difference between a top performer and a below-average performer at the same pay grade, expressed as a percentage. The average answer was 100 percent. When the managers were asked what the typical pay difference is between top and average performers in their companies, the answer was 5 percent to 10 percent.[1]

Figure 2-1 shows that there are really four critical linkages needed to connect performance with rewards.

A breakdown in one or more of these four linkages can occur for any of the following reasons:

1. Individual performance is difficult to measure in many jobs.
2. Managers are hesitant to evaluate employee performance.
3. The organization does not hold employees accountable for specific outcomes.
4. Traditional pay systems hinder performance recognition.

There are other complicating factors as well. In their attempt to rein in salaries, many employers continue to limit annual raises to a paltry

Figure 2-1. The Performance Measurement Cycle[2].

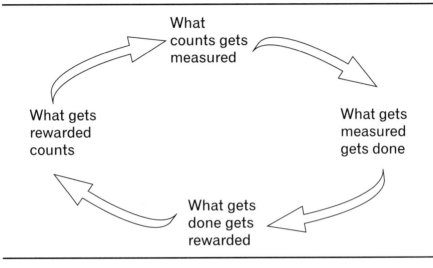

3 percent, on average. But in their frantic zeal to hire new people, they offer job hoppers 10–20 percent raises over their current salaries. Prospective job changers may even use their newfound leverage to finagle an even higher pay raise from their current employers. A classic dialogue between Dilbert and his boss captures the situation perfectly:

> *Dilbert:* I want a 10 percent raise.
>
> *Boss:* There's no budget for raises.
>
> *Dilbert:* I have an offer from another company that will pay 15 percent more.
>
> *Boss:* I'll give you 20 percent if you stay.
>
> *Dilbert:* I thought you said there's no budget for raises.
>
> *Boss:* Well . . . it's supposed to be a secret but . . . our policy is to give big raises to people who spend their time interviewing for other jobs.
>
> *Dilbert* (to his coworkers): Good news! The secret company policy is to reward disloyalty![3]

So, on top of cynicism about paying for performance, we now have the added resentment of many employees about pay inequities brought on by signing bonuses and stop-gap counteroffers to retain those who say they are quitting. This is what the market-driven war for talent has wrought. Worker satisfaction with compensation has slipped from 58 percent in the 1970s to a current level of 40 percent.[4]

The Variable Pay Approach

Because of increased global competition and the accelerating pace of change, more companies are realizing that they must look for ways to decrease fixed pay costs and begin to pay people in a more flexible way—in alignment with performance and profitability.

Many U.S. companies have switched successfully to "new pay" or "variable pay" options as a way of updating their compensation practices to fit current conditions. Here are some types of variable pay in use today:

- *Special Recognition Monetary Awards.* This method awards cash payouts to recognize unplanned, significant individual or group contributions that far exceed expectations. They are most effective if given when the contribution is fresh in the minds of all employees and with visible fanfare. Awards are not limited to the management team.

- *Individual and Group Variable Pay.* These are designed primarily for employees who don't normally participate in incentive compensation programs (traditionally reserved for executives, sales people, and piece-rate workers) but now are being implemented with scientists, programmers, quality control specialists, at-home workers, and others.

Individual variable pay works best for professions whose work is not highly interrelated with that of others. Group variable pay works best where two or more people must work together to achieve success or where the complexity of the organization demands interdependence. Many companies combine elements from both group and individual variable pay.

- *Lump Sum Awards.* These reward individual employee performance when base pay is already above the competitive market rate for the job. This allows the organization to reduce the money spent in annual pay base pay adjustments and to make up the difference by rewarding top performers. They can also be designed to reward group performance.

- *Gainsharing.* This method shares improvements in productivity, cost savings, and quality with employees who are members of a group that is instrumental in accomplishing these improvements. Awards are funded out of cost savings resulting from such improvements. The performance period can be monthly, quarterly, or yearly.

- *Winsharing.* Winsharing grants awards funded by the contributions of work groups that directly impact profitability. It pays out to all employees in the group on the basis of group performance compared to predetermined goals. While gainsharing typically focuses on productivity and quality, winsharing focuses on profit, quality, and customer value. Winsharing is different from profit-sharing in that winsharing uses group measures to determine funding.

■ *Cash Long-Term Variable Pay.* These payments are based on achievement of preset goals for periods longer than twelve months, in order to encourage sustained performance and a strong focus on strategic objectives. Because payouts are typically awarded at the end of a three- to five-year period, this type of pay also helps retain top performers.

■ *Stock Options.* Stock option plans offer employees the opportunity to purchase their for-profit common stock at some time in the future at a specific price. Stock options serve to tie the employee to the organization, as ownership tends to cause employees to be more aware of how their organization is performing. New plan designs tie the stock awards to the attainment of performance goals and make a wider range of employees eligible.

These different types of variable pay can be used in combination to create an overall pay program that not only reduces fixed-pay costs but enhances both performance and retention by truly allowing employees to be partners in the company's success. Every company must evaluate its current pay practices and business objectives and decide to what degree it wants to reinforce the achievement of individual results or group results. The key word is results. Rather than rewarding employees for seniority, bigger budgets, larger turf, and numbers of direct reports, these plans focus on the achievement of the right outcomes.

Organizations that construct true pay-for-performance compensation programs allow employees to know they will be rewarded for their contributions to business profitability. This is what creates commitment.

Who's Doing It

■ *Chick-Fil-A* gives restaurant managers a guaranteed base of $25,000 but lets them keep 50 percent of their store's annual profits. It doesn't transfer managers from store to store. Instead, the chain allows them to stay in one community and build local relationships that lead to increased business. This strategy has enabled Chick-Fil-A to maintain 10 percent to 15 percent annual revenue growth rates for ten consecutive years. The company also provides scholarships for employees who stay for two years at twenty hours per week. Retention results: Manager turnover rate of only 4 percent to 6 percent in the restaurant industry, which averages 30 percent to 40 percent. Employee turnover rate is 120 percent, compared to industry rates of 200 percent to 300 percent.

■ *Metropolitan Property and Casualty Insurance Co.,* moved to a broad-banding system for its 3,500 employees throughout the United States, replacing 738 job descriptions with 78 "broad function profiles" and complementing titles. The change was designed to rebuild the company's old compensation system into one that supported an environment based on individual contribution, not on the preestablished value of a job. Compensation is based on a combination of market values and budget and business objectives, and pay bands do not include minimums, maximums, and job levels.

■ *Lincoln Electric,* a Cleveland manufacturer of industrial electrical motors and welding equipment, pays employees a specific dollar amount for every acceptable piece they produce. Welders receive no salary or wages but can earn annual salaries of $100,000 or more on the basis of the quantity and quality of their piecework, plus bonuses. A year-end profit-sharing bonus approaches 100 percent of regular earnings and is based on group criteria such as output, quality, dependability, and suggestions.

Employees at Lincoln Electric are not entirely money-motivated, however. A strong sense of empowerment permeates the environment. Managers play the role of facilitator, helping the workers achieve their goals. Workers enjoy the intrinsic motivations of seeing their suggestions enacted, belonging to an elite group, feeling a sense of mission fulfilled, and realizing the fruits of tangible efforts. Retention results: 4 percent turnover and 2 percent absenteeism.

■ *Tyco Laboratories* allows each of its 250 profit center managers to run the business as if he or she owned it. This decentralized approach allows the company to put the financial resources of a $3 billion corporation behind the entrepreneurial drive and spirit of managers who think and act like owners. Incentive compensation is tied to each business unit's performance and not to corporate results or any factors beyond the manager's control. The company even encourages each unit's management team to share the unit's profits. In a time when many young managers are more drawn to entrepreneurial opportunities than to corporate life, this arrangement allows Tyco to attract and hold on to the right (and harder to hold on to) people.

■ *A.G. Edwards* pays branch managers on the basis of individual branch profits and actually pays its executives less than the competition. Branch managers are seldom rotated, allowing them to build local long-term customer relationships. The company shuns the practice of using up-front bonuses to lure brokers from the competition, believing it would attract the wrong kind of people and be unfair to its loyal employees. More than 90 percent of promotions come from within the company (see Retention Practice #12). Retention results: Broker turnover is less than half the industry average, with a 92 percent retention rate, where 80 percent to 85 percent is more typical.

■ *Texas Instruments* quadrupled the number of stock-option-eligible employees between 1993 and 1999. The company believes this has helped it to significantly cut turnover among technical workers over that same period.

■ *Wakefield Distribution* Systems, of Danvers, Massachusetts, is a small, family-owned company. John Lucey, the owner/president, wanted to "lock in" one key employee who brings great value—his CFO, Gabrielle Fecteau. To give her a long-term incentive to stay with the company, he designed a "phantom stock ownership" plan, allowing her to earn "stock" equal to 1 percent of the company's assessed value each year for ten years. At the end of that time, she may cash out over a ten-year period, collecting not more than 10 percent of her accumulated value each year. The phantom stock arrangement has been an ongoing source of motivation for Fecteau, giving her a vested interest in the company.

■ *North Mississippi Health System* made all 4,800 employees eligible to earn from 1 percent to 5 percent of their annual salaries as a performance bonus if their business units achieved certain patient satisfaction and cost-per-discharge goals. In two years, the system had eliminated a chronic absenteeism problem, flattened its cost-per-discharge, and raised its patient satisfaction rate to the 95th-plus percentile.

■ *Sony Electronics, Inc.,* a Park Ridge, New Jersey, unit of Sony Corporation, issues "performance shares" to hundreds of its California technical staff for achieving individual goals. The value of each share is linked to the performance of the business unit. The company reports that this practice has helped in attracting new recruits.

■ *Continental Airlines* gives each employee a $100 bonus check every time the carrier is the nation's number one on-time airline.

More rank-and-file employees at U.S. hotels are eligible for incentive compensation than ever before. In two years' time, the percentage of 350 hotels surveyed that included hourly workers, such as desk clerks and housekeepers, in their incentive plans jumped from 45 percent to 52 percent. The one measure most frequently used to determine awards was guest-comment cards.[5]

Best Pay Practices

The pay plans of most companies send employees the wrong message or a mixed message or no message at all.

Before you can even begin to fix your current compensation program or implement a new pay approach, most compensation experts agree, your company must address three other issues first:

1. Tell people exactly what is expected of them, not just in terms of results but how they must change their behavior in order to achieve those results (see Retention Practices #6, 11, 16, and 19).
2. Measure the results—by looking at key indicators and the behavior used to get those results (see Retention Practices #19 and 20). Determine key measures of organization, team, and individual success so that pay can be tied to real organizational outcomes, not just to the perceptions of supervisors. Targeted results should be within the employee's control, and the employee should consider the potential reward equal to the effort. Don't give ratings; assess and reward degree of attainment on key measures.
3. Make the commitment to reward your employees at a level that will actually reinforce the behavior change you desire. In short, link compensation directly to performance instead of to a "sense of entitlement" based on attaining a certain title or level of seniority.

Steven Kerr, who heads GE's world-renowned leadership development center, cites studies that show that to truly motivate people, you have to offer them an award that's at least 10 percent to 12 percent above their base salary, which is significantly more than the average—7.5 percent— that most companies pay.[6]

Here are some guidelines for implementing and maintaining a pay and performance management system that motivates and retains:

1. Allow those who will have to live under the new pay system to have a hand in creating it.
2. Don't overlay a new pay system on a performance management and compensation system that is outdated or incompatible with the new one.
3. Make sure managers see the performance management process as a tool to help them succeed, not as an empty annual bureaucratic exercise for dividing up small slices of so-called merit pay budgets.
4. Make sure senior management sets the example in using the system.
5. Hold line managers, not human resources staff, accountable for effective leadership of performance management efforts.
6. Measure and reward team performance (as in gainsharing and group bonuses) to reinforce teamwork. Too much emphasis on measuring and rewarding individual performance independent of peer success can undermine teamwork. Keep in mind that the greater the interdependence among various members of the organization, the more difficult it is to measure their separate contributions.

7. Disconnect pay from power and number of people supervised. Base it instead on creation of value. There are still too many baby boomers "chasing a shrinking number of slots in the hierarchy," says GE's Kerr. "If you continue to link rewards with rank, you're likely to create an army of malcontents."[7] GE dealt with this problem by cutting the number of different salary grades from twenty-nine to six, a technique known as "broad-banding."

8. Consider adopting a pay philosophy that pays excellent performers in lower-level positions more than managers or longer-tenured employees if their performance can be shown to contribute more to the value of the enterprise.

9. Offer profit sharing and stock ownership where possible. GE and many other companies have increased the number of employees eligible for stock options.

10. Recognize achievement when it occurs. Don't review people in July, then wait until January to reward them. GE invites employees to reward their peers on the spot—through a program called Quick Thanks! that lets any employee nominate any colleague to receive a $25 gift certificate.

11. Make rewards contingent on continuing performance. It is practically impossible to take back a raise. But if you give employees meaningful bonuses, instead of base pay increases, they know they will get bonuses the next year only if they keep performing.

12. If you can't give enough money, give something else. If you don't have enough cash on hand to give everyone a significant bonus, try using nonfinancial incentives (see Retention Practice #20).

13. Don't assume that the same pay plan will work overseas. If you have international operations, keep in mind that some countries, such as Japan, are not big on the idea of incentive pay. Instead of cash, many employees would rather have more time off or other nontaxable rewards.

14. Monitor the system to ensure fairness, consistency, and accuracy. Kerr's words to pay by: "When it comes to rewarding employees, the key is not how much more you have to give. It's how well you give what you already have."[8]

Retention-Focused Pay Strategies

Here are some ideas for new ways to structure your pay strategies.

1. Offer new recruits retention bonuses instead of signing bonuses, payable after a year or two on the new job. White Castle restau-

rants, for example, pays a retroactive increase of fifty cents an hour dating back to start date after employees have been on the job from thirty to ninety days, depending on the manager's discretion. The company has found that this practice increases the chances that employees will stay six months or longer.

2. Pay new or current employees "project completion" bonuses so that they will stay until a critical project is completed.
3. Pay retention bonuses or selectively grant stock options to employees who stay through a merger, acquisition, or plant closing.
4. For positions with very high turnover, consider creating a new, higher-paying position level into which employees in these positions can advance on the basis of completion of special training or achievement of set performance levels.
5. When you sense that an employee is beginning to look for another job, approach the person with the opportunity for a choice assignment or promotion into a higher-paying job.

To keep things in perspective regarding what pay can and cannot do to retain key talent, keep in mind the words of Peter Block: "It is difficult to use money to purchase loyalty. The people who join us, or stay with us, primarily for the money will leave us for the same reason. Unless the economy is on its back, some other organization can always afford to recruit our people for more money than we can afford to pay them."[8]

Now grade yourself and your organization on Retention Practice #2: "Measure What Counts and Pay for It."

How good a job is your organization doing on this practice?

Circle one: (A) Excellent   (B) Very good   (C) Good   (D) Fair   (F) Poor

How good a job are you as a manager doing on this practice?

Circle one: (A) Excellent   (B) Very good   (C) Good   (D) Fair   (F) Poor

How important do you believe this practice is to your organization's strategy to attract and retain the talent necessary to meet its business objectives?

Circle one: (A) Critical (B) Very important (C) Somewhat important
         (D) Not important

What can your organization do to improve on this practice?

What can you as a manager do to improve on this practice?

Retention Practice #3

Inspire Commitment to a Clear Vision and Definite Objectives

> Talented people want to be a part of something they can believe in.
>
> —Robert Reich

Recruiters have commented to me about how difficult it is to recruit people when they feel they are working toward specific, motivational objectives and believe they are making a difference in their current jobs. Offering these people more money will usually not budge them, but the opportunity to make an even bigger difference will.

Those who worked for the pharmaceuticals marketer Marion Laboratories, in Kansas City, in the 1970s and 80s, when the late Ewing Kauffman was building a strong culture of commitment there, still talk about the day when it became evident just how strongly Marion's employees felt about their ties to the company. One winter workday when snow and freezing rain blanketed the city, the local radio and TV stations issued bulletins warning commuters to stay home unless their jobs were considered absolutely vital to their company's operations. More than 95 percent of Marion's workers showed up that day!

The point is that people want more than just material rewards. They want to believe their jobs are vital to the company's success. They don't just want "something to do"; they want to "do something." What is that something that you and your fellow workers want to do for your organization? Is the sense of meaning and purpose you create within your culture enough to attract new workers and keep the right ones in place?

How "Cultures of Commitment" Use Mission, Vision, Values, and Ambitious Goals to Attract and Hold On to Talented People

Cultures of commitment have three things that many less successful and less committed organizations do not have:

1. *A Set of Guiding Principles or Core Values that Is of Intrinsic Importance to Those in the Organization.* Nordstrom, for example, values "service to the customer above all else, hard work and individual productivity, excellence in reputation, being part of something special, and never being satisfied."[1] United Parcel Service (UPS), after experiencing a traumatic drivers' strike in 1997, reinvented itself and doubled its net income by recommitting to some old and some new values—"reliability, technological innovation, procedural uniformity/efficiency, and attention to detail—all to achieve new standards in customer service.[2]

2. *A Mission that Captures the Organization's Reason for Being.* Wal-Mart's mission, for example, is "to give ordinary folks the chance to buy the same things as rich people." The mission of Mary Kay Cosmetics is "to give unlimited opportunity to women."[3] The mission of newly merged AOL Time Warner, in the words of CEO Steve Case, is "to build a global medium as central to people's lives as the telephone or television . . . even more valuable."[4] That company's competitor, Apple Computer, has a similar mission: "to marry the iMac and the Internet with an easy-to-use new operating system and free Web services for everything from your photos to your home page."[5] It will be interesting to see whether both companies can achieve their missions equally well or do so only at each other's expense.

The point is that these kinds of missions serve to attract, inspire, and keep valued employees motivated, unlike those such as "maximize shareholder value," which leave most employees cold. They capture what it is that makes the average worker want to put his or her heart and soul into serving the customer.

If the organization truly lives by its values and mission or purpose, it will attract the kind of talent that will fit, succeed, and stay, and repel those whose values are incompatible. At Southwest Airlines, for example, any job candidate who is not drawn to the company's mission to make flying a fun and pleasant experience will probably not even survive the company's careful screening process.

3. *An Envisioned Future Consisting of a Bold, Long-Range Goal, and a Vivid Description of What It Will Be Like to Achieve That Goal.* For example, in 1950 Sony set what some would have described as an outrageous goal—"to become the company most known for changing the worldwide poor-quality

image of Japanese products." As Collins and Porras noted, in their important book *Built to Last*, a company's goal should be audacious enough to make employees gulp and wonder how they will ever achieve it.[6] When that happens, the goal begins to have a magnetizing effect on team spirit and motivation.

The vivid description of the company's goal paints a picture that is so clear, compelling, and memorable that employees carry it around in their heads without ever again having to see it in writing. Here was Sony's vivid description in 1950:

> We will create products that become pervasive around the world. . . . We will be the first Japanese company to go into the U.S. market and distribute directly. . . . We will succeed with innovations that U.S. companies have failed at—such as the transistor radio . . . fifty years from now, our brand name will be as well known as any around the world . . . and will signify innovation and quality that rival the most innovative companies anywhere. . . . "Made in Japan" will mean something fine, not something shoddy.[7]

Never has a vivid description of one company's future been realized more perfectly and more astonishingly than Sony's. Painting such a detailed picture of an audacious goal has the power not only to inspire employee commitment but to clearly focus the entire organization on the kind and quality of talent needed to make it real.

Jack Welch, chairman of General Electric, was named "manager of the century" by *Fortune* magazine for taking an already successful company and making it the second most valuable company on earth, after Microsoft. Welch had a mission and a vision that actually stirred the emotions of employees when he took over as CEO in 1980—he would make every GE business either number one or number two in its industry. He proceeded to get into 118 new businesses and sold another seventy-one to get the company out of businesses where it held no competitive advantage. He also sent the message, and meant it, that GE's competitive edge would come from individuals and their ideas. He burned manager's guides that had been designed to tell managers what to do at every step and challenged them to think for themselves. He instituted "town meetings" between unit managers and their employees, where any question could be asked and new ideas were solicited for how to make the business run better. Those who spoke up and submitted good ideas were rewarded, along with those who implemented them. Every manager had to make written commitments and follow through on them. In short, Welch created a culture of commitment.[8]

Are your organization's values, mission, goals, and vision clear and compelling enough to attract and hold the right people?

Take a moment now to reflect on this question as you consider the components one by one.

List what you consider the key values of your organization:

- _____

- _____

- _____

- _____

- _____

Now write what *you* consider to be your organization's mission (not the mission statement):

_____

_____

Now list your organization's bold, long-range business goal:

_____

_____

Now describe in your own words, as vividly as you can, the exciting future your organization envisions for itself over the next several years:

_____

_____

_____

_____

_____

If you had difficulty describing any of these, then you as a manager are missing an important piece of the puzzle that you need to attract and keep the right people. You are the key link in communicating all these motivational elements to those who report to you; if you don't know or understand them, how can you expect your people and those you are trying to recruit to understand them?

You may be missing a piece of the puzzle if:

- Senior management has not clarified and communicated its values, purpose, goals, or vision for the organization.
- Senior management has clarified, but not communicated, the above.
- Senior management has written a mission statement, but it was an empty exercise, so the mission is now just "wallpaper." It does not inspire dedication or hard work. It exists only on paper and is not anchored in the heads and hearts of employees.
- Senior management has articulated its mission and values, but its actions are not consistent with its words.
- Senior management has communicated values, mission, goals, or vision that you do not agree with, or that employees did not help create, so they have no sense of ownership in them.
- You buy into the organization's values, mission, goals, and vision, but you have not involved your people in creating a meaningful subset of values, purpose, goals, and vision for your team.

No matter which of these possibilities is the case, there are actions you as a manager can take. If there are no clear goals coming from above, you can request them. If you don't agree with them, you can question them and propose different ones. You can involve your people in creating a vision that could spread upward and throughout the company. You can start a cross-functional strategic planning task force to create a new vision that takes your unit in a new or different direction. You and your people don't have to wait for senior management to decree the new vision—you can create your own, both as a team and as an individual. As discussed earlier, you do have the power to influence, if not control, the direction of the company.

Commitment or Compliance?

The problem with mission statements and strategies that are created from on high and then cascade down to the troops is that they evoke compliance, not commitment. As Peter Block says in his book *Stewardship*, "a statement crafted for a team to endorse is not owned by the team . . . creating a vision is an ownership function—each unit must create its own."[9]

Peter Senge, author of *The Fifth Discipline*, believes that "90 percent of the time, what passes for commitment is compliance."[10] Senge presents seven possible ways that employees may react to a vision set forth by the organization's leaders:

1. *Commitment.* Wants it; will make it happen.
2. *Enrollment.* Wants it; will do whatever can be done within the "spirit of the law."
3. *Genuine Compliance.* Sees the benefits of the vision. Good soldier; follows the "letter of the law."
4. *Formal Compliance.* On the whole, sees the benefits of the vision. Does what is expected and no more. "Pretty good" soldier.
5. *Grudging Compliance.* Does not see the benefits of the vision, but also doesn't want to lose job. Does enough of what's expected, but also lets it be known that he or she is not on board.
6. *Noncompliance.* Does not see the benefits of the vision and will not do what's expected. "I won't do it; you can't make me."
7. *Apathy.* Neither for or against vision. No interest. No energy. "Is it five o'clock yet?"

You may recognize these attitudes among members of your own team. Senge points out that "people in some organizations have never been committed to anything in their careers."[11] You have probably noticed that there are people, among those who are uncommitted, whom you want to keep. How can you increase their commitment?

How to Get Commitment from Your People

What really matters from a business standpoint is that you and your people are committed to achieving the right business results. As you know, in translating the vision into strategic objectives, frequently something is lost in the translation. As one front-line employee put it, "Top management says it wants an apple, but when the word gets to middle management, it's an orange, and by the time it gets down to us, it's a lemon."

They key thing to remember is that the vision drives the objectives, which drive the performance management cycle and reward system (see Retention Practices #16, 19, and 20). Here are some guidelines to get employee commitment to these objectives:

1. *Ask your people to help create goals and objectives from the bottom up.* If you want to get employee buy-in, the creation of objectives cannot just be a top-down process. Partnership environments create the most commit-

ment. If you want empowerment and not dependency, you will clearly articulate the organization's vision and the "subvision" you have for your unit, then involve your people in helping to define the key results and outcomes by which their performance will be measured. As Senge has noted, "My vision is not what's important to you. The only thing that motivates you is your vision."[12]

2. *Be committed to the vision yourself.* If you haven't bought into the vision yourself, how can you expect other people to buy into it? If you don't agree with the vision, either get clarification or influence top management to change it. Also, don't inflate the benefits or downplay potential problems with achieving the vision. Describe it as honestly as you can.

3. *Let your people know they have free choice.* If they feel coerced, you get compliance and a "victim mentality," not commitment. When it comes time to create a performance plan with each of your staff, give the person first shot at defining the appropriate measures, then try to negotiate agreement.

4. *Accept ongoing responsibility for creating alignment between the company's vision and the objectives of your unit.* As Collins and Porras summarized the challenge, "Building a visionary company requires 1 percent vision and 99 percent alignment."[13]

Who's Doing It

■ *3M* encourages visionary leadership among all employees by allowing those who develop new product ideas to take the lead in the development and marketing of those products. This practice has been instrumental in helping the company to produce more than 60,000 products!

■ *MindSpring's* internet customer-service center has linked its corporate vision to specific behavior to avoid—what it calls "The 14 Deadly Sins of MindSpring (or ways that we can be just like everyone else)." Sin #3, for example, is, "Make internal procedures easy on us, even if it means negatively affecting or inconveniencing the customer." Sin #8: "Show up at a demo, sales call, trade show, or meeting unprepared."[14]

Now grade yourself and your organization on Retention Practice #3: "Inspire Commitment to a Clear Vision and Definite Objectives."

How good a job is your organization doing on this practice?

Circle one: (A) Excellent   (B) Very good   (C) Good   (D) Fair   (F) Poor

How good a job are you as a manager doing on this practice?

Circle one: (A) Excellent   (B) Very good   (C) Good   (D) Fair   (F) Poor

How important do you believe this practice is to your organization's strategy to attract and retain the talent necessary to meet its business objectives?

Circle one: (A) Critical (B) Very important (C) Somewhat important
(D) Not important

What can the organization do to improve on this practice?

What can you as a manager do to improve on this practice?

THE SECOND KEY

Select the Right People in the First Place

Today's hiring mistakes are tomorrow's turnovers—it's as simple as that. Bad hires are the reason that 20 percent or more of the workforce are poor or marginal performers. Failure to select the right people in the first place is why only 50 percent of new hires last six months on the job.

Recruiters report that it takes much longer to fill openings than in years past, and one search firm reported that top executives may spend eleven or more hours per week on recruiting.[1] Yes, the job market is a major factor in all of this. But what about the factors you can control?

Whose Job Is It, Anyway?

Selecting the right person is the job of the one individual who has the most to lose if the wrong person is selected—the manager. Yet most managers have still not been trained in effective job analysis and in recruiting and interviewing techniques. Many say these are the responsibilities of human resources staff or the employment manager.

Managers say they don't have time to analyze and update job descriptions every time they hire. They don't want to have to prepare for a lengthy structured interview process or coordinate the involvement of several interviewers. With all the pressures on managers today, these objections are understandable. Yet, in all too many organizations, somewhere between line managers and human resources, the ball is being dropped.

You, the manager, need to reclaim primary responsibility for recruiting for a couple of reasons:

1. You are the person whose headache will be taken away if the right person is hired, or made worse if the wrong person is hired—you have the most to gain or lose. Therefore, you are the person most motivated to do the best job of selecting the right person.
2. It will keep you "plugged in" to the external community, business trends, and outside events. It will put you in touch with the diversity of the employment marketplace, what people think of your organization, what applicants know and expect, and changes in the competitive environment. If you leave recruiting to recruiters and your HR staff, you will become even more isolated.

How Your Organization Can Help You Select the Right People

Your organization can take a number of actions that will facilitate your search for the right person for the job. Among the steps it can take are these:

1. Your organization can provide you with training in state-of-the-art recruiting and interviewing techniques like those outlined in Retention Practices #4–13, especially those related to continuous sourcing, competency analysis, and behavioral interviewing.
2. By rewarding you for excellence in selecting the right people, your organization will be positively reinforcing you to do what only you can do best. At some companies, where hiring the right person is considered a key to reaching key business objectives, great hiring managers are celebrated as heroes, as we shall see.
3. Your organization can assist all managers in recruiting, as companies such as Hewlett-Packard and Cisco Systems have done, by involving all employees in the process, either by making them "scouts," or information resources for potential applicants, or by rewarding them for direct referrals of new hires.

Why Don't We Select the Right People?

There are so many obstacles to selecting the right person in the first place that it is a wonder that we get it right as often as we do. Making the right hire may be more a matter of avoiding predictable pitfalls than of doing it a certain "right way." Here are some of the most common mistakes managers make:

Pitfall #1: *Hiring for Experience and Expertise over Talent.* When listing job criteria, writing want ads, and screening resumes, hiring managers and recruiters often become so fixated on key knowledge areas required for entry that they overlook and screen out candidates whose talents and personality traits would, with some on-the-job training, enable them to become high performers. You may have heard the expression "hired on experience, and fired on personality." This often happens when the interviewing process is too focused on the resume and not on questions that uncover the true talents of the applicant.

Pitfall #2: *Hiring in a Hurry.* "I need someone in here now" is the familiar refrain in today's fast-paced business environments. But "warm body" hiring frequently precedes short-tenure turnovers. Then you have to take more time to do it again. That's how hiring in a hurry slows things down. Better to take the time to do it right the first time.

Another drag on the process is being in so big a hurry to fill the job that no time is taken to update the job description. By the time the people involved in the process realize they don't agree on the qualifications, it's already halfway through the interview process. Now candidates will have to be put on hold and possibly lost while the hiring team takes the time to do what should have been done at the front end—rewrite the job description.

Pitfall #3: *Hiring by Gut Feeling Alone.* "I know good horseflesh when I see it," I once heard a manager say. There's nothing wrong with trusting your intuition, but good decisions of all kinds usually need to be balanced with some analysis. This means taking time to analyze the job and ask key questions. How have conditions changed since we last filled this job? What results are now expected? With whom does this person now have to work? Again, you will need to slow down to do it right.

Pitfall #4: *The "Search for Superman" Syndrome.* When too many people become involved in listing requirements for the job, the resulting list is so long that few human beings would possess all the needed talents, traits, and areas of knowledge. This results in a screening process that weeds out many applicants who might actually excel at the job.

Pitfall #5: *Hiring in Your Own Image.* Any manager is vulnerable to the human temptation to hire those who are most like us. Hiring by similarity can encompass age, gender, race, religion, nationality, education, or personality type. One of the most common tendencies of managers is to hire only those who pursued the same career paths, or received the same degrees, or paid the same dues as they did. It may be more comfortable to hire those like you even though diversity of skill or personality or perspective may be what your organization needs more.

Pitfall #6: *"Politically Correct" Hiring.* This one is so common that we've all seen it operate. Someone higher in the organization returns a favor to a friend by asking the manager to hire the friend's nephew practically sight unseen. Politics often takes over in mergers and acquisitions when the best person for the job loses out to the one with the strongest sponsor.

Pitfall #7: *Underestimating the Power of Employee Referral.* There is no other recruiting source that produces a higher percentage of long-term hires (see Retention Practice #10).

Pitfall #8: *Hiring against Type.* The last person in the job didn't work out because of some outstandingly bad personality trait, so you decide to focus your search on finding a replacement with the opposite trait. The only problem is that you may be bringing on a totally different kind of outstandingly bad trait. Better to focus more on the current results expected in the job than on the predecessor.

Pitfall #9: *Hiring with No Proof of Performance.* Hiring managers fail to ask applicants to give examples of actual past behavior that give evidence of the needed talents (see Retention Practice #7). Instead, they ask softball questions like, "What are your strengths?" that are easy to fake. They call only the references given by candidates instead of seeking out others who may give more objective input. They engage in friendly, superficial chats with candidates that fail to uncover relevant qualifications. All these practices are avoidable, but, again, doing it right takes a little more time and effort.

Pitfall #10: *Overdelegating the Selection Process.* Managers, not human resources representatives and assistants, should create the job description, for reasons cited earlier. If you are too busy to do this key task, know that it probably won't be done right by the person to whom you delegate it. It can also be dangerous to allow your direct reports to conduct screening interviews without taking the time to thoroughly brief them on key qualifications.

Pitfall #11: *Failing to Describe the Job as It Really Is.* Fear of telling candidates the truth about the challenges and conditions of the job is the most common cause of short-tenure turnover. Telling the truth won't repel the right people (see Retention Practice #8).

Pitfall #12: *Overlooking the Inside Candidate.* We sometimes become so externally focused in our recruiting efforts that we fail to see that the ideal candidate lies right under our nose. Often it's a person in another unit who's ripe for a new challenge and equipped with just the right talent (see Retention Practice #12).

Pitfall #13: *Confusing Selling with Evaluating.* A manager may be so anxious to bring on someone who may appear to be a qualified candidate that she spends more time selling the candidate on the benefits of joining the organization than on conducting a thorough assessment against qualifications. Clear-eyed evaluation should happen prior to the sales pitch.

Pitfall #14: *Not Creating High Enough Hurdles.* One of the main reasons so many companies select the wrong person is that they fail to make the hiring process selective enough to weed out applicants whose values don't mesh with those of the company or whose desire is not great enough. Some organizations require candidates to complete a task, such as writing a one-page description of themselves or preparing a report on some aspect of the company or industry, before they will interview the applicants. A significant percentage of applicants will not even bother to complete the task. This allows these companies to conduct a more "fine-mesh screening" that helps them select from the candidates with the most desire for the job.[2]

Pitfall #15: *Not Thinking "outside the Box."* The war for talent has created a multitude of innovative and nontraditional practices for sourcing the right talent (see Retention Practice #13).

So much for the "don'ts" of selection. Now we turn to the "do's."

RETENTION PRACTICE #4

Understand Why Some Leave and Why Others Stay

> When a valuable employee leaves, it's a signal that something in the system may need fixing.
>
> —Frederick Reichheld

Why do good employees leave?

In addition to the six reasons presented earlier, one simple and over-riding answer is—because they can. Today's job market is healthy enough that employees in all job categories have options. Fewer feel "locked in" by anything more than their own inertia. They also know that they can no longer afford to believe that their company will be loyal to them, so certainly their own loyalty to their company no longer inhibits them from moving on.

What is most interesting is the difference in attitude among companies when an employee does resign and move on. There are basically two kinds of attitudes—one that says turnover is acceptable as a cost of doing business, and another that sees every instance of avoidable turnover as a defection, a disappointing failure to be analyzed, like the defection of a major customer.

The first attitude is exemplified by a company that was experiencing 31 percent turnover and that, instead of seeking to determine root causes, decided to spend lavishly on new recruiting efforts. A second attitude is prevalent among "loyalty leader" companies and among many high-tech companies in California's Silicon Valley, where the competition for talented technical professionals is fierce and the consequences of losing them can be financially damaging.

The CEO of one such company, Cypress Semiconductor, even sent out a memo to all his managers in which he announced a systematic process to be followed when a valued employee resigns, with the fervent hope of changing that employee's mind by correcting whatever "push factor" was involved. While this may seem too drastic a measure to many, it is difficult to argue with success: Cypress, by following the process, has managed to salvage more than 50 percent of those who resign. (The CEO's memo describing the process and its impact may be found in Appendix A.)

What does your company do to understand the causes of avoidable turnover? More than 95 percent of companies conduct "exit interviews," but 30 percent of them fail to follow through with remedies or action plans. Moreover, 42 percent of companies that conduct exit surveys say their interview process is not effective.[1] The information gathered is often superficial; answers usually describe external "pull factors" such as "better-paying job," "better opportunity" (whatever that means), "more challenge," "closer to home," to mention a few, without revealing the internal "push factors" that drove the employee to start thinking about leaving in the first place.

Many managers fail to consider that an employee's decision to quit is usually preceded by weeks or months of time spent thinking about quitting. An employee begins by evaluating the job and the company against what he or she had expected. If the employee then feels disillusioned, he or she may for the first time think about quitting. The employee may then spend time thinking about looking elsewhere, exploring other options, finding real options, evaluating those, and comparing them with the present job, all before finally making the decision to quit or stay.

When managers accept at face value such pat answers as "better opportunity" in exit interviews, they are missing an opportunity to understand the correctable issues that may have led to the decision to quit. The superficiality of exit interview information is made worse, of course, by the understandable lack of openness and candor on the part of employees in giving the reasons they are leaving the company, for fear of "burning bridges" if the information is not kept confidential. To overcome this problem, many companies have begun the practice of mailing exit surveys to the individual's home, then having a third-party consultant conduct an exit interview by telephone, often several days after the employee has already left, giving the employee time to sort out his or her feelings and to be a bit more objective.

The Art of Exit Interviewing

In-depth questioning can reveal those "push factors," or trouble spots in the organization, such as abusive or ineffective managers, insufficient challenge, lack of opportunity for advancement, problem coworkers, and out-dated HR policies. Some managers may actually resist knowing the unwelcome truth that it is their management practices and not the "better offer" that motivated the employee to begin looking in the first place.

To avoid "top of mind" responses that fail to get at the root cause, whoever conducts the exit interview must know how to ask probing questions, as follows:

Q: Why did you leave the company?

A: There was no challenge in the job.

Q: Why was there no challenge in the job?

A: Because my manager wanted to do all the most technically challenging assignments himself and wouldn't delegate (root cause).

Comments from exit interviews should be kept confidential to encourage openness and honesty. Push factors (root causes) honestly and precisely identified, combined with management's desire to deal with them, can help managers avoid hiring people who may later leave for the same reasons.

You may want to compare the exit interview you are using with the one in Appendix B. Some companies have begun setting up internal e-mail addresses to receive anonymous messages about the reasons people quit. Others have started using outside parties to conduct in-depth exit interviews with terminated employees as well as those who leave voluntarily. This practice acknowledges that the company probably has something to learn in avoiding future terminations (also see Retention Practice #23).

Keep in mind that whatever kind of exit survey you use should be appropriate to your organization and compatible with your purposes in using it. It is also important to ensure that the collected survey information is collected, analyzed, and shared with managers (instead of sitting in a file drawer for months) so that action can be taken to correct problems that contribute to avoidable turnover and to generate new ideas and tools that increase retention.

Analyzing Turnover in Your Organization

The more you know about the extent and cost of employee turnover, of course, the more effective you will be in securing funds, resources, and the organizational commitment needed to reduce it. Statistically, turnover is usually computed as the number of employee separations divided by the total number in the workforce expressed as a percentage. For example, an organization with twenty separations in a given month and that has 200 employees on the fifteen day of that month will have a monthly turnover rate of 10 percent.

Of course, turnover rates vary among industries, companies, geographic areas, departments, job categories, and employee characteristics such as age, education, and tenure in the organization. For example, younger, newer, unskilled, and blue-collar employees tend to have higher turnover rates. That's why turnover should be calculated and tracked by types of jobs, departments, and various demographic factors of interest to the organization.

If you have not been tracking avoidable turnover rates in your company or your department, you need to begin doing so, as it provides a benchmark for comparison and improvement.

To compute your monthly avoidable turnover rate, subtract the number of unavoidable separations during the month (e.g., decisions to return to school, spouse relocations, illness, deaths, pregnancies) from the total separations. The remaining figure is then divided by the total midmonth workforce to determine the avoidable separation turnover rate. For example, if six of twenty voluntary separations were unavoidable, the fourteen remaining separations divided by 200 employees yields a 7 percent avoidable turnover rate.

Because so much turnover happens among newer employees, it is important not to let the larger turnover rate mask this issue. One approach to tracking new employee turnover is to compute their "survivor/wastage" rates. For example, if you had hired twenty-five new employees in a given month and you wanted to track the number of new employee survival rate after three months, here's how it would work: If fifteen of them are still employed after three months, their survival rate is 60 percent (a wastage rate of 40 percent).

How One Company Used Focus Groups to Surface Turnover Issues

American Century Investments, a Kansas City–based mutual fund company, was challenged to reduce turnover among its four hundred information technology staff. Jerry Bartlett, senior vice president of human resources, cited the reasons: "The industry and technology changes so rapidly that it's hard to find people with those skills, and once you find them, you want to keep them."[2]

At its height in 1997, American Century's turnover rate was 16 percent, within the industry average range of 15–20 percent. Because this rate was higher than the company wanted, it decided to develop a strategy and approach to retain its people. It started with written surveys asking the IT staff what was important to them. The survey asked such questions as "What would keep you here?" and "What would make you leave?"

After conducting the surveys, the human resources department conducted focus groups to gain deeper insight into what the IT employees wanted. Discussions focused on what specific actions would make the biggest difference. The company created a special retention program in 1997 geared to IT staff, offering the following: flexible schedules with several options, training and development tailored to the competency deficits of each employee, and a specialized performance-based bonus.

The result: By the end of its first year in effect, the program had helped lower the turnover rate from 16 percent to 5 percent. Bartlett's advice: "Be sure that what you're doing is based on what people you are trying to retain."[3]

Did You Ever Think to Ask, "What Makes You Stay?"

Analyzing people who leave your company is looking at only one side of the coin, and the negative side at that. Many companies that take retention seriously are looking at the positive side of the motivational coin as well, by conducting "stay interviews" with employees whose performance is superior and whose tenure in the company is above average.

They may simply ask these "stayers" what keeps them in the company, or they may cover many of the same criteria used in an exit interview, such as why they joined the company in the first place, what they like most and least about their jobs, what they think of management practices and the company, what three things they would change to make theirs a better place to work, what they believe are the criteria by which other employees decide to stay or leave, and so on. These companies are discovering two things: first, that many keys to keeping the right people can be discovered by simply asking, and, second, that if the high-performing "stayers" are the kinds of employees they want to keep hiring, their responses to why they stay and what they like will reveal what to look for as the company recruits future candidates.

Taking the Pulse of All Employees

Employee surveys can be used, of course, to find out what all employees want that would make them stay longer if you could provide it. Often these are simple things. For example, Jack Stack, CEO of Springfield Remanufacturing Company, put together a fourteen-question survey and asked all employees to fill it out anonymously. The company then set up an Employee Satisfaction Committee to improve the lowest-rated items.

What they discovered at Springfield Remanufacturing was that there were loads of little problems (as opposed to a few big problems), and that most of these could be solved quickly and inexpensively just by bringing them to the surface and focusing on them. They included a discrepancy in the specifications for a fuel-injection pump in the pump room and the pumps in the dynamometer room. This problem was fixed the next day.

Stack uses the survey every six months as a "morale audit" to uncover actions that can be taken that will positively affect both performance and employee retention.

One final word to the wise about surveys—If you are not prepared to take action to correct problems, don't do the survey in the first place, because the very act of surveying will raise employee expectations that some corrective actions will be taken.

How to Turn Ex-Employees into Alumni, Ambassadors, Future Customers, and Rehires

Since it isn't realistic to expect to retain good people forever, smart companies are looking to stay connected with their former employees. Why? Because they know that maintaining a cordial relationship can lead to several positive outcomes—referral of future hires or future business, becoming clients or customers, or being rehired.

Who's Doing It

■ *In Focus Systems, Inc.*, a manufacturer of computer LCD projectors in Wilsonville, Oregon, ranks as the fourth best company to work for in the state. Though it loses 10 percent of its workforce per year, many of these former employers often end up in new positions with other companies where they can act as ambassadors for In Focus and champion the use of its products. One former employee, for example, influenced his new company to purchase 70 percent more In Focus projectors in one quarter than it had in the first quarter of the previous year.[4]

■ *Gensler,* a highly respected San Francisco–based architecture and design firm, has rehired many former employees and considers them among its most loyal and committed employees. Gensler's vice president of human resources has even added a new term—"boomerang rate"—the percentage of current employees who have returned after spending some time away. "Boomerangs are our most loyal employees," she told a *Fast Company* reporter. "They've inspected the grass on the other side of the fence, and found it not so green."[5]

Gensler's boomerang rate in 1998 was a remarkable 12 percent. Former employees who return to Gensler now receive an official company boomerang bearing the dates of the employee's first tenure and the date of return. Says company president Arthur Gensler, "There are only so many good people out there. If you cross off the ones who have already worked for you . . . that's very limiting."

Though they may not like it when an employee leaves, company officials can still joke about it. As the departing employee leaves, they often say, "You'll be back. We'll just let someone else use your desk for a while . . . this isn't goodbye, it's just see you later."[6]

Some advantages of hiring boomerangs:

- Their ramp-up time is quicker when they return.
- They already understand company values, culture, and policies.
- They bring back a wealth of new ideas to keep the company from getting stale.

- *Bain & Co.*, the Boston-based consulting firm, communicates more often with its "alumni" than most companies do with their current employees.[7] Bain employs more than 2,000 people around the world, but has more than 1,900 alumni in North America alone. The company even employs a director of career development and alumni relations who sees to it that these former employees receive frequently updated alumni directories, invitations to cocktail receptions or panel discussions, and biannual newsletters.

As one Bain alumnus put it, "Employees don't want to see you kicking ex-employees in the behind on the way out the door . . . because they'll know you'll do that to them when they leave." Instead, the company wishes them well and genuinely wants them to be successful in their new lives. Then it works to maintain the relationship and to let the former workers know they will be warmly welcomed back if and when the time comes. As a result, many do come back; in fact, in one eighteen-month period, more than half of the firm's new vice presidents were alumni.[8]

Now grade yourself and your organization on Retention Practice #4: "Understand Why Some Leave and Why Others Stay."

How good a job is your organization doing on this practice?

Circle one: (A) Excellent (B) Very good (C) Good (D) Fair (F) Poor

How good a job are you as a manager doing on this practice?

Circle one: (A) Excellent   (B) Very good   (C) Good   (D) Fair   (F) Poor

How important do you believe this practice is to your organization's strategy to attract and retain the talent necessary to meet its business objectives?

Circle one: (A) Critical (B) Very important (C) Somewhat important
             (D) Not important

What can the organization do to improve on this practice?

What can you as a manager do to improve on this practice?

Redesign the Job Itself to Make It More Rewarding

More often the person is too big for the job rather than the other way around.
—J. R. Hackman and G. R. Oldham, *Work Redesign*

Good people want good jobs. It really is that simple. When good people find themselves in bad jobs, they either disengage or they depart. In a healthy job market they are more likely to choose the latter.

What makes a job good or bad? There are two dimensions—first, whether the job fits the individual's talents and preferences (see Retention Practice #6), and, second, whether the job, because of the way it is designed, provides enough of the factors that make it "rich" in the kind of satisfactions that most workers want.

The employee motivation researchers J. Richard Hackman and Greg R. Oldham have documented that employees display strong self-motivation, high work satisfaction, high-quality performance, better customer service, low absenteeism, and reduced turnover when their jobs have five essential job characteristics:

1. *Skill Variety*. Skill variety means that an assortment of different skills and talents is required to carry out the work. Generally, the more skills and talents involved in doing the job, the more satisfying or meaningful it will be to the employee. But the critical variable is whether the job provides the individual with the opportunity to use the combination of abilities that the employee personally finds most satisfying.

You may have employees performing work so specialized and subdivided that this kind of variety is lacking. How could you change their tasks and responsibilities so that each person's tasks are more varied?

2. *Task Identity.* Task identity means that the job is undertaken as a whole, requiring the employee to complete a whole or identifiable piece of work from beginning to end, with a visible outcome. For example, it is more meaningful for a worker to assemble an entire computer than to solder electrical connections on computer after computer.

Do your employees have this kind of completeness in their tasks? How could the work be redistributed to make each person's tasks an integrated series of steps leading to an observable outcome?

3. *Task Significance.* Task significance means that the job has a significant effect on the lives or work of other people, either within or outside the organization. For example, a worker who assembles wheelchairs may feel more task significance than one who assembles picture frames. Many workers will not fully understand why their jobs are significant until someone does a good job of explaining it to them (see Retention Practice #15).

If the end purpose of your group's work is not evident to your people, how can you better convey to them its larger purpose? How can you regularly remind your people of the positive effects their work is having on the lives of others?

4. *Autonomy.* Having autonomy means that the employee has substantial freedom, independence, and discretion in scheduling the work and deciding how to carry it out. The more individuals feel personally responsible for deciding how to achieve the expected outcomes of the job, the more personal accountability they are likely to accept. This factor is covered extensively in Retention Practice #18.

Do you allow your people this kind of independence? Do you feel they need more training before you can feel comfortable giving them more autonomy? How can you provide more freedom and discretion in the jobs of those in your group who most lack this characteristic?

5. *Feedback.* This characteristic means that the job itself must provide continuous feedback, allowing the employee to gain the satisfaction of having immediate evidence of effectiveness on an ongoing basis, as, for example, when a mechanic turns the key of the car after fixing the starter, or when a sales clerk sells the right product to a customer, or when a doctor heals a patient with the proper care and medication. Some jobs do not provide this kind of feedback, as when an administrative assistant designs a proposal for a team of ad agency account executives, but is not there to see the client's reactions when it is presented.[1]

How can you build in ways for your people to receive more immediate feedback? How can you give them more immediate feedback yourself? (Also see Retention Practices #19 and 20.)

Rate Your Own Job First, Then the Employee's Job

You may want to first rate your own job on each of these five factors, using the Job Enrichment Rating form (Appendix C), before discussing them with your people. You may then decide to propose the redesign of your own job to make it more inherently rewarding. Then you will better appreciate what it takes to do the same for key employees you want to retain.

Before discussing job redesign with a key employee, give the employee the job enrichment form to rate his or her own job on the five factors. You should complete one as well, entering your perceptions of the employee's job, then compare and discuss your separate ratings. The differences may surprise you.

What obstacles are there to increasing some of these factors? Rigid job descriptions may be one. Another may be organizational cultures that are strongly founded on traditional ways, where people react to change by saying, "That's not the way it's always been done around here" or "We know the one best way to do the job." If the focus of people's jobs in your organization is on methods and not on outcomes, the redesign and enrichment of those jobs will be more difficult.

Guidelines for Redesigning and Enriching the Jobs of Your People

Managers sometimes struggle with ways to begin redesigning the jobs of their employees. Here are five ways that Hackman and Oldham recommend:

1. *Combining Tasks.* This method suggests that you take small tasks performed by separate people and combine them into a whole piece of work that one person can do. This serves to increase both skill variety and task identity, as when a nurse begins to provide many aspects of care and treatment for fewer patients instead of performing only one or two tasks for a larger number of patients.

2. *Forming Natural Work Units.* Allowing workers to arrange themselves into inherently meaningful or logical groupings increases both task identity and significance. One example is assigning systems analysts to a project team dedicated to one client instead of having them serve all clients. Natural work units can also be formed on the basis of any of several criteria—geography (giving salespeople their own territories), types of business served (assigning claims adjusters to certain industries), or work units (assigning clerical staff to certain departments).

3. *Establishing Client Relationships.* One way to increase job feedback is to put the employee into more direct contact with customers and to assign greater responsibility for managing customer relationships. For employees who want to exercise more of their interpersonal talents, the increased customer contact requires them to use these talents, thus also increasing skill variety. With increased responsibility for managing these relationships also comes a need for the added judgment required to negotiate due dates and priorities, troubleshoot problems, receive complaints, and make corrections, all producing a higher level of autonomy as well.

4. *Vertical Loading.* This concept means giving the worker increased autonomy by pushing down the responsibility and authority formerly held by the manager, for example, allowing teachers to select their own books and create their own lesson plans instead of requiring them to use books and lesson plans selected by the principal. There are many ways to vertically load a job—giving employees discretion in setting schedules, determining work methods, deciding when quality standards have been reached, and deciding when to start and stop work, when to take breaks, and how to assign priorities. (Caution: Beware of "horizontal job loading"—adding more and more tasks to an employee's job without adding to any of the key job enrichment factors.)

5. *Opening Feedback Channels.* The key here is to remove whatever is standing in the way of the employee's receiving direct feedback about how he or she is doing. There are many ways to do this. One is to establish more direct interaction with customers, as already discussed. Allowing workers to do more of their own quality control is another. Many organizations also post performance results for all to see rather than having these results kept only by the supervisor and transmitted up, not down. And, of course, much performance feedback information is now immediately available by computer, if we only take care to design our systems so that workers have access to it. However employees receive feedback, they should receive it as directly, as immediately, and as regularly as possible.

Who's Doing It

■ *United Parcel Service* knew it had to do something to reduce the turnover rate among its drivers. The company was all too aware of the costs involved in finding and training replacement drivers, who typically take months to learn their new routes. UPS first looked into the real reasons it was losing so many drivers and found that many had left because they so disliked the onerous task of loading packages at the beginning of each run.

The company made the decision to assign the loading task to a new group of workers. This caused a significant drop in the turnover rate of drivers. Although the turnover rate for the loaders was quite high, the company was willing to accept this, because these workers were much easier to replace than the drivers. This is a classic example of a company targeting and selectively retaining the workers it can least afford to lose.

- The CEO of *Maids International*, Dan Bishop, focused on identifying the factors that were causing burnout, fatigue, and sky-high turnover among his house-cleaning crews. After studying the way the crews did their jobs task by task, Bishop decided to increase skill variety by allowing them to rotate tasks from house to house and even built in a scheduled time for them to chat during drives between customers' houses. The average worker tenure increased to nine months, four months better than that for one of their main competitors for labor—McDonald's.

What obstacles do you see to increasing each of the five job enrichment factors in your own group and in your organization as a whole? Challenge yourself and your company to find ways to overcome those obstacles, and optimize the inherent satisfaction in the jobs of those people you most need to keep.

Bear in mind that job enrichment may not be the answer in keeping all employees. For example, job enrichment may not be enough to overcome an employee's dissatisfaction with pay or an important aspect of the work environment. More often than not, however, the right kind of job redesign will work to humanize and enrich the working lives of your people.

Now grade yourself and your organization on Retention Practice #5: "Redesign the Job Itself to Make It More Rewarding."

How good a job is your organization doing on this practice?

Circle one: (A) Excellent   (B) Very good   (C) Good   (D) Fair   (F) Poor

How good a job are you as a manager doing on this practice?

Circle one: (A) Excellent   (B) Very good   (C) Good   (D) Fair   (F) Poor

How important do you believe this practice is to your organization's strategy to attract and retain the talent necessary to meet its business objectives?

Circle one: (A) Critical (B) Very important (C) Somewhat important
             (D) Not important

What can your organization do to improve on this practice?

What can you as a manager do to improve on this practice?

RETENTION PRACTICE #6

Define the Results You Expect and the Talent You Need

When you recruit and hire for task X, it won't be long before the employee will be asked to do A, B, C, and D as well.
—Joanne Jorz, vice president,
program development, Conceptual Systems
(quoted in *HR* magazine, December 1996)

If you are like many managers today, you may be moving so fast to fill job vacancies that you don't stop to think about how the job has changed since you last filled it. Because everything is changing so fast, the job has probably changed as well. Changes in the outside marketplace and in customer relationships, technical innovations, downsizing, the use of outsourcing, and team dynamics all combine to change the way the job should now be defined. The continuing use of outdated job descriptions stands in the way of understanding the work that now needs doing and, ultimately, of your hiring the right person for the new job.

Here's a common scenario: For whatever reason, a manager is in a hurry to fill a position. As it happens, the demands and results expected of the person who fills this position have changed since the last time it was filled. Nevertheless, because getting a person to fill the position quickly is so important, the same old job description is used to write the help wanted ad and to screen in applicants.

Only when the interviewing starts do the various interviewers realize that they do not agree on the knowledge, talents, self-management traits, motivations, and "fit factors" needed for the job. Finally, one of them calls "time out" on the interviewing process so that the hiring team can discuss what is really needed and try to reach agreement before continuing to interview. In an attempt to speed up the process, the company has actually slowed it down and increased the risk that frustrated applicants will go elsewhere. This is a classic case where "doing it right the first time" shortens, rather than lengthens, the process.

In today's world, the whole concept of defining work in terms of jobs is now being questioned. In his book *JobShift*, William Bridges argues that companies now need to stop hiring people to do jobs as they have traditionally done. Instead, he proposes that "we must start helping people to refocus their energy on the work that needs doing; start helping people to rethink what they can do best and how to recycle those basic abilities into activities the organization needs doing."[1]

Bridges even goes so far as to say that, in the future, organizations will become "dejobbed." He cites the current trend among faster-moving, more successful organizations to use the following alternatives to the traditional one-job, one-person concept:

- *Contract-based hires*, where professionals who are not regular employees do the work
- *Cross-trained project teams*, where assignments are too time-limited for job descriptions to be written
- *Ad hoc groupings*, where reporting relationships are too brief to be finalized by a place on the organizational chart
- *Temporary hires*, where the work does not justify long-term employment
- *Entrepreneurial external vendors*, who take over some of the organization's work from its employees

Managers must now begin to think in terms of transferable talents deployed to meet present organizational needs. This acknowledges the reality that talent is the common denominator of all jobs and that needs are what creates jobs. After all, think about what a job really is—a talent that meets a need.

Many large companies are now defining and describing jobs in terms of competencies, not just in terms of duties and tasks or simply the knowledge required, as they have done in the past. One multinational food company lost twelve out of twenty-four presidents it hired over a three-year period before realizing it had failed to analyze the unique competencies required in each situation. When it began to conduct the proper competency analysis process for its next twenty-four hires, only two of them did not work out. Competencies can be knowledge, talents, motivations, or personality traits that can be measured and shown to differentiate between superior and average or poor performers.

When you start identifying what you want in a job candidate, you will want to focus first not on competencies but on the work that needs doing and, more relevant, on the results you expect from that work. You must state these results clearly and specifically. Another important consideration is that the results must be achieved in such a way that the employee's relationships with customers, vendors, peers, direct reports, and manager are not damaged.

Try this exercise. Write in the space below the immediate and ongoing results expected of you in your job, including the quality of those results. Another way of getting at these results is to ask yourself, "What would success look like six months or a year (or more) from now?"

_____

_____

_____

_____

_____

_____

The First Type of Competency—Talents

In the late 1970s, a young man named George Willig climbed the World Trade Center in New York City by inserting metal devices of his own design into the building's window washing channels. When the media descended on George's mother to get her perspective on her son's accomplishment, she recalled the times she had taken George and his sister to the amusement park as children. While his sister simply enjoyed the roller coaster ride, George always seemed more interested in how it worked mechanically. She further commented that he continued to make good use of his "eye for mechanical design" in his job as a toy designer for the Ideal Toy Company.

Most people are like George Willig, at least in the sense that they have natural talents they like to express, whether through their work or in some other way. Research on job satisfaction over the years has consistently revealed the use of one's innate abilities to be a more important satisfier and motivator than either money or status.

Talents are not rare and precious. Everyone has talents—too many to possibly name them all. Talents are behavior; they are the things we do more easily than the next person. We speak of "natural-born" talent, but those with a gift, knack, ability, or flair for something can refine and develop that talent through experience. Talents cannot be taught, however, so you have to select for them. As someone once said, "You can teach a turkey to climb a tree, but it is easier to hire a squirrel."

When selecting for talent, you must keep in mind that a person may have a talent, yet not enjoy using it. The ones we do enjoy using are called "motivated talents," meaning we find ourselves naturally self-motivated to use them. When given the opportunity to take on a challenge, we will prefer using our "motivated talents." As a career coach, I often ask people to make a list of "twenty things I like to do," or ask, "What do you do when no one is telling you what to do?" The answers to these questions often reveal a person's motivated talents.

The real trick is to match the right motivated talents to the right role, challenges, and expected results, while not forgetting that the person needs to mesh with the styles and complement the talents of you and of the others on your team in achieving the objectives of your unit. Another key to remember is that people with different motivated talents can achieve the same expected result in their own unique ways.

In spite of this last admonition, it is still helpful to use a checklist of the talents you hope the candidate will possess.

Now, using yourself as a "guinea pig" in this process, look back at the results expected of you in your current job, as you previously listed them. In the Talent Inventory (Appendix D), check and/or write in the twenty most important talents that you believe are needed to achieve these results:

Compare the talents you checked and wrote in on the Talent Inventory to the talents described or implied in your job description. Are they substantially different? Now go back and circle the ten abilities you consider most important to success in your job.

The Second Type of Competency—Knowledge

The next type of competency to consider is the knowledge necessary to achieve the results. In other words, what do you need to know about or have experience with that will help you get the required results? Unlike talents and personality traits, knowledge can be taught or self-taught by study or practice.

Examples of knowledge include computer programming languages, foreign languages, manufacturing operations, the insurance business, the contacts or customers you know, the geographical territory where you live or have lived, the classroom knowledge areas you have acquired, the tricks of the trade you picked up in your first couple of jobs, or whatever you may have learned through a hobby or leisure pursuit, such as photography, woodworking, or managing your investments.

Over the years, hiring managers and human resources staff have made countless hiring mistakes by overemphasizing the importance of technical knowledge requirements in screening candidates for the job. This happens because we tend to think of knowledge as a minimum requirement for qualification, or "ticket to entry." Some managers are too quick to screen out applicants with just the right talents, personality traits, and motivation for the job just because they may lack a perfectly trainable knowledge. The fact is, knowledge can be transferred, and new hires can be trained.

Now, list the areas of knowledge (Appendix D) you consider necessary to achieve the results expected of you within the next year and beyond, as if you were preparing to hire your replacement.

Now go back and place an "R" next to those that are required (the candidate "must have") and a "P" next to those that are preferred but not required. Next, place a "T" next to those for which your company is willing or able to provide training to the candidate who is qualified in every other way but lacks a key knowledge.

The Third Type of Competency—Self-Management Traits

The third major type of competency is self-management traits—the personality characteristics and attributes of temperament that were formed early in life and are not likely to change significantly. Many companies are now focusing on such traits as elements of "emotional intelligence" that, in a business environment that puts a premium on self-directedness, teamwork, and interpersonal skills, are more important than ever to individual and organizational success.

Because self-management traits are resistant to change, they are important to consider when trying to match candidates with your company's culture or unit subculture, including the type of manager to whom they will report. Self-management traits are often the key "fit factors" that determine whether or not there will be "chemistry" or compatibility between two coworkers or whether a new hire will be accepted by others on the team. When some companies say they "hire for values" or "hire for attitude and train for skill," they are actually hiring for character traits such as confidence, integrity, tenacity, trustworthiness, and courage.

The Self-Management Trait Inventory in Appendix D can help you focus on the self-management traits needed to achieve the results you expect and the cultural fit you believe to be necessary for success. Use it to describe your own traits, as if you were preparing to hire your replacement:

You may have noticed that many of these self-management traits come close to the wording of talents in the talent inventory. This is because self-management traits are talents in the broadest sense, and the two frequently cannot be separated. If you feel that you have checked traits and skills that mean the same thing, then you may want to substitute one for the other.

Now go back and circle the ten self-management traits that you believe would be most important for your replacement to possess.

The Fourth Type of Competency—Motivations

If we define competency as an underlying characteristic of an individual that can be shown to be connected to superior performance, then we must include motivations. In listening to the most satisfying achievements of hundreds of workers in transition during the past twenty-five years, I have consistently been able to identify a variety of motivations that drive them to achieve.

They were all naturally self-motivated to meet some kinds of challenges, but not the same kinds of challenges. They were looking for opportunities (often without even knowing it) to achieve a certain kind of result or intrinsic reward for their efforts. Analysis of a person's most satisfying life and work achievements, such as might be conducted in a behavioral interview, will reveal that person's prime motivators.

As you look over the Motivation Inventory in Appendix D, check those that you believe would be most fully engaged by your potential replacement, as you consider the results now expected of you.

If you were hiring a manager to come in and turn around a department in disarray, for example, you might look for a candidate whose most satisfying accomplishments revealed motivations such as "to respond to a challenge," "to overcome adversity," "to be a change agent," or "to have an impact." For a manager who would be starting up a department you might look for different kinds of motivations, as might be shown in past successes where the candidate repeatedly "built enterprises" of some kind or "realized visions" (see Retention Practice #6 for guidelines on how to structure questions to uncover these motivations).

Now, go back and circle three motivations that you believe would best suit the challenges involved in reaching the results currently expected of you if you were selecting your replacement at this point in time.

Questions to consider:

- Does your job description accurately reflect the talents, knowledge, self-management traits, and motivations required to achieve results expected of you now and in the future?
- If you had to hire your replacement, would you still use the job description as the basis for writing a recruitment ad?

You may now want to meet with your manager and explain what you have checked and written about the talents, knowledge, traits, and motivations needed in your present job. Have your manager ask you questions until you are both sure you understand the results fully and why these competencies are important to the achievement of those results.

Check your new list of competencies against those in your current job description. Update your job description with your human resources representative. Meet with your boss to revise your current performance plan, if appropriate. Then, repeat all the same steps for each of those who report to you.

Of course, before using any of these four competency inventories, check within your company to see if you should be using competency assessment instruments that your company has specifically developed for you to use with the people you manage.

How to Use These Competency Inventories to Increase Retention

Before making your next hire or filling a position on your team internally, first list the specific results you expect the new person to achieve within the next six months, one year, and beyond, if appropriate. Think about the changes taking place in your company, industry, marketplace, and competitive environment. Consider the key people with whom the new person will have to interact. What special circumstances and constraints are they likely to encounter?

Using the Talent, Knowledge, Self-Management Trait, and Motivation Inventories in Appendix D, check the competences you believe will be needed. You may want to have all those involved in the hiring decision complete the inventories separately. You can then get together to discuss what you are looking for, resolve differences, and complete a Candidate Profile/Evaluation (Appendix E) to use as a guide to creating interview questions. As you do so, remember that the results you expect as a team are the most important thing to be clear about.

Despite all your efforts to define what talents, knowledge, traits, and motivations will be needed to achieve those results, you cannot take all the guesswork out of the process. It is possible that candidates without all the competencies you specified can be successful as well. This is not an exact and foolproof process, but, if you will take the time to go through it when you hire, it will reduce your percentage of bad hires significantly, and that in itself will assure you of a higher retention rate.

Hiring with Success by Studying Your Best

Building templates of your "water walkers" (people who are so consistently outstanding it seems they can do no wrong) is another effective, more sophisticated technique for determining the real competencies necessary for success, especially for positions with large numbers of occupants where openings recur frequently.

'Water walkers" are your most successful performers in any given job category. You know who your top performers are, but have you ever stopped to ask yourself what they do that makes them successful?

Many companies have created profiles of their most successful employees to use as a "template" for identifying and hiring more employees like them. Other companies train their less-effective employees to do the things that top performers do.

There are many top consulting firms that assist organizations in selection and training using these methods. The Doubletree Hotel organization, for example, had a consulting firm conduct interviews with 300 employees to analyze the personal attributes of "standouts" and "washouts" and is using the results to create a database of success factors for various jobs. The company has identified the dimensions of success for reservation agents such as sales ability, attention to detail, adaptability/flexibility, and motivation. There are specific definitions for each of these, and the company has designed interview questions to uncover them.

The psychologists John Flanagan, during World War II, and, later, David McClelland, the Harvard professor who studied high achievers and motivation almost his entire career, were pioneers in doing "competency assessment" for organizations. The technique typically begins with "behavioral event" interviews with "water walkers." These top performers are asked to provide step-by-step accounts of critical incidents where they performed in a superior manner. A list of competencies is distilled from these interviews and then used for selection and training.

Fast-growing companies that are bringing in many new hires and want to be more confident about the characteristics they look for in hiring are getting a great return on their investment from this process.

Who's Doing It

■ One major retailer complained about excessive turnover among its mostly male sales staff: 40 percent of all new salespeople were leaving within six months. The company planned to open several new outlets and would have to hire many more salespeople. It wanted top performers who would also stay.

Using sales figures and peer ratings (important in eliminating superstars who may be selling at the expense of other salespeople), the company identified its top performers. In-depth behavioral event interviews uncovered fifteen competencies, including energy (but not aggression, as they had predicted), an intense concern for customer wants, the ability to manage time efficiently, and the willingness to use spare time to do sales-related tasks. Job applicants in one region were then given one-hour versions of the behavioral-event interviews (see Retention Practice #7), which resulted in the company's starting to hire more applicants in that region with nonsales backgrounds and more women. After three months, the newly hired salespeople in that region were achieving sales revenues 15 percent higher than those achieved in other regions, and their turnover rate was only 12 percent, compared to a rate of 40 percent in the other regions.[2]

Competency assessment, to be successful, should be customized to the needs of a given organization. The customization and validation process (including the use of standardized personality surveys to document the traits of actual top performers) takes time and expertise. Additionally, because of fast-changing conditions, the organization may be required to reward new success-related behavior rather than the behavior it has rewarded in the past. Keep in mind that, when identifying competencies for the purpose of selection, the company should define competencies as special characteristics of the people who do the job best.

Suggested assignment: Think of the top performers in your department or organization. Do you really know what they do differently from their less effective peers? Write down the competencies you think make them successful, then ask them what competencies they think make them successful.

Consider collaborating with a human resources representative or consultant trained in competency assessment to interview these individuals in detail about the steps they took to accomplish several recent successes. Better yet, observe them at work.

The competencies you identify may surprise you, but remember, competency assessment must be done on several top performers before a template of critical competencies can be considered valid and reliable. You may also want to use a consultant trained in assessment to use normed and standardized personality surveys to supplement competency analysis and further validate the profiles of successful versus average performers.

Now grade yourself and your organization on Retention Practice #6: "Define the Results You Expect and the Talent You Need."

How good a job is your organization doing on this practice?

Circle one: (A) Excellent (B) Very good (C) Good (D) Fair (F) Poor

How good a job are you as a manager doing on this practice?

Circle one: (A) Excellent (B) Very good (C) Good (D) Fair (F) Poor

How important do you believe this practice is to your organization's strategy to attract and retain the talent necessary to meet its business objectives?

Circle one: (A) Critical (B) Very important (C) Somewhat important
            (D) Not important

What can your organization do to improve on this practice?

What can you as a manager do to improve on this practice?

RETENTION PRACTICE # 7

Ask the Questions that Require Proof of Talent

I aspire to create an enterprise where at least 80 percent of everybody's job consists of doing things they love.
—CEO, First USA Corporation

Contrary to the quotation, it has been estimated that 80 percent of American workers are mismatched with their jobs in terms of the natural abilities required or the self-motivation needed to perform them well.[1] There are many reasons for this; perhaps you have had experience with a few of them:

- The company was in such a hurry to fill the position that it did not take the time to define the required competencies.
- The applicant was more interested in getting a job than in asking questions to find out whether it was the right job.
- The company's decision to hire was based primarily on the requirement of an educational degree or credential, or of a technical capability, and not on the real ability to do the job.
- The company's decision to hire was based primarily on the candidate's charming manner and ability to interview well, despite the lack of the natural abilities and motivation necessary to do the job well.
- The company's decision to hire was based primarily on someone's personal relationship with the candidate or on the recommendation of a friend or colleague, with little effort invested in evaluating the individual.
- The manager was never trained in effective interviewing techniques.

All these factors combine to create an alarming rate of turnover in the first three to six months on the job. And yet many companies continue to make these mistakes, continue to endure the frustration, continue to pay the costs of turnover—including customer service disruption, reemployment, and training—rather than taking the time to learn a more effective way. The good news is—there is a more effective way.

Let's assume you have followed the guidelines in Retention Practice #6 for defining the key results expected and the four types of competencies required for the next position you are about to fill. Before starting to interview candidates for the job, what do you do first? Now that you have invested the time in defining the job, it stands to reason that you would think up some questions that would require candidates to present evidence that they actually possess those competencies and are motivated to achieve the expected results.

These would not be the traditional pet questions, such as:

- Tell me about yourself.
- What are your strengths?
- What are your weaknesses?

Or hypothetical questions, such as:

- How would you go about finding new office space?
- What would you do if two of your employees weren't getting along?

Or, even worse, leading questions, such as:

- You do have good presentation skills, don't you?
- Working long hours doesn't bother you, does it?

The problem with all these questions is that they do not elicit answers that give actual evidence that the candidate can do and will do the job.

To hire the right people in the first place, you will need to ask behavior-based questions. This style of interviewing—"behavioral interviewing"—is now being used by an estimated one-fourth of all U.S. companies. Behavioral techniques are growing in popularity each year because companies are discovering that they take much of the guesswork out of the hiring equation.

Behavioral interviewing is based on the premise that the best predictor of future behavior is past behavior. Unless you can audition, have the individual work for a trial period, or go through an "assessment center simulation," behavioral interviewing is the best available technique for uncovering what are known as the "can do" (knowledge and experience) and "will do" (the talents you are self-motivated to use) factors in a given job. Behavior-based questions require the applicant to give examples of actual past behavior that reveal evidence that either proves the existence of motivated abilities or reveals the lack of them.

Motivated talents, as previously noted, are simply the abilities we especially enjoy using and prefer to use when we have a choice. They are usually action verbs, such as "leading," "training," "planning," "listening," "repairing," and "analyzing," as shown in the Talent Inventory in Appendix D. Sometimes the same traits are described differently, as in "willingness to take charge" or "reacts well in emergencies." In some cases, candidates can be tested for these abilities, such as finger dexterity, visual acuity, or even conceptual ability.

We are internally self-motivated to use certain motivated talents. That is, we do not require any outside motivation to use them other than a challenge that engages them. Because this select handful of talents is intrinsically satisfying to use, we gain tremendous satisfaction in using them and seek opportunities to use them again, regardless of whether we receive recognition, praise, or a monetary or material reward.

Here's how you would go about preparing the right kinds of questions if you were about to hire a new receptionist. First, you would simply list the results you expect as discussed in Retention Practice #6, for example:

- Be on time and have a good attendance record.
- Elicit very few caller or customer complaints.
- Maintain composure under the stress of simultaneous callers.
- Elicit positive caller or customer comments on patience, friendliness, and helpfulness.
- Remember caller/customer names.
- Have good working relationships with other office staff.
- Communicate information accurately.
- Follow up promptly on customer inquiries.

Next, you would list the competencies required to achieve these results, such as:

- Punctuality and reliability for showing up at work
- Strong customer service attitude and orientation
- Ability to remain calm and composed under stress
- Patient assertiveness with rude callers
- Natural interest in people and friendliness
- Good memory for names
- Ability to work a strong team member with other staff

- Persistence in getting accurate information to the right person in a timely manner

Now you are ready to make a list of behavior-based questions. Instead of asking a leading question, such as "Are you good at handling rude callers?," which almost always elicits an answer such as, "Yes, I happen to be quite good at that," you come up with a question that requires some proof that the person has demonstrated that ability in the past, such as: "Tell me about how you handled a particularly rude customer in your last job."

Other behavioral questions you might ask a receptionist candidate:

- Describe a time when you had to be persistent in answering a caller's question.
- Tell me about a time when you had to remember callers' names.
- Tell me about a situation where you had to work in close cooperation with coworkers.
- Can you recall a time when you were under a lot of stress from an overload of callers and how you handled it?
- Tell me about a time when you were going to have to miss work because of outside or personal issues other than illness; how did you deal with the situation?

These questions force the candidate to come up with the only kind of answer that truly convinces—actual past behavior. As the behavioral interviewer, you will have to be patient and give the candidate the time to think of a past situation, even if it takes several seconds. You must learn to say, "Take your time," and be comfortable with the silence as they reflect.

Keep in mind that past decisions made by candidates are also behavior and can reveal a great deal about both fit and motivation, especially the reasons the candidate took each new job and what the candidate liked most and least about each new job and about previous managers.

Behavioral interviews are almost impossible to fake. Candidates have a very difficult time coming up with convincing untrue stories on the spur of the moment. This technique can even be used to determine which candidates stand the greatest chance of fitting into your particular work culture. For example, if your work culture requires employees to use their own judgment with minimal supervisory input, you would ask the obvious question, "Tell me about a time when you had to use your own judgment to handle a tough problem without being able to consult your supervisor."

Of course, you will need to judge for yourself whether the candidate's stories and examples are as persuasive as they need to be to really prove that the person has the talents, traits, and motivations you are seeking. The longer your list of behavioral questions, the more likely you will get the evidence you need to make the right selection. It is also important not to allow candidates to ask questions about the position at the beginning of the interview, as this gives them the ability to gear their answers to what they think you want, just so they can get to the next step.

When you ask a behavioral question, you will want to listen for three parts of the story:

1. Circumstances, setting, and challenge
2. Specific actions taken by the applicant
3. Outcomes or results of those actions

Often, the applicant will simply give the circumstances, and it will be up to the interviewer to ask follow-up questions to get the rest of the story. Follow-up questions are critically important in interviewing, as the applicant may not provide the behavioral response you requested. Some examples:

Interviewer says: "Tell me about how you handled a particularly rude customer in your last job."

Applicant gives a hypothetical response: "If I had a rude customer, I would be cordial but persistent."

Interviewer persists in getting a behavioral response: "Actually, I'd like to hear about a specific time when you had a rude customer. I want to know exactly what steps you took and what the results were." Interviewer waits in silence while applicant recalls an incident.

Applicant may tell only the circumstances and not the actions or results: "Well, one time I had a mad caller who had received the wrong part for a critical machine in his production line."

Interviewer says: "Go on, tell me what happened."

Behavioral interviewing can also be used to determine whether a red flag, such as a resume that indicates "job-hopping," is the result of an inability to get along with managers, customers, or coworkers or is due to mitigating circumstances, such as a plant closure, relocation of spouse, or aggressive recruitment by a competitor. In this situation, in addition to asking why the person left each job, you might also ask, "Tell me about a time you were faced with a personality conflict at work and how you handled it" or "Have you ever been terminated from a job?" and, if so, "Tell me the circumstances leading up to it, what happened, and how you responded to it."

Another important thing to remember about behavioral interviewing is that if a talent or trait is strong and self-motivated, it will recur throughout the candidate's life. This means you shouldn't have to probe more than once in order to get the candidate to come up with a specific example. If you do, then chances are that the talent, trait, or behavior is not part of a strong and recurring motivational pattern.

To use behavioral interviewing to identify the key motivations you are looking for, ask candidates what they liked and disliked about each of their past jobs, why they made key career decisions they have made so far, why they left each of their past jobs to take the next job, and, most important, what was the most satisfying thing about each of their most satisfying life and work accomplishments. All these questions get at the underlying gratification in the candidate's real past behavior, but, in order to uncover a predictive pattern, you must pursue all these lines of questioning.

If you have taken the time and trouble to identify the talents, traits, and behaviors of your most successful performers (as discussed in Retention Practice #6), you will know what behavioral questions to ask in hiring future applicants for those positions.

To be done well, behavioral interviewing requires training, practice, and the discipline to slow down, analyze the job, prepare questions, and be patient with the process during the interview. You must be sure to ask all candidates, both external as well as internal, the same questions. The benefits you will gain will be worth the preparation time you invest. This powerful tool will help you to significantly reduce your mis-hire rate, a key factor in reducing turnover.

Try this exercise. Review your top twenty talents, your top ten self-management traits, and your top five motivations, the ones you previously selected as most important to success in your job (from the Talent, Self-Management Trait, and Motivation Inventories in Retention Practice #6). Now, write in the spaces below some behavioral questions you would ask if you were interviewing your replacement tomorrow:

_____

_____

_____

Repeat this process for the next position you may need to fill.

Other Reliable Ways to Evaluate Job Candidates

Behavioral interviewing is not the only way to assess and select job applicants, though it is probably the most practical and affordable for most managers. Many organizations supplement the behavioral interviewing process by having applicants take batteries of standardized personality inventories that help to predict applicant success. Such inventories should be used only when they have been validated, that is, taken by already successful employees and proven to be predictive of success in particular job roles.

Many other companies, such as BMW and Cessna, use simulations. At its factory in South Carolina, BMW has built a simulated assembly line where job candidates get ninety minutes to perform a variety of work-related tasks. Cessna has developed an elaborate role-playing exercise for managers that simulates a day in the life of a harried executive. A job candidate may spend an entire day in an office with phone, fax, and an in-basket stuffed with files and letters. The company will even have someone call the candidate and pretend to be an irate customer, to see how the candidate responds to that situation.

At Nucor, the steel manufacturer, the company carefully watches the construction crews that build its plants, looking for the work habits it values, then hires the best to work in the plants. Many companies hire temp workers and college interns with the same intent and find that getting a sample of their actual performance reduces the risk of hiring. Companies that use simulations and behavior observations swear by these methods, and understandably so, as the same principle holds: Behavior predicts behavior.

Now grade yourself and your organization on Retention Practice #7: "Ask the Questions That Require Proof of Talent."

How good a job is your organization doing on this practice?

Circle one: (A) Excellent   (B) Very good   (C) Good   (D) Fair   (F) Poor

How good a job are you as a manager doing on this practice?

Circle one: (A) Excellent   (B) Very good   (C) Good   (D) Fair   (F) Poor

How important do you believe this practice is to your organization's strategy to attract and retain the talent necessary to meet its business objectives?

Circle one: (A) Critical (B) Very important (C) Somewhat important
            (D) Not important

What can your organization do to improve on this practice?

What can you as a manager do to improve on this practice?

Retention Practice #8

Give a Realistic Job Preview

Generally, job satisfaction is the result of an individual's expectations of, and what is received from, different facets of the work situation. The closer the expectation is to what is actually received, the greater the job satisfaction.
—Gene Milbourn and G. James Francis

It's an old story—a new recruit discovers, perhaps on the first day, or in the first week, or maybe not until months later, that the job is not what he expected, and quits. When this happens, the recruiting process must begin again, followed by training, lost productivity, and expenses that might have been avoided.

This is an especially common scenario among entry-level employees, whose lack of work experience necessarily produces unrealistic expectations. New recruits are frequently disappointed in the lack of initial challenge on the job, the slow rate of advancement, the routine aspects of the job, the management style of the boss, the lack of a window, and on and on. They are often not even aware that they have expectations about these things until after they have been on the job for a while.

On the other side of the equation, inexperienced hiring managers are often reluctant to discuss aspects of the job or organization that might seem unattractive for fear that the applicant might not want to take the job. After losing a few disillusioned new employees, these managers may eventually learn that discussing the less desirable aspects of the job prior to the hire actually serves to screen in those who are most likely to stay and succeed.

Experienced managers also realize that they need to discuss the results and standards they expect before the applicant has accepted the position, not afterward. One of the main reasons that expected results are not discussed in the hiring process is that the manager hasn't given much thought to her expectations in the first place. If you have taken the time to define the results expected and abilities required, as discussed in Retention Practice #6, you need only to discuss these expectations straightforwardly with each candidate.

What both employers and prospective employees overlook is that they are engaged in forging a "psychological contract" with each other that may be unwritten but is no less binding than a legal contract. It is an implicit contract between the individual and the organization that specifies what each expects to give and receive from the other in the relationship. When expectations match, then there is a good chance the parties will be happy with the situation. For example, when a new hire expects an office and gets an office, then the reality matches the expectation. However, when the new hire expects an office, then finds that he must share a cubicle, there is a mismatch that can create disillusionment and contribute to an eventual resignation.

In his classic article "The Psychological Contract: Managing the Joining Up Process," John Paul Kotter pointed out that there are really four sets of expectations—what the employee expects to give and receive, and what the organization expects to give and receive.[1] As a manager representing the organization, you may expect an employee to occasionally work on Saturdays, but if the employee did not hear you state that expectation, she may come to resent giving up time with her family and begin looking for another position.

Kotter's research showed that psychological contracts in which both sides have similar expectations are more likely to result in greater job satisfaction, higher productivity, and reduced turnover. However, when there are several mismatches in expectations, the opposite results are more likely.

Of course, either party can and will break the contract if important expectations are not met. In a job market where the supply of entry-level jobs exceeds the demand, the disappointed new hire is the party more likely to break the contract. New hires frequently don't leave the company until there is a series of perceived let-downs or disappointments that serve to "push" or motivate them to consider resigning. Thinking the company has broken its promise, individuals react by slowly breaking their part of the bargain. The new hire may begin to disengage, perhaps by coming in later or going home earlier or even by stealing from the company ("they owe me!").

Some areas where new hires frequently expect more than the company is prepared to give are:

- Opportunity for rapid advancement
- Level of responsibility
- Personal growth and training
- Job security
- Opportunity to operate independently
- Coaching and mentoring
- Opportunities to exercise creativity

Some areas where organizations frequently expect more than new hires are prepared to give are:

- Willingness to work long hours
- Ability to work effectively in teams
- Willingness to conform to the organization's culture
- Willingness to travel or relocate
- Willingness to accept pace of work
- Willingness to adapt to rapid changes

The possibility of mismatches is increased by the manager's hurry to fill the position, which forces hasty "contracting," leading to career dissatisfaction and, ultimately, a high rate of attrition.

Many companies have responded in recent years by initiating the practice of giving "realistic job previews" before the applicant has accepted the job. Such previews may be given in the form of straightforward discussions, videotapes, observation of the work being done, or unpaid "internships." Some managers even allow recruits to "shadow" a current employee for a day so they can see for themselves what the work is really like. It is just as important to dispel unrealistic expectations as it is to provide factual information about the daily realities of the job and the working conditions.

Do you give "realistic job previews" to the people you recruit? Have you lost employees during their first few weeks on the job because they discovered something about the job that they hadn't expected? Are you afraid you will scare off attractive candidates if you tell them what the job is really like?

No job is perfect. But you want to hire the people who fall in love with the job in spite of its imperfections. Just keep in mind that you must also describe the attractions and satisfactions of the job as well. It's one thing to sell a new recruit on the new job, but it's even better to sell them and have them stay sold.

Who's Doing It

- *Jiffy Lube.* Jiffy Lube was experiencing unacceptably high rates of turnover, as high as 180 percent in many of its stores, among entry-level service technicians. Many had accepted these positions without giving a thought to the extremely hot summertime conditions and the extremely cold wintertime conditions that are inevitable when working in the service bay areas, and they were quitting to take indoor jobs with other companies.

Jiffy Lube decided to recruit high school juniors for trial internship positions in the bays. These internships can lead to part-time jobs and carry the promise of partial assistance with college tuition for those who stay with the company for two years. This system allows the interns to "preview" the conditions firsthand. Those who cannot endure the extreme conditions are allowed to drop out before the company has invested very much in bringing them aboard and training them as full-time employees. The turnover rate among these recruits has been significantly reduced.

■ *Wells Fargo Bank.* In order to reduce its high first-year turnover rate among tellers, Wells Fargo began using a technique that served to screen candidates by assessing their customer relations ability, while simultaneously giving them a realistic preview of the job, all in the same process. Here's how it works. The bank requires all teller applicants to sit at a video screen with keyboard and to watch an interactive CD-ROM, with actual customers appearing on the screen before them with various complaints. When an irate customer is seen complaining about a miscalculation of her balance, the frame freezes and the applicants have to choose from four multiple-choice responses, indicating how they would respond to the customer. This technique has helped the bank reduce its turnover rate among tellers by screening out those who realize through this experience that a teller's day-to-day work activity would not be their cup of tea.

■ *GeoAccess.* This Kansas City company takes pride in its entrepreneurial spirit. Its motto is "Let results rule!" Employees wear shorts to work and take pains to keep things nonbureaucratic. The communication style of the company is direct, frank, and spontaneous. In meetings, employees give one another feedback that is honest but may hurt. "We lay it on the table," says the human resources director, Greg Addison. "Things move so fast here. . . . We have no time for meetings after the meetings." Addison makes sure that all job applicants are made aware of this aspect of the company's culture so that they won't be surprised once they are on board. The company also tells candidates that they must be comfortable in a role that will be undefined except for results expected. "Many companies don't understand their own culture," he says, "so they select misfits."

There are also special circumstances when being truthful in prehire situations is critical, as when an organization is downsizing or experiencing a disruptive culture change, such as a merger or acquisition. Candidates will have questions about job security, possible limitations to advancement opportunities, and rumors they have heard. These concerns should be addressed in a frank and open manner.

When hiring in uncertain times, it also makes sense to look for candidates who have had a variety of work experiences and have shown they can be flexible and handle more than one role at a time as well as those with a willingness to accept the truth and take the job anyway.

The key here is to minimize surprise. Resist the temptation to tell only the good things about the job and the work environment.

Questions to consider:

- What are some things about your workplace you would be reluctant to tell a job applicant?
- What are some of the most common unrealistic expectations among new hires that lead to turnover in your organization?
- What can you and your organization do to eliminate or reduce these unrealistic expectations?
- What obstacles do you face in carrying out these actions?

Now grade yourself and your organization on Retention Practice #8: "Give a Realistic Job Preview."

How good a job is your organization doing on this practice?

Circle one: (A) Excellent   (B) Very good   (C) Good   (D) Fair   (F) Poor

How good a job are you as a manager doing on this practice?

Circle one: (A) Excellent   (B) Very good   (C) Good   (D) Fair   (F) Poor

How important do you believe this practice is to your organization's strategy to attract and retain the talent necessary to meet its business objectives?

Circle one: (A) Critical (B) Very important (C) Somewhat important
            (D) Not important

What can your organization do to improve on this practice?

What can you as a manager do to improve on this practice?

RETENTION PRACTICE #9

Use Multiple Interviewers and Reference Checking

Hire fast, suffer slow.

—Anonymous

When it comes to selecting the right person, the more inputs you can get, the better—up to a point. Think about who needs to have a say in the hiring decision—possibly your manager, key peers, a human resources manager, perhaps a technical expert, or even a customer. Three to five interviewers seems to be the optimal range to increase the likelihood that the right person will be selected without the selection process becoming too time-consuming for all concerned.

You must remember, of course, to make sure that all interviewers have reached agreement about key results expected of the candidate and the talents, traits, knowledge, and motivations needed to achieve them (see Retention Practice #6). You may want to use the Candidate Profile/Evaluation form presented in Appendix E to summarize the key competencies you are seeking. Reaching agreement is not easy, considering the usual pressures to hire quickly and the difficulty of getting all the parties together at the same time.

One way to do multiple interviewing is to have all interviewers meet with the candidate one-on-one, a technique known as serial interviewing. Each interviewer pursues his or her own line of questioning, incorporating different behavioral questions, as previously described. Interviewers meet beforehand to decide who gives what information about the company, the job, the benefits, and so on in the "selling" phase at the end of each interview. When the interviews are over, the primary interviewer then checks with the other interviewers for their impressions and/or meets with them as a group.

Interviewers should be cautioned not to share their impressions with one another between interviews, giving each other the thumbs-up or thumbs-down or commenting about what they liked or disliked. It's best if each person reaches an independent assessment.

Another multiple interviewing method, recommended especially for star prospects, is to have two or three interviewers huddle after meeting with each candidate to compare notes. They can then decide what other questions need to be asked and perhaps what other information to pass on to the candidate, such as selling points, key facts about the company, or a realistic job preview. The next step is to brief the final interviewer, who will then conduct the more focused closing interview.

While many companies use a panel of interviewers, which uses less time, such panels are often not conducive to building rapport and creating an atmosphere of openness. Panel interviews can come across as interrogations with no apparent or logical pattern to the questioning. They tend to work better when the interviewing team has planned the questioning sequence and coordinated beforehand, or when one person conducts the interview while the others sit in and listen.

It can even be good strategy to include skeptics and naysayers in the group of interviewers, whether the format is a panel or serial, especially with managerial candidates. If candidates can pass muster with the severest critics, this can often accelerate their assimilation as word gets around and may even turn the critics themselves into strong advocates.

Whichever multiple interviewing method you choose, you will enhance your chances of hiring the right person when you bring several different perspectives to the table.

Who's Doing It

▪ *Old World Spices and Seasonings, Inc.* This Kansas City custom blender of food seasonings wanted to reduce turnover and maintain high morale by getting everyone involved in the hiring process. After an initial screening interview, all job candidates interview with a five-person committee that rotates quarterly, with each department represented on the committee. The only fixture among the five is the human resources manager.

Before each candidate's second interview, the committee reviews materials, and the human resources manager reminds them of questions they can and cannot ask. Interviews typically last two hours. If the committee votes to hire a candidate, the human resources manager consults with the department manager, then makes the offer.

After coming aboard, new hires go through extensive training and receive weekly performance reviews and more formal monthly reviews for the first three months. The committee then reviews the new hire's performance and recommends whether to make the person a permanent employee.

The company's president is satisfied that the process has helped ensure the hiring and retention of good people. The process has also built a sense of teamwork and pride among employees in having done a good job in making an important company decision. Besides giving new hires a feeling of acceptance before they even start, the process allows them to feel comfortable asking a panel of their future peers what it is really like to work there. This reduces the likelihood they will have unrealistic expectations about the job environment (see Retention Practice #8) and become turnover statistics later.

▪ *The Taylor Group.* This systems integrator in Bedford, New Hampshire, puts job candidates through a rigorous screening process that typically involves four separate visits and eight or more separate interviews over the course of a month. Each interview is designed to probe a different aspect of the candidate. The screening process begins with preliminary e-mail questions and a phone interview, by which 25 percent of applicants are usually eliminated as not good fits for the culture. In subsequent rounds, managers share detailed written reports of their notes to brief the next interviewer and take part in post-interview debriefings.

The ultimate hiring decision is based on consensus, but one serious objection by any one of the interviewers is all it takes to eliminate a candidate. The company's human resources manager, Laurie Murphy, reports that if a candidate becomes impatient with the process "and pressures us for a quicker response, we don't succumb." The company maintains a mere 6 percent turnover rate. "Getting it right the first time is the best approach to retention," says Murphy. "In this market it's easy to lose candidates, but it's worse to lose employees."[1]

Creative Screening Tactics

There are a number of ways to get a handle on the personality characteristics of job applicants that go beyond the traditional office interview and setting. Here are some ideas:

▪ Ask candidates to lunch and suggest they do the driving. The best candidates will have clean cars and usually do well conversing in the informal restaurant environment.
▪ Place help wanted ads that show your company's name but not the phone number. Candidates with initiative will look up the number.
▪ When unsure about a candidate after an interview, instruct the person to follow up with a phone call, then don't return the first two calls. Those with persistence will keep calling.[2]

The Lost Art of the Reference Check

Reference checking is yet another way to bring depth to the candidate assessment and selection process. Many employers believe that an honest reference check is the most reliable piece of information they can get to help them get a well-rounded picture of a future new hire.

Yet, many managers do not contact references, because they:

1. Prefer to trust their own intuition about candidates (which often turns out to be wrong).
2. Believe that all references are only going to say positive things anyway.
3. Are not willing to spend the time contacting references.
4. Don't believe that references will tell them anything more than the person's job title and dates of employment. because of HR policies that restrict what they can say.

The time problem is especially frustrating, because managers think they are saving time by rushing through the hiring process when they are really risking that they will have to repeat the process all over again, thus losing twice the time. During a seminar for a restaurant chain, one hiring expert quipped that "most interviews for crew employees today last roughly twenty minutes and consist of only three basic questions: 'Is your heart beating?,' 'Will you promise not to steal too much?,' and, most importantly, 'Can you work this weekend?' "[3]

You need to believe that checking with references is worth the time it takes. Getting the impressions and evaluations of those who have worked with the candidate in previous organizations is in some ways superior to behavioral interviewing, as the input you get, although delivered indirectly, is based on direct observation of real past behavior.

The checking of references has become more difficult because of the chilling effect lawsuits have had on the willingness of past supervisors to speak candidly. On the recommendation of attorneys and human resources departments, many managers will not divulge anything about past employees except job title and dates of employment. This reluctance stems from the fact that many companies have been sued by rejected job candidates for defamation of character.

Meanwhile, other employers have been sued because they failed, during reference checks by hiring companies, to give information about past criminal records of former workers who later committed crimes against their new coworkers. In reaction to this problem and the ongoing need for employers to have the benefit of information only references can provide, thirty-two states have enacted statutes that offer protection from liability

for employers who give references in good faith—that is, factual information given without malice.

Be aware of the laws in your state concerning immunity from lawsuits
for former employers who relay truthful reference information about employees to prospective employers. In spite of the threat of suits, many references will still speak openly if approached with politeness and persistence.

In a recent survey, 74 percent of executives polled at *Fortune* 1,000
companies said they have policies to confirm names and employment dates
only. However, the survey also found that half of the executives surveyed
were willing to disregard their policies in order to give a boost to the careers
of top-performing former employees.[4]

Another obstacle to reference checking is the fact that more than 90
percent of job applicants are currently employed, making it unlikely that
their current supervisors will be available as references.

More companies than ever are using background checking services to
check on things like criminal records, financial stability, and the validity
of college degrees and other credentials. Because of intense job market
competition, many applicants put fraudulent information on their resumes. Many reference checking software companies now offer the capability of gaining access to applicant data such as education, previous
employment, personal and financial references, professional licenses, driving records, and drug screening results, all by inputting the applicant's
name and social security number. A release signed by the applicant is required before these services can be engaged.

> The percentage of executive candidates who misrepresent their ed-
> ucational credentials on their resumes has increased to 16.7 per-
> cent, from the prior three years' average of 14.6 percent, according
> to the Milwaukee executive search firm Jude M. Werra & Asso-
> ciates.[5]

Tips for Better Reference Checking

Here are some ways to improve your reference checking:

1. First, inform all applicants that you have a "no reference, no hire"
   policy. This will help to filter out those with something to hide.
2. Ask leading candidates for a signed release relieving their former
   employers of liability for information they provide to you. You can
   fax the signed releases directly to former employers. Also, ask all

applicants for their written approval to check with any additional references of your choosing.

3. The most important references to check are usually the candidate's previous managers, assuming they supervised the candidate long enough or closely enough to feel comfortable offering their evaluations or to have valid observations.

4. Ask the previous managers for the names and work phone numbers of two of the candidate's peers and two direct reports, if applicable, so that you get a full-circle view of how the person was viewed by others.

5. Expand your universe of possible references by contacting coworkers who don't officially speak for the company, business contacts outside the company, customers, project partners, vendors, colleagues from professional associations, and former coworkers now at other companies.

6. You can usually assume correctly that the references given to you by the candidate will be favorable, which is why many interviewers do not contact them. The best hiring managers contact them anyway, knowing that skillful questioning can increase their frankness and willingness to provide behavioral vignettes of how the candidate either performed or did not perform in the past.

7. The human resources department of the candidate's previous employers will usually tell you very little, as it may have policies that safeguard information on previous employees.

8. Prepare and follow a checklist of behaviorally oriented questions to use for all references, each question designed to uncover proof of key competencies listed on your Candidate Profile/Evaluation (Appendix E). Ask for real-life on-the-job examples of instances when the candidate exhibited the talents, traits, and motivations you are seeking. Using the Candidate Profile/Evaluation will also help ensure the consistent and fair evaluation of all candidates against the same criteria.

9. If you are the hiring manager, make the calls yourself instead of depending on human resources staff or passing the job off to others. You are the one with the greatest vested interest in the new hire's success. Moreover, your references are more likely to open up if they know they are talking with a peer or counterpart.

10. Approach your calls to references not as a mechanical exercise or "necessary evil" duty that you must complete. Do not use the words "reference check" when you state your purpose, as this can make the person defensive. Instead, introduce yourself, ask if it is an appropriate time to talk, and keep the conversation friendly.

11. Explain that you have interviewed the candidate, then describe in

your own words how important it is that you hire the right person for the job in question. Say that you are calling to reduce the risk and vulnerability involved and that you are sure the contact has had to make similar decisions. Try to enlist the person's sympathy for your purpose, one human being to another.

12. Begin with open-ended questions that the contact is most likely to want to answer. This will get the person comfortable talking. Examples include: "Would you describe her greatest strengths?" or "What were her greatest contributions?" Stay with open-ended questions as you move on to behavioral questions (see Retention Practice #7) designed to uncover proof of key competencies. Save questions on dates of employment and actual job title until the end.

13. If the reference is reluctant to answer your questions, try reading the part of the resume that describes the candidate's job with the organization, just to confirm the facts about job duties and accomplishments. This can help to uncover dishonesty and exaggeration and sometimes even prompt the reference to offer additional information.

14. If the reference continues to be reluctant, before giving up ask, "Are you sure there is absolutely nothing you can say that will help me make this decision?"

15. Listen carefully for voice tone changes, hesitations, deep breaths, and other audio cues that may suggest a reluctance to endorse the candidate. "Faint praise" is almost always a red flag as well. Remember, if the employee was a good performer, the reference should feel no vulnerability or reluctance to talk; people will generally want to say good things when they have good things to say.

16. If the reference seems receptive, ask for more names within the organization, and contact those individuals as well.

17. If you cannot reach the most recent supervisor, ask the candidate for the names of former supervisors as well.

18. If you are to have a policy of reference checking before hiring, you must do it for all candidates, not just special categories, such as women or minorities or those who were terminated from their last jobs.

Hiring authority Dr. Pierre Mornell recommends a simple and effective technique—calling all references during lunch or after hours so that you reach an assistant or voice mail. Request that the reference call you back if the candidate is outstanding. If the candidate really was outstanding, eight out of ten people will respond quickly. However, if only two or three of ten references return the call, "the message is loud and clear."[6]

Who's Doing It

■ *Amazon.com.* This internet leader, which went from being an idea to being an industry giant in four years, with a staff of 3,000, challenges its managers to hire people who are more talented and skilled than they are in an ongoing effort to constantly raise standards for entry and improve its workforce. One technique the company uses to maintain high standards is to ask at least twenty-three questions of each reference. The goal is to learn not just what a candidate has done but "how he has done it," says Amazon's senior vice president, Alan Risher.[7]

Now grade yourself and your organization on Retention Practice #9: "Use Multiple Interviewers and Reference Checking."

How good a job is your organization doing on this practice?

Circle one: (A) Excellent   (B) Very good   (C) Good   (D) Fair   (F) Poor

How good a job are you as a manager doing on this practice?

Circle one: (A) Excellent   (B) Very good   (C) Good   (D) Fair   (F) Poor

How important do you believe this practice is to your organization's strategy to attract and retain the talent necessary to meet its business objectives?

Circle one: (A) Critical (B) Very important (C) Somewhat important
              (D) Not important

What can your organization do to improve on this practice?

What can you as a manager do to improve on this practice?

RETENTION PRACTICE #10

Reward Employee Referrals of Successful New Hires

> Around the world, our current employees are our best recruiting source. They understand the soul and spirit of the company.
> —Thomas A. Morelli, vice president of human resources, Solectron

Studies of the recruiting process show that the best hires come from employee referrals. Some companies have conducted an analysis of employee defection rates broken down by the recruiting methods used to bring in the employees in the first place. One study showed first-year turnover rates as follows:

- 67 percent for employees recruited from the competition
- 55 percent for those recruited from newspaper ads
- 45 percent for college recruits
- 30 percent for candidates referred by other employees[1]

Why the significantly higher retention rate for employee referrals? There are three main reasons for this:

1. Current employees are usually realistic in the way they describe the job/environment.
2. Current employees tend to know the person they are referring and can make a reasonable guess as to how well the person will fit into the job and culture.

3. Current employees have a strong self-interest in seeing the right people hired; they want to have competent coworkers on the team.

There is one exception to this last point: when poor or marginal performers are referring other poor and marginal performers. If there are too many employees in this category, it is usually better to weed them out before starting an employee-referral rewards program.

Many companies offer incentives for referring employees who are hired, payable when the new employee has been on the job at least six months, sometimes a year. Incentives range from movie tickets to cash bonuses to extra vacation days to parking spaces to free meals in the company cafeteria. There are companies, usually recruitment advertising agencies or incentive consultants, who design, sell, and systematically implement formal employee referral programs.

Who's Doing It

■ *Career Track*, a management seminar company in Boulder, Colorado, gives employees a half-day off with pay if they recommend a person who is hired and makes it past the ninety-day probation period.

■ *GE Medical Systems*, a Waukesha, Wisconsin, unit of General Electric, awards $5,000 bonuses and airline tickets in its effort to recruit software personnel.

■ *Cambridge Technology Partners*, of Cambridge, Massachusetts, rewards current employees with bonuses of from $1,000 to $5,000, depending on the company's degree of need at the time for key high-tech computer specialists. The company paid out $389,000 in one year—a savings over normal annual agency fees.

■ *United Parcel Service*, concerned about depleting the labor supply in Louisville, Kentucky, where it needs overnight-package sorters, bases referral rewards on how long the new employee stays with the company.

■ *Software Technologies Corporation* (STC), a Los Angeles–based provider of integration technology, offered employees who made successful referrals chances to win a new blue BMW Z3 sports car.

■ At *Tellabs*, in Ashburn, Virginia, one software engineer made more than $6,000 by referring two friends who were hired and stayed with the company for ninety days.

■ *Brooktrout Technology Inc.*, of Needham, Massachusetts, pays a $1,000 bounty to nonemployees who help the company fill key positions and has set up a web site, www.brooktrout-cash.com, for that purpose.

■ *American Century Investments* offers bonuses of $250 to $10,000 for helping the company fill positions. The upper figure goes to those who refer critical-need specialists such as architecture and data warehouse technicians. Employees earned $400,000 in one year for successfully suggesting

270 persons for job openings in the mutual fund company. One employee earned $2,500 in one year for referring five new employees. The company's senior vice president of human resources, Jerry Bartlett, believes that employee referrals offer "far and away the most cost-effective return on our investment" in terms of finding and hiring workers. [2]

■ At *Juniper Networks* in Mountain View, California, all persons who join the company are expected to bring an additional person with them. As a result, almost 90 percent of new hires at Juniper come via referrals. As their reward, the referrers can choose between a free ski weekend or a visit to California's wine country.

■ *Ask Jeeves*, the Emeryville, California, internet information company, estimates that half its hires are friends of other employees. The company recently quadrupled its referral bonus to $2,000.

■ *GeoAccess,* of Kansas City, pays employees $2,000 for each successful referral regardless of the level of the job filled. GeoAccess filled 62 percent of its hires from employee referrals in 1999.

■ *Net Perceptions*, of Eden Prairie, Minnesota, initiated a bonus program in which employees who bring in referrals that lead to interviews, even if those referred aren't hired, can enter a drawing for a pair of round-trip airline tickets to Hawaii.

■ At *Direct Lease*, in Portsmouth, New Hampshire, during one three-month period, employees earned one point for recommending a qualified candidate, two points if the referral led to an interview, and another three points if it led to a hire. The winner chose from a list of prizes valued at $2,000 apiece, including a trip to Bermuda and a TV. The runner-up chose from a list of $1,000 prizes. Third prize was a set of golf clubs.

■ Employees at *SafeNet Consulting,* in Minnetonka, Minnesota, can earn an extra dollar an hour for every successful referral they make. One referral can equate to about an additional $2,000 a year, and the salary increase stays in effect for as long as the recruited employee works at the company. Some employees have made six or seven referrals. The program is expensive, but its CEO believes it makes more economic sense than paying a headhunter $20,000 to $40,000 per hire.

■ *Quad/Graphics, Doubletree Hotel, Southwest Airlines, Motorola,* and *Solectron* all encourage the hiring of current employees' relatives, usually with the caveat that one family member cannot supervise another. Of the 8,416 employees at Quad/Graphics, 4,848 are related by blood or marriage. These companies believe that talent and good work habits run in families and that family ties make for more enduring bonds between people and the company, which results in longer-term retention.

■ *Cisco Systems*, the San Jose–based, $8.5 billion technology leader, has launched what it calls a "Friends Program" to help prospective employees make a friend at the company who can describe the benefits of working there. More than 1,000 thousand Cisco employees have volunteered for the program, attracted by a generous referral fee (starting at $500) and a lottery ticket for a free trip to Hawaii for each prospect they befriend who is ultimately hired. Through its website, the company matches up employees with people who have approached them as prospects and who have similar backgrounds and skills. The employees then call the prospects to tell them in their own words about life in the company.

Cisco receives 100–150 requests per week from applicants who have seen the program advertised in local movie theaters and who want to be introduced to a friend in the company. About one-third of all new hires now come through the program.[3]

There are several key questions you should consider when implementing a new hire referral program:

- Is the incentive offered sufficient to motivate employees to make the referral?
- Are you prepared to publicize the program well inside the company?
- Are you prepared to offer rewards for referrals of all kinds and levels of employees, and will you vary the amount of the rewards by level?
- Will you offer cash, merchandise, time off, or vacations as the reward?

Now grade yourself and your organization on Retention Practice #10: "Reward Employee Referrals of Successful New Hires."

How good a job is your organization doing on this practice?

Circle one: (A) Excellent   (B) Very good   (C) Good   (D) Fair   (F) Poor

How good a job are you as a manager doing on this practice?

Circle one: (A) Excellent   (B) Very good   (C) Good   (D) Fair   (F) Poor

How important do you believe this practice is to your organization's strategy to attract and retain the talent necessary to meet its business objectives?

Circle one: (A) Critical (B) Very important (C) Somewhat important
           (D) Not important

What can the company do to improve on this practice?

What can you as a manager do to improve on this practice?

RETENTION PRACTICE #11

Hire and Promote Managers Who Have the Talent to Manage People

> What becomes clear from this investigation is that while we tend to celebrate "great" companies, in reality, there are only great managers. In fact, it is on the frontline that the hard work of building a stronger workplace gets done.
>
> —Gallup Organization[1]

While managers hold most of the keys to employee retention, many managers are either incapable of using them or unwilling to do so.

There is no doubt that you, the individual manager, have the power to override negative factors within the larger culture and influence your employees to stay with the organization despite those factors. One study found that 50 percent of work-life satisfaction is determined by the relationship a worker has with his or her immediate supervisor.[2]

In interviews with more than 20,000 U.S. workers who were leaving their companies, the Saratoga Institute, in Santa Clara, California, found that poor supervisory behavior was the top reason in their decision to leave.[3]

For years exit interviews have consistently surfaced some variation on the theme "my boss was a jerk" among the top three reasons people leave companies. Employees complain that their bosses didn't communicate, didn't provide feedback, didn't recognize their contributions—all the things good managers are supposedly expected to do.

Dr. John Sullivan, chief talent officer at Agilent Technologies, has suggested that companies need "a bad manager identification program" by which the bottom 10 percent of the poorest performing managers are transferred out of managerial jobs. "Everybody knows who the bad managers are," says Sullivan. [They say], "Would you please fire those idiots? It's embarrassing to be around them."[4]

Sullivan has also proposed that companies tell all managers that "excellence in management is a condition of their employment, and part of that responsibility is that employees are satisfied." He also recommends that at least 10 percent of each manager's pay be made contingent on how well the individual manages his or her staff and retains key performers.[5]

Retention-focused companies are now beginning to adopt such policies, because they realize all too well the negative impact bad managers can have. Steve Wynn, CEO of Mirage Resorts, went so far as to insist that "if managers and supervisors can't explain why they are asking employees to do something, then the troops don't have to snap to."[6]

Management experts are now saying that companies that manage people in the right way will outperform, in terms of profitability, those that do not by 30 percent to 40 percent. If you have ever had to work for a manager who had little interest or skill in managing people, you will understand instinctively the negative impact such a manager can have on morale and productivity.

Why, then, are so many companies still hiring and promoting managers of people with so little people management ability? There seem to be three main reasons:

1. Good technical specialists—doers—are still being promoted into management positions as a reward for technical competence, without any assessment by management of their talent for or interest in managing people.
2. Managers who achieve bottom-line results and skillfully "manage up" continue to be promoted despite the fact that they may have abused many of their staff and caused many good people working under them to leave the company.
3. Those who hire managers feel they are too busy or hurried to do the preparation work that hiring good managers requires.

Research on succession planning has revealed that organizations would rehire only 62 percent of their managers and that 44 percent of companies report that they don't evaluate or compensate managers for their efforts to develop new talent.[7]

Regarding technical skills and good management, Hagburg Consulting Group found, in a twelve-year study of more than 2,500 senior managers, that 25 percent of those on the rise in high-tech companies lacked people skills, such as the ability to motivate teams or open-mindedness. The study also concluded that technical executives are 50 percent more likely to be poor leaders than executives in other industries.[8]

On the issue of managers who achieve bottom-line results at the expense of their people, General Electric chairman Jack Welch has stated that "GE is quite willing to toss out managers who don't sign on to the culture, even if they produce good results." Part of GE's culture includes taking seriously the softer interpersonal side of the manager's responsibilities.[9]

According to a survey of HR directors of *Fortune* 1,000 companies, these were the top ten skills managers need for organizational success:

- Interpersonal
- Listening
- Persuasion/motivation
- Presentation
- Small group communication
- Advising
- Interviewing
- Conflict management
- Writing
- Reading[10]

As you can see, eight out of ten are people-related.

Many *Fortune* 500 companies now list leadership competencies needed by current managers, and rank the importance of competencies needed in filling managerial positions. Here is an example, with people-related competencies in boldface:

Leadership Competencies

- **Oral Communication**
- Written Communication
- **Customer Focus**
- Entrepreneurial Orientation
- Integrated Functional Perspective
- International/Global Perspective
- Strategic Thinking
- Planning/Organizing/ Prioritizing
- Envisioning the Future
- **Coaching and Teaching**

- Results Orientation
- **Tolerance of Uncertainty**
- Technological Literacy
- **Flexibility/ Adaptability**
- **Community/Social Focus**/ Responsibility
- **Empathy**
- Learning Focus
- **Ethical Behavior**
- **Interpersonal Skills**
- Initiative
- **Ability to Manage a Diverse Workforce**

- **Confidence and Self-Esteem**
- **Conflict Resolution**
- **Judgment and Decision Making**
- **Delegating**
- **Motivating**
- **Influencing and Persuading**
- **Stress Tolerance**
- **Team Skills (Leader, Member, Facilitator)**
- Time Management Skills
- **Project Management Skills**
- Reliance on Quality Methods
- Goal Setting Skills
- Creativity and Innovation
- Financial Management
- **Building Followership**

While these types of competency listings are useful, there are two problems with them. First, they don't allow for the fact that every manager is going to use the talents, traits, and motivations that combine to create his or her unique management style. Not every successful manager of people is going to manage people in exactly the same way. Very few managers will achieve at equally high levels in all these competencies. Second, in each organization, and in each subunit of that organization, some of these competencies will simply be more important than others, depending on the team dynamics and business objectives.

What we do know is that the greatest people managers do things differently and more effectively than the average managers of people, as documented in Gallup's study of 80,000 managers, *First, Break All the Rules*, written by Marcus Buckingham and Curt Coffman.

What Great People Managers Do

I believe that companies interested in retaining the right people need to be concerned with selecting as people managers those whose motivated talents lie in the areas covered by most of the practices in these pages, especially those covered in Retention Practices #14 through 24.

Buckingham and Coffman came to a similar conclusion. Their research revealed that great people managers act as catalysts who concentrate on doing four activities:

1. "When selecting someone, they select for talent . . . not simply experience, intelligence, and determination." (See Retention Practices #6 and 7.)
2. "When setting expectations, they define the right outcomes . . . not the right steps." (See Retention Practices #15 and 18.)
3. "When motivating someone, they focus on strengths . . . not on weaknesses." (See Retention Practices #19 and 20.)

4. "When developing someone, they help them find the right fit . . . not simply the next rung on the ladder." (See Retention Practices #21 and 22.).[11]

More Do's and Don'ts of Great People Managers

Here are some other practices of successful people managers:

1. They don't always hire the best, but they do hire the "best fit." They know that focusing on hiring the most intelligent, or the top college graduates, or only those from the best universities totally ignores the fact that there must be a matching of motivated talents and traits with the specific job challenges and that the "fit factors" and motivations must be matched to the situation as well.

2. They have the insight to realize that, however menial a job might be, not just anyone can do it well. Great hotel maids have special motivated talents, just as great hotel managers do. Bad people managers tend to hire "anyone who can fog a mirror" for these entry-level jobs, then try to "idiot-proof" them by dictating the methods by which the job must be done. Good managers study their best people at all levels and know what to look for when they hire.

3. They focus on matching a person's strengths to the right challenge and the right role, not on improving weaknesses to the point that every employee is well rounded. Bad managers put people in the wrong jobs, basing their decisions on what they need them to do (not on what the employees want to do), then continually remind them of the talents they are lacking.

4. Good managers realize there is a limit to how much they should keep rotating people in and out of new assignments. This practice does prepare people for higher-level assignments, improve team versatility, and make the group less vulnerable to turnover and absenteeism. Eventually, however, high performers want to settle into the type of role where they can do what they do best and enjoy most.

5. Good managers realize there is more to be gained in performance improvement and retention by spending more time with their already-good performers than by spending more time with poor performers, challenging them to be great and supporting them in reaching ever-higher levels of contribution.

6. They establish a culture of trust by giving people free rein to achieve outcomes in their own way, instead of insisting they do things the way the manager would do them (a culture of compliance).

7. They manage different people differently, according to the Platinum Rule—"do unto others the way they would like to be done unto," knowing that not all people have the same motivations.

8. They see themselves as serving their people, not the other way around.

9. They are tolerant of diversity but intolerant of nonperformance.

10. They are not afraid of strength in their associates and are confident enough to seek to surround themselves with the most talented direct reports possible without feeling threatened.

11. They care about their workers and take a personal interest in what is going on in their lives.

12. They let their subordinates move on to growth assignments outside their team instead of selfishly blocking the move, because they know that these people might otherwise leave the organization.

13. Good managers give feedback, praise, and recognition on the spot. Bad managers isolate themselves to the point that they are not in a position to observe employee performance or withhold feedback until performance appraisal time.

14. Good managers know when to confront nonperformance and either redesign the job so that it fits the individual, reassign the person to a better-fitting job, or terminate when necessary (see Retention Practice #23).

How to Select Managers with the Talent to Manage People

Here are some tips on selecting managers with the know-how to manage people effectively:

- Prepare for the interview by listing the results you expect them to achieve, then check the competencies needed on the inventories in Appendix D (from Retention Practice #6), paying special attention to the people talent categories (e.g., Human Relations, Influencing Others, Leadership, and People Management) and to self-management traits such as empathy, openness, tolerance, and patience.

- List several questions that will elicit examples of past behavior when candidates were challenged to use people-related talents (e.g., "Tell me about a time when you helped one of your people to grow and develop on the job" or, "Tell me about a time when you rewarded or reprimanded one of your people"), designing a question for each people management talent that is needed.

If employee retention is a particularly important issue in your organization, you may even choose to ask questions based on some of the twenty-four retention practices in this guide, such as "Tell me about a time when you recognized one of your people in a creative way" (see Retention Practice #20).

- If candidates' answers to these questions are not detailed enough to prove the required abilities, ask them to go into more detail on exactly how they spoke to their employee and recall the steps they took in the process.

- Behavioral interviewing, when used in conjunction with standardized personality and leadership surveys that have been administered by a certified practitioner, and validated with your best people managers, can reveal areas of concern prior to hiring and can also be used to address areas for improvement and coaching for internal managerial candidates.

- Don't be misled by strong technical ability. This is a classic mistake hiring managers make when selecting prospective supervisors. Technical ability may be necessary, but it is not enough to make an individual contributor an effective manager of people.

- Check references, especially those who previously worked for the candidates as direct reports. Ask them behavioral questions like the ones suggested earlier so that they will describe incidents that demonstrate whether the candidate has the various people talents needed.

- Before hiring, let finalists for the job know that effective people management and retention are so important that a major piece of their performance evaluation and monetary rewards will be based on performance in these areas. Tell them they are expected to achieve results without alienating their people in the process. Then, back up your words with action.

Who's Doing It

- *Entex Corporation* launched a major retention initiative that reduced turnover costs by $3 million in just one year. One of the highest-impact steps the company took was to base 20 percent of each manager's bonus opportunity on how well the manager maintained low turnover in his or her department or reduced turnover from an earlier high level.

Can Great People Managers Be Made?

What can be done about managers in your company who seem to lack the talent to manage people effectively? Can these talents be developed? The answer is yes and no. Many management consulting companies have built significant practices in coaching managers and executives to become more effective leaders of people. Right Management Consultants frequently uses 360-degree (multirater) feedback and standardized personality surveys to help managers of their client companies gain a better understanding of themselves and how they are perceived on a variety of behavioral dimensions and abilities, including people management. Most organizations harbor managers who are "long and strong" in the tasks of implementing, following through and achieving results, but, because they lack competencies in areas such as coaching, team building, fostering of trust, emotional self-control, and empathy, they may be driving employees to leave the company.

Often it is the frank feedback these managers get from the 360-degree process that serves as a "wake-up call" and causes them either to change their management practices or move into a position where they no longer have to manage people at all. Some cannot make those behavioral changes, and others will not make the effort. It should be noted that it typically takes nine months or more of expert coaching to change habitual behavior and for managers to adopt new people management attitudes.

Who's Doing It

■ A large agriculture company retained the Kansas City office of Right Management Consultants to provide assessment and coaching to several of its managers and executives. One manager—we'll call him Don—had been a star individual contributor his entire career until he was put in charge of a key department. In his new role, Don became bossy and domineering in meetings and frequently interrupted others, squelching their ideas. Moreover, he was perceived as a "brown-noser" because he seemed to spend more time with certain senior managers who would seek him out for his expert opinion.

After receiving 360-degree feedback, which summarized his strengths as well as areas for improvement, Don was devastated at first—he was so affected by how others perceived him that he wept while reading the report to his wife. The feedback was the wake-up call he needed. For several days he seemed to withdraw, but, after he received further assessment and coaching, his behavior began to change dramatically.

He assigned his direct reports to take turns being in charge of meetings, began to listen without interrupting, appointed one of his staff to monitor his behavior and provide him with candid daily feedback, and gradually learned to be less dependent on the approval of the senior leaders. A year later, Don was leading his division, and the people in it, much more effectively, taking great pride in his improvement and enjoying the challenge of managing people.

Another Way to Select and Keep the Right Managers

Federal Express has launched a program for evaluating and selecting rank-and-file employees who apply for managerial positions. The program is called LEAP, which stands for Leadership Evaluation and Awareness Process. Every year, about 3,000 FedEx employees decide they are ready for the managerial track and enter the LEAP program.

Company president Fred Smith initiated LEAP when he realized that 10 percent of first-time managers were leaving the company within just fourteen months of taking on their new assignments. That is why the first LEAP module involves an eight-hour class called "Is Management for Me?" These sessions, taught by senior FedEx executives, change lots of minds. Fully 20 percent of the people who take the class drop out of LEAP to pursue other aspirations.

The dropouts have received a realistic preview of the life of a manager, with its longer hours, increased workload, and headaches relating to people management and discipline, plus the fact that managers are never "off-the-clock."

The self-evaluation phase of the LEAP process screens out another significant segment of aspiring managers at FedEx—in fact, only 20 percent of those who start LEAP ever make it to the final stage of the process. "Too many people get into leadership for all the wrong reasons," said Steve Neilsen, managing director of the FedEx Leadership Institute. "They want power. They think it's the only way to advance. LEAP is a gate that everyone has to pass through. And those who pass through it are attuned to what it means to lead and to work effectively with other people."[12]

Now grade yourself and your organization on Retention Practice #11: "Hire and Promote Managers Who Have the Talent to Manage People."

How good a job is your organization doing on this practice?

Circle one: (A) Excellent   (B) Very good   (C) Good   (D) Fair   (F) Poor

How good a job are you as a manager doing on this practice?

Circle one: (A) Excellent   (B) Very good   (C) Good   (D) Fair   (F) Poor

How important do you believe this practice is to your organization's strategy to attract and retain the talent necessary to meet its business objectives?

Circle one: (A) Critical (B) Very important (C) Somewhat important
          (D) Not important

What can your organization do to improve on this practice?

What can you as a manager do to improve on this practice?

Retention Practice #12

Hire from Within When Possible

In most industries it takes employees two weeks to find a job outside the company and two months to find a job inside the company.

—Doug Merritt, co-founder of Icarian, Inc.,
a Sunnyvale, California, maker of staffing software

Here's a story that can be told by almost every major search firm: A company advertises in a major newspaper to fill a key position but is not impressed enough with the applicants' backgrounds to bring any of them in for an interview. So, it retains the outside search firm and pays it a fee somewhere in the $20,000–$30,000 range to find and present the best available candidates. Here's the kicker—the search firm completes an exhaustive nationwide search and concludes that the best available candidate is right under the company's nose. The company, embarrassed but unable to disagree, accepts the search firm's recommendation that it promote from within to fill the key position.

The main problem in this scenario is the assumption made by the company—that the best person for the job had to be outside the company, not within. This knee-jerk response too often results in the unnecessary expenditure of both money and time, not to mention the embarrassment. It can also be extremely frustrating to talented internal applicants when they apply for positions, only to be kept waiting for weeks and even months before they are interviewed; then, after they interview for the position, they are kept waiting several weeks more, only to be told they were not selected and without any feedback as to the reasons. Unfortunately, this sequence of events happens all too frequently, and not just in large companies, creating a "push factor" that can cause valued employees to begin looking elsewhere.

Traditionally, the best companies have looked first within the organization before recruiting from the outside. Why? Because it accomplishes all of the following retention-related results:

1. It shows all employees that the organization is committed to them, which must be demonstrated before companies can ask employees to commit to the organization.
2. It focuses the attention of employees on growth from within instead of outside alternatives as a viable route to advancement.
3. It serves as a key reward for consistently high achievement and focuses the attention of other employees on the attitudes, abilities, and behaviors that are valued by the organization.
4. It saves the company time and money that would otherwise be spent going through a third-party recruiter or running a help-wanted ad.
5. It maximizes investments already made in current staff, such as training, on-the-job experience, and familiarity with the culture and ways of the organization.
6. It saves money that the company might otherwise spend on signing bonuses when it hires from the outside.

The question is not whether to have a hire-from-within policy, but when to make exceptions to it by hiring from the outside, and how to implement and make best use of such a policy.

When to Hire from the Outside

Companies need to hire from outside in certain circumstances. These include:

- When an internal search has uncovered no one with the degree of technical ability, specialization, or overall competence to fill the position
- When a fresh perspective and new approaches are needed to revitalize a stagnant department or work group
- When the long-term use of a hire-from-within policy has had the unintended effect of increasing employee complacency and mediocrity

Questions to Consider

- How do you deal with internal candidates who feel they should have been chosen instead?
- What can you do to prevent their departure and to remotivate them to stay, assuming you want to do so?

You may have noticed that the phrase "promote from within" has not been used here. That is because, as mentioned before, promotions are not as plentiful as they once were. Employees who are productive but not promotable must be given some hope for their own professional growth, which can often be found through reassignments, transfers, team projects, or special projects, all of which can provide greater challenge. Providing challenge, not necessarily promotion, is the way to motivate and retain the majority of those who work for you—including the solid citizens you depend on.

How to Hire from Within More Effectively

Here are some ways you can improve your ability to hire from within:

1. Conduct internal searches first, not as an afterthought.
2. Spread the word about unmet needs in your area to other areas, using e-mail and other methods, before going through the formal job requisitioning process.
3. Look for plateaued employees as internal candidates; they may respond with more energy and enthusiasm than others to an opportunity to contribute to a new, more important assignment.
4. Scrutinize employees from other departments the same way you would an outside candidate, using action steps described in Retention Practices #4–9.
5. Promise yourself and your organization that you will confront your poor performers and either coach or terminate them instead of recommending them highly and passing them off to other departments.
6. Be willing to let your best people move on when it serves the interests of both the individual and the organization as a whole.

Who's Doing It

- *Advanced Micro Devices*, a microprocessor manufacturer in Sunnyvale, California, found that allowing workers to change jobs within the company, rather than hiring from the outside, saved both time and money. The company believes it is more efficient to move workers within rather than start from scratch with new hires. "We can get to market quicker by leveraging inside talent," says its director of staffing.[1]

■ At Netscape Communications, a unit of America On-Line Inc., one employee moved from the sales department to a position in product development. "Netscape was exactly the place where I wanted to be," he said. "but I was looking around for the position I wanted to be in."[2] The company has found that moving insiders is cost-efficient, in that the employee is already fully functional, knows the players, and knows how to use the e-mail system.

Many large companies have begun creating internal recruiting units who coordinate with external recruiting staff but focus on surfacing suitable internal candidates for all open positions. Most of these companies hope to fill at least six out of every ten openings internally.

Now grade yourself and your organization on Retention Practice #12: "Hire from Within When Possible."

How good a job is your organization doing on this practice?

Circle one: (A) Excellent   (B) Very good   (C) Good   (D) Fair   (F) Poor

How good a job are you as a manager doing on this practice?

Circle one: (A) Excellent   (B) Very good   (C) Good   (D) Fair   (F) Poor

How important do you believe this practice is to your organization's strategy to attract and retain the talent necessary to meet its business objectives?

Circle one: (A) Critical (B) Very important (C) Somewhat important
             (D) Not important

What can your organization do to improve on this practice?

What can you as a manager do to improve on this practice?

Retention Practice #13

Creatively Expand Your Talent Pool

You can't hire people who don't apply.

—Anonymous

The competition for workers of all kinds and all levels has become so fierce that companies have to think "outside the box," as the saying goes. This means tapping the imaginations of their managers and recruiters to expand the pool of potential candidates in ways they have never before tried.

Mammoth Lakes Ski Resort in California, for example, has begun hiring Australian college students as winter ski lift operators, because the students' summer vacations coincide with the winter months in the United States. Restaurants and hotels hire disabled workers from sheltered workshops to fold silverware into cloth napkins and have even begun hiring homemakers and retirees as part-time wait staff to work one two-hour period per day.

In communities where there is a shortage of entry-level workers due to high housing costs—in Johnson County, Kansas, for example—chambers of commerce and business and government leaders have joined forces to influence the building of low-income housing and the creation of new public transportation programs.

Bold new thinking is called for. Still, many companies have yet to use some of the tried-and-true techniques that have been proven to be effective over the years. Here are some of the tactics that have been proven to be effective in helping creative companies win the war for talent.

Old and New Ways to Expand Your Talent Pool

1. Begin recruiting at high schools instead of colleges.
2. Begin internship or apprenticeship program for high school or college students.

3. Place recruitments ads in out-of-town newspapers or small local ones.

4. Use part-time workers for jobs where they have not previously been used.

5. Begin or increase usage of radio, TV, and movie advertising, now used by 40 percent of all companies. These media can be especially effective in reaching Generation X'ers, many of whom seldom read the newspaper.

6. Begin or increase usage of job postings on the internet, now used by more than 75 percent of all companies. Consider: While fewer than 60 million people see a daily newspaper, more than 90 million have internet sites.

7. Use temporary help firms, not just for lower-level positions but for management-level as well. Many of these firms specialize in supplying management and executive talent for interim projects or assignments.

8. Interview applicants who may lack traditional qualifications, such as degrees or years of experience, but have the right "motivated abilities" and can be trained (e.g., career changers, homemakers, ex-military).

9. Begin an employee-referral-and-reward program (see Retention Practice #10).

10. Host an open house and tour.

11. Recruit from among clients, customers, and suppliers.

12. Set up your own training center, and pick from among the best graduates.

13. Work with the local chamber of commerce to have them keep a resume book of new arrivals.

14. Hire a biplane to fly over crowds at sporting events with a trailing banner (a less expensive alternative than billboards).

15. Ask current successful employees what they do in their leisure time. If you find that many of them have similar interests outside work, such as attending car shows, set up a booth at those events.

16. Hire more disabled workers, as employers such as Olsten Staffing Services and Manpower Inc. have done.

17. Send managers and human resources people to speak at church job clubs in your area. Also encourage them to speak at high schools, on college campuses, and on military bases.

18. Register to list your open positions with the state employment service.

19. List open positions with outplacement consulting firms where you can hire talented individuals from a variety of fields and functions without having to pay a fee. Such firms, with offices worldwide,

will list your positions on international computer-accessible job banks at no charge.

20. Offer a cash bounty to anyone who defects from a competitor.
21. Hire and train entry-level workers through the federal "Welfare-to-Work" program, as Marriott hotels has done. Marriott has retained 75 percent of these workers for more than 300 days, helping to keep Marriott's turnover rate well below those of its rivals.[1]

    Other companies with successful welfare-to-work programs include Sprint, United Airlines, Salomon Smith Barney, and Cessna Aircraft. Sprint recruits call center operators from one of Kansas City's poorest neighborhoods and has maintained a 77 percent retention rate, which is more than twice that at its suburban location.[2] The federal program prepares welfare workers for employment by teaching soft skills such as showing up on time, maintaining an appropriate appearance, and getting along with coworkers. Of the top 100 U.S. companies, thirty-four had such programs in 1999, and thirteen more were planning them.[3] The for-profit private company AmericaWorks also helps get people off welfare and into entry-level jobs, and keeps them on their payroll for the first four months.

22. Set up and publicize your own job hot lines and websites.
23. List open positions on job hot lines and websites of professional associations.
24. Set up booths at community job fairs.
25. Recruit a more diverse workforce by setting up booths at minority fairs and on college campuses known for their diversity.
26. Hold on-site career fairs. Provide childcare during interviews if possible.
27. Constantly remind customers that you have jobs open, as restaurants such as Chili's have done by printing "Would you like a job with that?" on their drink coasters. Winstead's hamburger chain also prints invitations to work there on its sacks and napkins.
28. Offer cash compensation to all candidates who come in for interviews, a technique that has worked successfully to help Thompson's Nutritional Technology, of Kansas City, Kansas, attract shift workers.[4]
29. Let it be known in your help wanted ads that you value older workers. Workers over fifty now make up 40 percent of the workforce and will be a source of reliable and experienced talent for years to come. Some companies actually include in their ads the phrase "Age is no factor." Of course, you have to really mean it.
30. If your business is a retail store, hold a special "discount day" exclusively for employees of competing stores, allowing them to

buy your product or service at a discount and bringing a group of qualified candidates through your front door.

31. List job openings on the websites of companies such as discover-me.com. that allow prospective candidates to take personality inventories, and screen them for profiles compatible with available jobs. (Keep in mind that personality assessments performed to select those with certain qualities need to be validated for predicting success in the jobs for which you are selecting, or you may be exposing yourself to lawsuits.)

32. To recruit entry-level service workers, stop in at community centers, introduce yourself and say, "I'm looking for workers."

33. Create a first-name relationship with state welfare and job service officials so that they will remember to refer candidates to you.

34. Create a public-private partnership with local transit officials to subsidize a bus that will pick up workers where they live and bring them across town to your work site.

35. Cultivate relationships with community organizations such as clubs and churches and ask them to refer promising applicants.

36. Ask your best people to give you the names of three other first-class people they know who might be persuaded to join the company. Ask these employees to help the organization strike up relationships with them.

37. Train all managers to capture the names and e-mail addresses of impressive people they meet at conferences. Over time, create a talent database and send the people in it a monthly newsletter by e-mail.

38. Don't just check the references that talented applicants provide. Consider people who offer references as job candidates in their own right, and capture their names as well.

39. Ask new hires which people they would recruit from their former companies and colleges, because talented people tend to recognize other talented people.

40. Stay in touch with talented people who leave, and use them as sources for new talent leads.

41. Create a list of talented people you would love to have on board, and send them your monthly e-mail newsletter. (See #37.)

42. Ask talented people at other companies whether they could work for you as a consultant over a weekend.

43. In advertising, or through your website, invite prospective employees to chat by phone or by e-mail with current high performers to find out what they like about working in your company.

44. Make the top 10 percent of star performers at other companies the unusual offer of "prequalifying" them for jobs. One company

actually mailed a coupon with the message "The day you want to come work for us, you're hired. You don't have to go through our HR bureaucracy. We will hire you instantly."

45. Encourage high school and college seniors to apply for part-time jobs so that they can make some spending money.

46. Consider recruiting internationally. Software start-up companies recruit software engineers from India, Eastern Europe, Turkey, and Siberia. Using programmers who live halfway around the world who work while their U.S. counterparts sleep allows these firms to develop new projects quickly.

47. Have your company's publicity people arrange for a company representative to throw out the first pitch at a baseball game, as National Semiconductor has done.

48. Develop a recruiting public relations kit that provides candidates with an insider's view of what the work entails and what kind of environment the company provides.

49. Change your advertising message and location to attract more attention. One bank stopped advertising in the banking section of the classifieds and instead ran an ad in the retail section saying, "Life after retail. Get Sundays off," which drew a great response.

50. Consider relaxing company policies that forbid hiring relatives, and ask employees to refer family members for jobs in other departments.

51. Contact career transition firms and relocation companies that may be looking for positions for displaced spouses.

51. Contact firms like IMCOR, which can supply your company with management and executives for short-term assignments, which often become full-time ones.

52. Use firms such as Experiencenet.com, an e-commerce business-to-business company that uses a web database to connect independent professionals with companies who want their services.

53. To attract retail workers, post specific hours of work shifts available on store windows and doors.

54. Stop limiting your recruiting to "the best" universities and big-company candidates. Many of the best hires are "diamonds in the rough" found at state colleges and at smaller firms.

Who's Doing What

■ *Microsoft* has developed a strong e-recruiting and e-training process for reaching out to universities. The company's website features a substantial amount of information designed to attract talent and a series of interactive screening interactions.

■ *Humana*'s e-recruiting software searches the web for resumes and matches qualified candidates to appropriate openings. The company e-mails qualified candidates using a tracking system, updating their resumes as it updates the company's database. Humana cut its spending per qualified resume from $128 to 6 cents! Annual savings were $8.3 million per year, and recruiting process efficiency has improved significantly.

■ Responding to a sex-discrimination class-action lawsuit, *Home Depot* designed an automated hiring and promotion system called the Job Preference Program, or JPP. The company installed computer kiosks in every store where a broader pool of applicants, including women, would be invited to apply. By March 2000, the new computerized staffing system had increased the number of female managers by 30 percent and the number of minority managers by 28 percent (see "Keeping *All* the People Who Keep You in Business").

The JPP system requires applicants to call an 800 number where they connect with a forty-to-ninety-minute basic skills test that helps weed out unqualified candidates before any time is invested in live interviews. The computer even upgraded one woman's stated job objective from cashier to sales associate and hired her for that position after the computer prompted her to state her longer-term objective, which was sales. The system is networked so that all applications go to stores within commuting distance, ensuring managers of a larger pool of candidates. Other companies that have automated their application process include *Target, Publix Supermarkets,* and *Hollywood Video.*

■ *Cisco Systems*, the San Jose–based technology leader, has grown from 250 people to more than 15,000 and has achieved a turnover rate of around 8 percent, compared to an industry rate of around 15 percent, by creating a digital system that expands its pool of the right kinds of applicants, then prequalifies them.

The company's other recruiting activities, such as placing ads in Silicon Valley newspapers, setting up tables at upscale social gatherings, and using strategically placed cards in the stands at football games, all refer prospective job seekers to the Cisco website. The entertaining website features information in Cantonese, Mandarin, and Russian.

Cisco's recruiters hold focus groups to learn about the social interests, hobbies, and lifestyles of the company's most successful engineers and managers. Using this information, the company identifies the most popular and influential websites on which to post recruitment ads. The company also goes on the Net to places where the right kinds of prospects are most likely to hang out, such as The Dilbert Zone.

On its website, Cisco posts hundreds of detailed job descriptions that are easily searchable by keywords, fields of interest, and locations around the United States and the world. On its special "HotJobs@Cisco" page, the company lists unique positions it is especially eager to fill. The website also gives recruits a window on life at Cisco by linking them up with current employees who share similar backgrounds and skills.

In 1999, Cisco was receiving around 35,000 resumes per quarter, 80 percent electronically, and had automated 70 percent of its recruiting process. At the same time, the company has been building a database that can predict the qualities and characteristics that will make a star employee. The database will be used as a screen for the company's Profiler system, in which a prospect will submit information on-line, responding to relevant questions, thereby creating a specialized resume that Cisco recruiters can match to job openings.[5]

Now grade yourself and your organization on Retention Practice #13: "Creatively Expand Your Talent Pool."

How good a job is your organization doing on this practice?

Circle one: (A) Excellent   (B) Very good   (C) Good   (D) Fair   (F) Poor

How good a job are you as a manager doing on this practice?

Circle one: (A) Excellent   (B) Very good   (C) Good   (D) Fair   (F) Poor

How important do you believe this practice is to your organization's strategy to attract and retain the talent necessary to meet its business objectives?

Circle one: (A) Critical (B) Very important (C) Somewhat important
            (D) Not important

What can your organization do to improve on this practice?

What can you as a manager do to improve on this practice?

THE THIRD KEY

Get Them Off to a Great Start

Sara, a skilled technical writer, had moved from one Midwestern city to another to take a higher-paying position with a computer products company. Her husband had resigned his job to make the move with her.

When she arrived for work on her first day, no one seemed to be expecting her. Sara's manager was out of town on business and had apparently forgotten to set up her new office. She spent the morning sitting in a makeshift cubicle with no telephone, reading through company policy manuals and marketing materials. Everyone was so busy that only the receptionist cared enough to find out that no one had invited her out to lunch.

When her manager returned later that afternoon, he apologized for not being there that morning and asked if she could stay late to meet with him. He explained that he was under pressure to complete a project and would need her to start entering research findings into a database. It would be at least a two-week project. "After we get that done, we'll talk about your job description," he told Sara, "but there's plenty to do around here to keep you busy for now." The next morning, when she suggested a new way to organize the data, he told her, "Don't try and get creative with this . . . just do it the way I showed you."

The day after that, Sara's manager told her that she could expect to be doing a series of less-than-challenging assignments for the foreseeable future. This would be her way of "paying her dues." After talking it over with her husband, who was still looking for work in the new city, she decided to resign from her job. Within three days they had moved back home.

In this story, almost everything that could go wrong in an employee's first few days on the job did go wrong. We need to remember that for many employees it takes only a little disillusionment for "buyer's remorse" to set in. In Retention Practice #8, "Give a Realistic Job Preview," we looked at ways to reduce turnover by openly discussing mutual expectations with job prospects prior to hire. Yet, even if we have made expectations clear, we can still drive away talented employees by failing to manage the "joining up" process—-the new hire's critical first few days and weeks on the job.

Only One Chance to Make a Good First Impression

One study reported that 50 percent to 60 percent of employees change jobs in the first seven months of employment—as soon as they are hired, they begin looking for "better opportunities" that continue to be available in a "buyer's job market."[1] Another study of 1,000 executives revealed that 40 percent of new management hires fail within the first eighteen months.[2]

Experienced managers understand that they are most vulnerable to losing employees during their first six months on the job. When asked to reflect on their own past jobs, most managers would agree with the research that shows that early on-the-job experiences have a significant impact on job satisfaction, employee attitude, productivity level, and turnover.[3]

For an organization that hires twenty-five college graduates a year, paying them an average of $30,000 each, the difference between managing the joining-up process and mismanaging it can total $750,000 in annual turnover costs. Yet most organizations do a poor job of getting new hires off to a great start. Either they are preoccupied with doing business as usual, or they don't realize it's a problem, or they don't realize the magnitude of the problem, or all three.

The situation is only made worse by the quickened pace in most organizations brought on by rapid technological change and the bare-fisted competition for market share. Many companies are impatient with new hires. They expect them to hit the ground running and are unwilling to spend the time needed to properly coach and train them.

The Questions New Hires Are Asking Themselves

Taking a new job is like almost any major decision, such as buying a new house or getting married; after the decision is made, we look for reassurance that the decision was the right one. When we begin to see even small pieces of evidence that our expectations are not being met, we may feel a sense of betrayal and fear that a contract has been broken.

Although a new hire's expectations may cover a wide range of issues, most have a handful of fundamental questions that need to be answered during their first few days or weeks on the job:

- Do I feel welcome and valued here?
- In what way is my job important to this organization?
- Exactly what is expected of me?
- Will I learn, grow, and be challenged here?
- Will I get to exercise independent judgment and creativity?

As we saw in Sara's story, none of these questions was answered in a positive way. As we shall now see, there is much you can do to make sure your future new hires can answer these questions positively.

Now that the new hire is on board, your power to influence that person's success and retention is at its peak. Here are the practices that will make a difference.

RETENTION PRACTICE #14

Give New Hires the Red-Carpet Treatment

In terms of investment dollars, how much of the money we spend on hiring the right people do we waste by pouring cold water on their enthusiasm on that very first day?
—Ron Lebow and William L. Simon, *Lasting Change*

One day while walking down the street, a highly successful executive woman was tragically hit by a bus, and she died. Her soul arrived up in Heaven, where she was met at the pearly gates by St. Peter himself.

"Welcome to heaven," said St. Peter. "Before you get settled in though, it seems we have a problem. You see, strangely enough, we've never once had an executive make it this far, and we're not really sure what to do with you."

"No problem, just let me in," said the woman.

"Well, I'd like to, but I have higher orders. What we're going to do is to let you have a day in Hell and a day in Heaven, and then you can choose whichever one you want to spend eternity in."

"Actually, I think I've made up my mind . . . I prefer to stay in Heaven," said the woman.

"Sorry, we have rules." And with that St. Peter put the executive in the elevator, and it went down-down-down to Hell. The doors opened, and she found herself stepping out onto the putting green of a beautiful golf course. In the distance was a country club, and standing in front of her were all her friends—fellow executives she had worked with—and they were all dressed in evening gowns and cheering for her.

They ran up and kissed her on both cheeks, and they talked about old times. They played an excellent round of golf and at night went to the country club, where she enjoyed an excellent steak and lobster dinner. She met the Devil, who was actually a really nice guy (kinda cute), and she had a great time telling jokes and dancing. She was having such a good time that, before she knew it, it was time to leave. Everybody shook her hand and waved goodbye as she got on the elevator.

The elevator went up-up-up and opened back up at the Pearly Gates. She found St. Peter waiting for her. "Now it's time to spend a day in Heaven," he said. So she spent the next twenty-four hours lounging around on clouds and playing the harp and singing. She had a great time and, before she knew it, her twenty-four hours were up, and St. Peter came and got her.

"So, you've spent a day in Hell and you've spent a day in Heaven. Now you must choose your eternity," he said. The woman paused for a second and then replied, "Well, I never thought I would say this . . . I mean . . . Heaven has been really great and all, but I think I had a better time in Hell."

So, St. Peter escorted her to the elevator, and again she went down-down-down to Hell. When the doors of the elevator opened, she found herself standing in a desolate wasteland covered in garbage and filth. She saw her friends were dressed in rags and were picking up the garbage and putting it in sacks. The Devil came up to her and put his arm around her.

"I don't understand," stammered the woman, "yesterday I was here and there was a golf course and a country club and we ate lobster and we danced and we had a great time. Now all there is a wasteland of garbage and all my friends look miserable."

The Devil looked at her and smiled. "Yesterday we were recruiting you . . . today you're an employee." (As told by Pat Perkins, 11/11/99.)

We laugh at this story because we recognize the truth in it—that organizations all too often stop putting energy into the wooing and welcoming of new employees and begin taking them for granted as soon as they come on board. The following true story is a good example:

A software engineer who had recently moved from the West Coast, where he was in the aerospace industry, to the Midwest, where he had just taken a job with a major utility, felt that he had been totally abandoned during his first few months on the job. "I felt like an expensive piece of equipment that had been put away in a storeroom, still in its box, and left to gather dust," he told me. "No one spent any time with me, telling me about the company culture or coaching me on how to be successful." As a result, he made some mistakes that almost cost him his job.

As the saying goes, you will never get a second chance to make a first impression. And if that first impression is a negative one, the new employee will never fully recover from it.

Common Mistakes Employers Make When "Welcoming" New Hires

There are a number of mistakes that employers make during new employees' first days on the job that can leave them with bad feelings about the new job. They include:

- Having assembly-line orientations—during which new hires attend long lecture sessions and fill out forms
- Not having the new employee's desk, phone, computer, and other office supplies in place prior to the first day
- Ignoring the new hire or leaving the person to read manuals without one-to-one contact
- Making new-hire orientation a strictly HR–run affair with little involvement of the new hire's manager and department
- Failing to have the new hire's manager set specific performance objectives

Most of these mistakes happen because managers are distracted by pressing matters and don't put forethought into how to welcome the new hire. You must decide that welcoming the new hire properly is an investment in long-term retention and simply must often take precedence over other urgent or seemingly more important concerns.

Red-Carpet Guidelines

Here is a list that you should review prior to welcoming each new employee to your team:

Prior to a new employee's first day:

_____ Provide key written material, such as an employee handbook and other relevant pieces, prior to the first day on the job if possible.

_____ Arrange for office furnishings and supplies ahead of time so that the employee is not bogged down by these concerns during the first week.

_____ Consider taking the new hire to lunch prior to the first day on the job.

_____ Plan how you want the new hire to spend his or her first day, and arrange for person-to-person guidance from one or more of your team.

_____ Make sure to let all staff know that the new employee is expected, and ask them to make him or her feel welcome.

_____ Leave your own calendar open at the beginning and end of the employee's first day, and make sure someone takes him or her to lunch.

Day one:

_____ Consider having a surprise welcoming party in the new hire work area, with coffee and pastry, or arrange a potluck lunch with all employees bringing a dish (why do we give parties for employees only when they are leaving the company?!).

_____ Meet with the employee early in the day to reaffirm the importance of the employee's job to the organization's success and to finalize a performance agreement with specific results and mutual expectations made clear (Retention Practice #16).

_____ Introduce the new employee to as many team members as possible, or have the team members drop by to introduce themselves. Don't tell new hires what you think of each co-worker; let them form their own impressions.

_____ Have someone show all new hires around the facility, making sure they are properly oriented to the location of supplies, copier, fax, restrooms, coffee machine, file cabinets, and phone directory, and introduced to the company phone system, expense account procedure, and so on.

_____ Schedule group orientations when several new employees are there for their first day. Conduct these sessions in the afternoon. Cover company history, an orientation to the business/industry, the organization's culture, and mutual expectations. You may want to have a few experienced employees present to give their input on company culture and what it takes to succeed. Consider producing a video that a single new hire can view prior to or on the first day, or, as many companies are now doing, place orientation information on an internal website to be viewed later in a piecemeal fashion at the new hire's convenience.

And finally . . . one simple retention-focused action that, among all those you can take on day one, will have the greatest return for the amount of energy expended:

Ask the employee to promise that he or she will come and talk with you before deciding to leave the organization.

During week one:

_____ Introduce the employee with enthusiasm during a group meeting, if there is one scheduled.

_____ Pair up the new employee with a respected peer or senior coworker to be a mentor or buddy who will serve as coach, re-recruiter, caretaker, and encouraging presence during the new hire's first six months. The buddy will meet with the new person weekly during the first thirty days, and periodically during the first 180 days, to ask such questions as:

- "How's it going?"
- "Do you have the resources you need to do the job?"
- "Do you need any assistance in dealing with anyone in the organization?"
- "Is the job/organization what you expected it would be?"
- "What more can we do for you?"

_____ Encourage the employee to schedule one-on-one meetings with co-workers, getting their various perspectives on things.

_____ Give appropriate and challenging assignments during the first week (see Retention Practice #17).

_____ Schedule the employee for appropriate in-house or outside training, as needed.

_____ Check in with the employee from time to time during the first week, and have an informal end-of-the-week review session.

Through month three:

_____ Meet regularly to discuss the employee's performance and development and to clarify expectations during the first three months (see Retention Practices #19–22).

_____ On the three-month anniversary, have your first quarterly progress review of the performance agreement you made on day one. Set new goals as described in Retention Practice #16.

_____ Allow the employee to rewrite his or her job description if it is outdated and no longer matches current and ongoing activities and challenges.

Through month six:

_____ Conduct a midyear review, using the same performance agreement. Create a new one if necessary.

_____ Conduct a more formal career development checkup discussion, using guidelines in Retention Practices #21 and 22. The time and energy you put into continuing informal "checkup" or "course correction" sessions with the new hire convey the message that he or she is critical to team success. This must be true, or you wouldn't have hired this person in the first place. The attention you pay them says, "I value you so much that I want to make sure you are happy and successful here."

Frequent communication with your top performers will also provide you with early warning of any disillusionment or dissatisfaction they may be feeling. This type of meeting may begin with the simple question, "How's it going?"

Who's Doing It

■ At *BHA*, a Kansas City industrial supply company, all 300 of the company's employees are encouraged to come by to personally introduce themselves and welcome all new hires during their first week on the job.

■ *Data Processing Resources Corporation*, of Newport Beach, California, helps new hires across the United States find housing and cars and learn where to shop for groceries.

■ *Sun Microsystems* gets new hires into the spirit of teamwork quickly by having them assemble into teams and build a container that will keep an egg from breaking when dropped from a height of six feet. The company also assigns all new employees a "buddy," called a "SunVisor."

■ *Right Management Consultants*, of Philadelphia, which provides new employee assimilation consulting for their corporate clients, provides a thorough orientation process for the administrative staff it hires in its offices worldwide. In addition to a detailed assimilation interview with the new manager and meetings with all staff, the process includes having the new administrative hires take the same self-assessment surveys and attend the same training as the firm's career transition clients.

■ At *Greet Street*, a San Francisco–based company that makes personalized greeting cards and other multimedia products over the Web, day one is informal and creative. There is no personnel manager, no personnel office; and there are no job titles. Everyone in the thirty-employee company works in the same large, open room, and everyone has the same first assignment—to open a large box containing a desk, computer, and phone. The first thing each employee does is to set it all up.

Phase two of the company's ritual is to have the new hire talk to every other employee and get acclimated by sitting in on other people's meetings, talking with new colleagues, and learning how things work in an informal way.

Step three is to have new employees come up with their own snappy job titles, a tradition that started with the company's two cofounders, Tony Levitan, "creator of chaos," and Fred Campbell, "creator of substance."

■ Intel, which added 31,000 employees in a three-year period, created a six-month "integration" curriculum for all new hires. Prior to day one, each new employee receives a packet of materials with the headline "Welcome to the World of Intel," with a passport that doubles as a workbook. On day one, new hires view a video starring chairman Andy Grove and receive a briefing from a senior manager on the company's business strategy, mission, and objectives.

Then it's on to a no-nonsense meeting with the direct manager where each new employee's "deliverables" are discussed—the tangible results the employee is expected to achieve during the first performance-review period.

One month later, new employees attend an eight-hour class called "Working at Intel," which offers a more thorough introduction to the company's culture. This piece of the orientation process is taken quite seriously; yearly bonuses suffer if all new hires don't complete the course.

Finally, at the six-month point, new hires meet individually with a senior executive staff member who runs them through a structured, two-hour question-and-answer session, concluding with, "What do you think it will take to succeed at Intel?"

■ *Quick Solutions* sends lavish gift baskets filled with pasta, wine, and other gourmet goodies to the homes of the newly hired. One new hire's wife commented, "The basket was a really nice welcome. I worked at an insurance company for fifteen years, and they never included spouses."[1]

■ *Persistence Software*, of San Mateo, California, serves bagels and bran muffins on mornings when a new recruit joins the company. To encourage other employees to come by and meet the new person, the company places the tray of breakfast food near the new hire's desk, and an e-mail goes out to all 110 employees inviting them to come by for a breakfast greeting.

■ All 350 employees at *MetaSolv Software,* in Plano, Texas, are invited to a keg party at its offices during happy hour every Friday. New employees are invited to work the tap.

Now grade yourself and your organization on Retention Practice #14: "Give New Hires the Red-Carpet Treatment."

How good a job is your organization doing on this practice?

Circle one: (A) Excellent   (B) Very good   (C) Good   (D) Fair   (F) Poor

How good a job are you as a manager doing on this practice?

Circle one: (A) Excellent   (B) Very good   (C) Good   (D) Fair   (F) Poor

How important do you believe this practice is to your organization's strategy to attract and retain the talent necessary to meet its business objectives?

Circle one: (A) Critical (B) Very important (C) Somewhat important
            (D) Not important

What can your organization do to improve on this practice?

What can you as a manager do to improve on this practice?

RETENTION PRACTICE #15

Communicate How Their Work Is Vital to the Organization's Success

> When people feel they are being of service to something larger than themselves, then something happens—an alchemy—that transcends logical thought and possibilities; the undoable gets done, the impossible is possible.
>
> —Craig Neal, The Heartland Institute

Believing that their work is important to your organization's success is one of the most essential requirements in whether employees stay or move on. The lack of "task" significance, as already mentioned in Retention Practice #5, "Redesign the Job Itself to Make It More Rewarding," is one of the five main causes of employee dissatisfaction.

While some jobs are more important to the organization's mission than others, all jobs, if properly designed, have some degree of meaning. This does not automatically ensure, however, that the employees who hold those jobs fully appreciate why their jobs are important. This is where you can make the difference—by communicating the significance of the job to each new jobholder.

In Sara's story, her manager failed to do this. He assigned her to a project without explaining to her how the organization would be better or worse off if the job were done well or poorly. He missed the opportunity to motivate by engaging Sara in the mission of the organization.

Who's Doing It

■ Cheryl Hanks, a highly regarded nursing supervisor at *St. Luke's Hospital* in Houston, put it this way: "I share with my staff the vision and mission of the hospital . . . and then we talk about how we fit into it."[1] Hanks described how she shares the organization's standards for quality care, but also the hard-nosed financial and productivity objectives for the hospital, the unit, and the individual.

■ *Harley-Davidson* puts up large full-color posters of celebrity "Harley Hog" owners standing with or sitting proudly on their motorcycles so that plant workers are constantly reminded that they play an important role in customer satisfaction.

■ At the pharmaceutical maker *Aventis*, patients who have benefited from the company's allergy medication describe how they were helped in an orientation video.

Tell the Company's Story

The entrepreneur who founds a company that becomes successful has a success story to tell. These stories often involve struggle, humble begin-nings, courage, vision, faith, and sacrifice, and they are inspiring to new employees. Are you telling your company's story to your new hires?

Nighttime Pediatrics Clinics, which runs five after-hours clinics in the Salt Lake City area, has gathered reminiscences from doctors, nurses, clerks, and parents into a small book called "Nighttime Stories" to capture and express the special significance employees feel about working there. "They spoke of a doctor who bent the clinic's rules to treat a disoriented old woman; a payroll manager who persuaded management to trash an expensive investment in flawed new software; a nurse who drove a teenage mother and her sick child home on a snowy night."[2]

Workers in a coal mine, who operate machines that grind coal to pow-der, can feel their work has a higher meaning. Though the work may be noisy and dirty, they tell stories to their families about how the coal dust fires boilers that make electricity, how their work contributes to making electricity more cheaply, and how that helps their families and neighbors.

I once worked for an ad agency whose owner decided to announce that he was retiring and turning over the reins to the agency to his son. He did so by sending out a press release announcing this without telling his son what he was planning to do. The son did not know he was in charge until someone showed him the article in the paper the next day. The son rose to the challenge and over the next ten years built the agency into one of the largest and most successful in the Southeast.

Years later I conducted a career change workshop attended by a human resources executive who had lost his job. He was filled with hurt, anger, and fear. But, in taking inventory of his assets, he realized he had the "right stuff" for starting his own one-man outplacement consulting firm, which he did, selling his new car to help finance the start-up.

A year later he hired me as his first consultant and went on to build one of the most successful career transition consulting firms in southern California. His success and dedication were driven by his empathy for the plight of the displaced professionals he served, and I was motivated by his sense of mission, as were the other new employees we attracted to the team.

I have always enjoyed telling these stories. They are examples of how the mythology and legacy of the company's founding "hero" has the power to motivate future employees.

What is your company's story? Do you make it a point to tell the company's story to each new employee?

Why Is Their Work Significant?

In these days when so many jobs have been eliminated, the justification of each worker's job is an open issue. Assuming an employee's job has withstood scrutiny and is still considered vital to the company's mission, you must understand that mission and communicate it to the employee in a compelling way, preferably on day one.

Your organization, if it is like most organizations today, is probably asking you and all employees to do more with less. Why should your people work so hard? Your job is to give them a good reason to be dedicated.

It begins with you. Are you dedicated to achieving your organization's "vivid description" of future success as you described it in Retention Practice #3, "Inspire Commitment to a Clear Vision and Definite Objectives"? If you still can't describe your company's future in a vivid way, that's a problem. If you don't believe your company can realistically achieve that future as described, that's another problem. But if you do understand the company vision, and you are committed to it yourself, you must communicate it with passion to your new people.

The mission and vision you describe should be something more inspiring than "increase market share" or "enhance shareholder value." As discussed in Retention Practice #3, the most motivational company missions and visions are usually linked to achieving a new level of value for the customer, and only secondarily reaching new heights in profits and recognition for the organization.

Communicating job significance makes the difference between just holding down a job and believing you are "building a cathedral." Even those who flip burgers can see themselves as key contributors to customer satisfaction and company success.

On each new employee's first day you must fully explain the difference that excellent performance in that job can make in achieving customer satisfaction, and how that leads to the success of the organization.

To Communicate Effectively, Prepare to Communicate!

Begin the process of communicating your company's special mission by reviewing your organization's business goals and the vivid description as you wrote and understood them in Retention Practice #3. Assuming you buy into this desired future for the organization, describe to each new employee the future you envision for your team or work unit as you see it, incorporating your own unit's goals.

Next, describe to the new person the significance of your own job to the organization's achievement of the envisioned future and goals you have described.

Finally, think of one of your most valued employees and how you see that person contributing to the achievement of your team's envisioned future and goals.

If you have never actually sat down and discussed the significance of a valued key employee's job in some detail, you may want to do it before it's too late. Or, if you have not done it lately, do it again. For new employees, day one is not too early. (The first interview is an even better time to start talking about job significance. If the mission and larger meaning of the job do not resonate with the employee, that employee is probably not the right person for the job.)

It is especially important that you sit down in private with your most essential people—star performers and those with critical skills—during times of crisis or intense change. Tell them they have a crucial role to play in the change, whether it be a turnaround, new strategy implementation, downsizing, or reorganization.

Your Next Challenge—Make Sure They Keep Feeling Needed

Communicating to employees about the significance of their jobs isn't just a one-time event. You must keep telling them, or else they will begin to feel ignored, taken for granted, or even expendable. If it matters whether they do their jobs halfheartedly or with excellence and enthusiasm, let them know it.

Remember—commitment comes when people feel they are vitally important to the organization's cause.

Now grade yourself and your organization on Retention Practice #15: "Communicate How Their Work Is Vital to the Organization's Success."

How good a job is your organization doing on this practice?

Circle one: (A) Excellent   (B) Very good   (C) Good   (D) Fair   (F) Poor

How good a job are you as a manager doing on this practice?

Circle one: (A) Excellent   (B) Very good   (C) Good   (D) Fair   (F) Poor

How important do you believe this practice is to your organization's strategy to attract and retain the talent necessary to meet its business objectives?

Circle one: (A) Critical (B) Very important (C) Somewhat important
                (D) Not important

What can your organization do to improve on this practice?

What can you as a manager do to improve on this practice?

RETENTION PRACTICE #16

Get Commitment to a Performance Agreement

If you don't measure it, people will know you're not serious about delivering it.
—James Belasco, *Teaching the Elephant to Dance*

Once the new employee fully appreciates the significance of his or her job assignment, the next question that naturally arises is, "Exactly what is expected of me?"

As you may recall, "cultures of commitment" are characterized by "clear communication of the corporate mission, strategy, goals, and expected results." As the employee's manager, you are the link that must be counted on to communicate these expected results. You are the one your company must count on to create the link between "what counts gets measured" and "what gets measured gets done," as diagrammed in Retention Practice #2.

This practice is about how good you are at managing the performance of all your people, not just the newly hired. Your effectiveness in using performance management techniques to keep your best people will be determined by the degree to which you accept and utilize a partnership model, rather than the traditional model. Here are the main differences:

Traditional Model	*Partnership Model*
■ Manager sets objectives, or there may not be any.	■ Objectives set with employee's input.
■ Manager evaluates performance subjectively, writes up appraisal.	■ Manager and employee agree on whether objective measures were met or not. Employee may write own appraisal.

■ Process driven by HR as bureaucratic exercise.	■ Process owned by line managers as tool to help employees succeed.
■ Strongly influenced by personality issues.	■ Focus on objectives minimizes subjectivity and bias.
■ Objectives may be vague.	■ Objectives are specific and measurable.
■ Appraisal process is a yearly event.	■ Performance discussions occur on a daily or weekly basis, with quarterly reviews.
■ Performance appraisal done to force-rank employees to determine who gets pay increases.	■ Employees rewarded for achieving "stretch" objectives connected to organization's "stretch" objectives.

The traditional model reflects an outdated "parent-child" relationship in which the boss is the sole, arbitrary, and all-powerful judge of performance. The partnership model, on the other hand, reflects an adult-to-adult relationship where two partners forge a mutual agreement.

As we know, a bank lender signs an agreement with a borrower to repay a loan. The banker does not usually need to badger and control the borrower into repaying the loan, at least in most cases. The same should be true for managers and their employees. If there is agreement between adults, there should be no reason for coercion, especially if the employee understands the possible rewards of achieving his or her end of the bargain.

The Agreement Starts with Getting the Employee's Input

The employee is much more likely to buy into the performance agreement if he or she has had a chance to contribute to the setting of performance objectives.

One simple and practical model for setting performance discussions in general is the "Get-Give-Merge-Go" process, which works like this:

Step 1. Get: The employee's understanding of the purpose of the discussion and expectations of you, including the employee's ideas, questions, and concerns.

Step 2. Give: Your ideas, questions, and concerns.

Step 3. Merge: Your perspective and ideas with theirs, agreeing on specific action steps.

Step 4. Go: Set dates to review progress toward completion of agreed-on objectives.

Who's Doing It

- P. J. Smoot, learning and development leader at *International Paper*'s Memphis office, redesigned the company's performance review process to allow employees to review themselves, as many companies now do. Instead of passing judgment on everything their staff members do, managers at International Paper now reach a mutually agreed-upon performance agreement by actively soliciting employees' ideas.

"Listen for understanding," she advises managers. "And then, react honestly and constructively. Focus on the business goals, not on the personality." The manager then should use questions to guide the reviewee to a mutual understanding: "What about this? Would this have been more effective?" Ms. Smoot wishes managers would drop the tough-guy approach to reviews and adopt the qualities of a good Little League coach.[1]

The company has also instituted the practice of using "accountability partners," where each employee identifies others they work with who may be contacted for input by their manager at review time.

- Another company that has brought its performance management system up to date is *Electro-Mechanical Corporation,* of Bristol, Virginia. The company switched from annual to quarterly reviews to keep employees from being surprised at appraisal time. "If there are surprises," says Roger Leonard, Electro-Mechanical's general manager, "it is the manager who should get the negative evaluation."[2]

Mr. Leonard also has employees guide the review process and keep the performance agreement so that they can look at it from time to time to see where they stand.

- James Sauter, former CEO of several newspapers in the Ann Arbor, Michigan, area, changed his approach to performance reviews one year when he and one of his vice presidents couldn't agree on the overall rating. "We were miles apart on his performance. I thought it was adequate at best, he thought it was outstanding."

After that experience, Mr. Sauter stopped ranking and rating his people and now reaches an agreement on clear and measureable performance goals.[3]

Set S-M-A-R-T Objectives

To craft a mutually acceptable, motivational, and indisputable performance agreement, use the following formula in the setting of objectives. Performance objectives should be:

Specific
Measurable
Achievable
Results-oriented
Time-bound

A performance agreement such as the one in Figure 16-1 can be used as a guide (a blank agreement form is presented in Appendix F).

How Can Progress Be Measured?

One of the most difficult aspects of setting performance objectives is reaching agreement on which measurable objectives to use, as some employee's jobs lend themselves to measurement more easily than do others. Here is a list that can help you and your people set mutually agreeable objectives in four main areas:

1. *Quantity.*

- Number of customers/clients serviced per month/quarter, etc.
- Number of items processed (orders, forms) per week, month, etc.
- Average backlog of orders per day, month, etc.
- Number of cases handled (referrals, complaints) per period
- Number of customer complaints per period
- Percent employee participation in specific programs
- Number of person hours lost to absenteeism per period

2. *Quality.*

- Error rate (by department, project, etc.)
- Production hours lost due to injury (severity rate) per period
- Percent orders without error
- Percent avoidable voluntary employee turnover
- Percent procedures, tests repeated
- Percent work redone (or rejected completely)
- Percent work repeated
- Percent downtime or unproductive time

3. *Time.*

- Number or percent of deadlines missed
- Number or percent of complaints resolved within _____ days

Figure 16-1. Sample performance agreement.

To:	James Edwards, District Manager
	Date: <u>3/1/2XXX</u>

From: Meredith Wilson, Store Manager

Within the period <u>4/1–6/30</u> , the following will be accomplished:

I. Key Result Area: <u>Customer Service Improvement</u>

OBJECTIVES:	DATE
1. Install new computer system	4/30
2. Conduct customer service training	5/15

II. Key Result Area: <u>Increase Sales</u>

OBJECTIVES:	DATE
1. Increase revenues 15 percent through new quarterly promotion: 6/30	
2. Increase community involvement	

III. Key Result Area: <u>Cost Reduction</u>

OBJECTIVES:	DATE
1. Increase orders without error by 10 percent	6/30
2. Reduce waste by 10 percent	6/30
3. Reduce employee turnover by 20 percent	6/30

Progress toward these objectives will be reviewed at weekly meetings.

I understand that meeting these objectives will be the most significant factor in my performance evaluation and compensation.

Employee's Signature _____

Manager's Signature _____

- Number of days to complete
- Number of working days after end of month, quarter
- Time elapsed (turnaround time)
- Frequency each month, quarter

4. *Cost.*

- Percent variance from budget
- $ as line-item in budget (e.g., overtime)
- Dollars saved over previous period, quarter
- $ cost per contract or order received
- Number of hours to complete task each time

With a little thought and determination, you and your employees can set SMART objectives together, as partners in the planning process. Meeting quarterly will help you stay on target, avoid surprises, and, most important in employee retention, make sure you both understand exactly what results are expected.

Now grade yourself and your organization on Retention Practice #16: "Get Commitment to a Performance Agreement."

How good a job is your organization doing on this practice?

Circle one: (A) Excellent   (B) Very Good   (C) Good   (D) Fair   (F) Poor

How good a job are you as a manager doing on this practice?

Circle one: (A) Excellent   (B) Very good   (C) Good   (D) Fair   (F) Poor

How important do you believe this practice is to your organization's strategy to attract and retain the talent necessary to meet its business objectives?

Circle one: (A) Critical (B) Very important (C) Somewhat important
            (D) Not important

What can your organization do to improve on this practice?

What can you as a manager do to improve on this practice?

RETENTION PRACTICE #17

Challenge Early and Often

The role of leaders at all levels is to demonstrate to people that they are capable of achieving more than they think they can achieve.

—John Browne, CEO, British Petroleum

Which kind of employee do you want to keep more—the one who wants to be challenged and tested on the job, or the one who would rather be brought along slowly?

Most managers would say they prefer those who are eager for a challenge, because they usually turn out to be the top performers. And yet, hiring and keeping these "eager beavers" presents challenges for which you may not be ready.

Why Challenging High Performers Is a Challenge in Itself

- You're not sure how big a challenge it will take to keep them challenged.
- They may not be able to handle the challenge you give them.
- You're afraid they will screw things up.
- You believe they need to "pay their dues" first, as you did.
- You need them to clean up those odds and ends that have been accumulating.
- You want to give them a good long time to settle into their new jobs before assigning them anything really big.

We know that most employees do not feel challenged enough in their jobs. One attitude survey revealed that only 45 percent of employees feel their present jobs provide the chance to do challenging, interesting work.[1] Not being challenged enough, or not having the right kind of challenge, consistently ranks high as a reason employees resign their jobs.

Recently hired college graduates, in particular, have always been impatient to be challenged in their first jobs. They are used to being stimulated and tested, and the best and the brightest among them have high hopes for the challenges their first jobs will bring.

But their managers may have grown up in an earlier time, when young graduates were expected to pay their dues before being trusted with a major assignment. Some "old school" managers even speak proudly about how tough it was to break in in the old days and complain about how young people today expect too much too soon.

That new hires feel entitled to too much too soon is a problem, and always will be. But two key things have changed in recent years. First of all, many workers born since 1960 have watched their dues-paying parents be downsized after years of hard work and have little faith that their patience will pay off. Says the Generation X expert Bruce Tulgan, "The logic behind dues-paying is that, in the long run, there will be a reward. . . . But these days, investing in those kinds of long-term rewards is risky, since the 'Lifetime Job Club' isn't admitting too many new members. It's easy to imagine paying those dues now and never cashing in."[2]

Second, there are, and will be for the next ten years, fewer of these workers in the workforce than there are "baby boomers," and there will be more jobs available for them than there are young workers to fill these jobs. This means that the companies that stand the best chance of keeping these younger workers will be those that are willing and able to keep them challenged.

Who's Doing It

■ *Trilogy Software Inc.*, of Austin, Texas, one of the fastest-growing software companies in the United States, has more than 700 employees and annual revenues of $200 million and growing. Trilogy feels the key to its fast growth has been "to recruit the best people it can find, get them up to speed as fast as possible, then to turn them loose so they can make an immediate impact."[3]

"At a software company, people are everything," says company co-founder Joe Liemandt. "You can't build the next great software company—which is what we're trying to do here—unless you're totally committed to that. Of course, the leaders at every company say 'people are everything.' But they don't act on it."

To make the dream a reality, Trilogy created "Trilogy University," an intense and unusual orientation program for the new college graduates it hires, amounting to a crash course in software, in business, and in the company's culture. "It's more boot camp than business school," says Liemandt. He can be found at the office at 10 P.M. on weeknights quizzing recent hires on the company's products and customers.

In 1998, Trilogy received 15,000 resumes, conducted 4,000 on-campus interviews, and hired 262 college graduates whom it considered the best technical and cultural fits. But, rather than bring its new hires along gradually, as many of its competitors do, Trilogy "tosses them the keys to the car and tells them to step on the gas . . . for three exhausting and exhilarating months, they 'ramp up' at TU." The new recruits learn about the software industry from Liemandt and are challenged to improve the company's existing products or create new ones. Liemandt assures them that the company "will push them to the limit and then reward them accordingly."

"You don't have to sit around here earning tenure before you see a customer," says Jeff Daniel, the company's chief recruiter. "One of our TUers . . . is already working on accounts in France. I go out and tell my recruits, 'A kid your age was here for a month and a half, and now he's in Paris.' "

Says one new recruit, "I wasn't ready for college to end. None of us were. Now it doesn't have to." Says Liemandt, "They just came out of school and they're like, 'I studied a lot. Now I want to work a lot. So don't bore me, and don't spoon-feed me. Give me really hard stuff and lots of responsibility, and I'll go deliver.' "

It should be noted that Trilogy is growing fast enough that it has plenty of challenging and exciting work to offer its new hires. The company is a prime example of an organization whose recruitment and retention strategy is well suited to its business goals.

■ *FreeMarkets OnLine, Inc.,* is a booming Pittsburgh start-up company that organizes interactive online events in which suppliers bid for customers' raw materials business. Emily O'Brien works there as an "assistant market maker," a job that combines marketing, customer service, and sales. She responds to problems that occur when the on-line bidding gets out of hand. When a client wants millions of dollars worth of whatever product, she sources suppliers until she finds enough to fill the bill.

"It's a great job, offering lots of responsibility and autonomy," says O'Brien. "There are no artificial barriers to promotions here. . . . There's no thought control, and no vertical hierarchy." It's also O'Brien's first corporate gig. She's twenty-four years old.[4]

By putting many of its entry-level hires into jobs like O'Brien's, FreeMarkets Online makes itself exceptionally attractive to talented college graduates.

- *Charles Schwab* has designed a new-hire job rotation program called Wings, in which new recruits take on a series of short-term assignments of their own choosing before they apply for permanent positions within the company.

"Schwab is a big company, and there's no reason to suspect that twenty-two-year-olds will know what department they want to work in," says Laura Stepping, who helped create the program. "By letting them select various interim assignments, we're telling them that it's all right to explore, that it's okay not to be sure what you want to do."[5]

One twenty-three-year-old graduate with a degree in economics, whose background in technology was limited to a weeklong course in HTML coding, chose to pursue a web design assignment. She developed an online reference tool to help Schwab employees understand the securities handled in its nonstandard assets department.

What Schwab did right, of course, was to give credence to the idea that young workers can be trusted to choose the right kind of challenge—one that is motivating to them, appropriate to their talents and of value to the organization.

- *Enterprise Rent-A-Car* hires more new college graduates than almost any other company in the nation, assigning them to be field-office entrepreneurs. Tim Hutchins, twenty-five years old, had interviewed with large companies, but none offered as much growth potential as Enterprise.

He was hired as a management trainee making about $10,000 less than his contemporaries at other companies. They told him he was crazy. But he showed them. He was promoted to assistant branch manager within thirteen months, and, with performance bonuses, he made close to $50,000 in his second year.

Now, when Hutchins sits around drinking beer with his friends, they realize that he has surpassed a lot of them in both salary and responsibility. He has even recruited many of them to come to work for Enterprise.

"Think of it this way," says author Ron Leiber, who profiled Enterprise, Schwab, and FreeMarkets Online for *Fast Company.* "You can make entry-level jobs exercises in mediocrity. Or you can give recruits real tasks, tangible resources and support, and room to move. If the rookies fail, maybe you don't want them anyway. But if they pull it off, you can give them even more responsibility. And once the word gets out that your company offers high-quality entry-level jobs, more of the prospects will look your way for work."[6]

At a time when the first-year turnover rate for college graduates has doubled in recent years, rising to 11.6 percent for the class of '97, companies that are looking to hire and keep the best young talent will need to offer them unprecedented opportunities for challenge.

Guidelines for Challenging All Employees—New and Experienced

Here are some suggestions that will help you ensure that both your new hires and your longtime employees don't leave your company because they haven't been challenged sufficiently:

1. Pay enough attention to make sure that all employees are appropriately challenged, whether they are twenty-two or sixty-two, new hires or twenty-year veterans, college grads or high school dropouts.
2. Keep in mind that all your direct reports have different needs, depending on their performance levels and length of time in the organization, as shown in Figure 21-1, "Who Gets Developed . . . and How" (see Retention Practice #21).
3. Match the challenge to the person's level of ability. Ask employees what talents they would most like to use and what kind of challenge they would like. Use the Talent Inventory (Appendix D) if they are not sure which talents they most want to use.
4. Challenge your people to "find a need and fill it." Give them your ideas about where the "unmet needs" lie within your area, and ask for volunteers to take on these challenges as new assignments.
5. Break down the challenges in your area into achievable, specific results. A challenge may be too big for one person but may offer job enrichment possibilities to several members of the team. Remember, it's not the "bigness" of the challenge but the "fitness"; that is, how well it fits the employee's interests and abilities, that matters.
6. To increase challenge in an employee's job, look for opportunities to link the individual job more directly to customer problems.
7. Be mindful not to stunt the growth of your best people by keeping them in jobs they have outgrown, even though they continue to perform them with excellence. "We need you to keep doing what you're doing" are often the words that trigger the resignations of valued employees.
8. Update your performance agreement with the employee by adding new results you expect, as needed, to reflect any new challenges or assignments that arise.
9. Be sure to provide training and resources necessary for the employee to meet the challenge.
10. Remind the employee of possible rewards for meeting the challenge.
11. Follow through with timely and appropriate rewards.

Now grade yourself and your organization on Retention Practice #17: "Challenge Early and Often."

How good a job is your organization doing on this practice?

Circle one: (A) Excellent (B) Very good (C) Good (D) Fair (F) Poor

How good a job are you as a manager doing on this practice?

Circle one: (A) Excellent (B) Very good (C) Good (D) Fair (F) Poor

How important do you believe this practice is to your organization's strategy to attract and retain the talent necessary to meet its business objectives?

Circle one: (A) Critical (B) Very important (C) Somewhat important
          (D) Not important

What can your organization do to improve on this practice?

What can you as a manager do to improve on this practice?

RETENTION PRACTICE #18

Give Autonomy and Reward Initiative

> The leader who does not trust enough will not be trusted.
> When actions are performed without unnecessary speech
> The people say, "We did it ourselves."
>
> —Lao Tsu

Did you hear the news report about the supervisor at a publishing distribution company in Nashville, Tennessee, who chained and padlocked an employee's leg to his workbench after the employee got up and walked ten feet to offer a coworker a piece of gum?[1]

This true story is so outrageous you have to laugh, unless, of course, it happened to you. It is an extreme example of the impulse to control that lies within the heart of many a supervisor. Yet, this impulse is not the only factor involved in the reluctance of many managers to give their employees more freedom and the opportunity to use their creativity and independent judgment in the way they do their jobs.

When Todd Conger was promoted from his production job to manufacturing process coordinator at Morton International, the airbag manufacturer based in Brigham City, Utah, he fell into the age-old new manager's trap. When he saw his eleven-member team slipping behind schedule, he'd step in and start doing the work himself.

But the more work he did, the less work seemed to get done—and the less motivated his team became. Instead of just jumping in to tackle obvious problems, they would wait for specific instructions from him. Conger finally realized that his "help" was actually perceived as insulting. "I thought I was helping them," he said. "But they thought I was telling them they weren't working fast enough: 'Look, I can do it faster than you.' '' Conger learned what many new leaders learn the hard way—never do what you can delegate.[2]

Other managers appear to simply want or need control over their people and the work process. At a Michigan municipal utility, one supervisor was well known for ordering work to be redone, apparently for no other reason than to have it the way he wanted it, even when it made more sense to do it in a new or different way. His electricians quickly learned that taking the initiative was the shortest route to frustration. "Whatever entrepreneurial tendencies they may have had evaporated, and they settled into a survival strategy. Sit back and wait for the supervisor to explain exactly how he wants each step done. If you don't invest, at least you won't feel any pain when solid work is torn out and redone for no good reason."[3]

Why Managers Don't Give Their People More Autonomy

There are several reasons managers don't delegate and empower their people more, which makes it all the more remarkable when we hear about those who do. Here are some of the reasons:

- They enjoy the work too much to give it over to someone else.
- Managers promoted from a nonmanagement role may not know how to change from doing to delegating.
- They are afraid they will give away their power if they empower their people.
- They are afraid the employee will mishandle the assignment, making everyone look bad.
- They say they have no time to train their employees to the point where they can trust them to make more decisions about how the work gets done.
- They don't believe their workers really want autonomy.
- They think they, not the employees, are supposed to be the authority on how things are done and should be consulted frequently.
- They don't trust the competence or judgment of their workers.
- They fear they will be outperformed by a more competent member of their staff.
- They mistakenly believe that delegation is an all-or-nothing arrangement.
- The manager's manager may expect him or her to know every detail of a project, thereby making it difficult to delegate.
- They are cynical about the "E-word," believing that worker empowerment is just another halfhearted management fad.

Do you identify with some of these? Most managers do, because all of them are either understandable or legitimate reasons for reluctance. And yet, we also know that the desire to make judgments about how one's job is done is one of the five strongest factors in job enrichment and satisfaction (see Retention Practice #5). The fact is, today's flatter, more responsive workplaces require workers who can take the initiative, act quickly, and deal promptly with customer needs.

Still, only 48 percent of U.S. workers say they are given the authority to make decisions about how to do their jobs.[4] In another survey, only 55 percent of U.S. employees say they hold the power to make decisions to satisfy customers. Said one respondent, a magazine circulation manager, "The company stifles ideas, and you don't feel you're accomplishing anything."[5]

Younger workers especially are seeking out more autonomous careers. About 70 percent of workers age 21 to 32 would prefer having their own business to working for someone else.[6] Big companies, now realizing that they are competing with start-ups for the services of Generation-Xers, are learning to mimic small companies by creating smaller, more autonomous units. Clearly, organizations that are serious about retaining top talent understand that their best performers are the ones who want the most autonomy and freedom to take the initiative. They are also discovering, interestingly enough, that average performers can transform themselves into top performers when given the chance to have more say.

Who's Doing It

■ Duane Delp, owner of *Mechanical Mann*, a Laguna Hill, California, auto repair shop, does a lot of management by walking around. While making his rounds, he asks his employees to carry a note pad for writing down potential changes in the workplace. That's how he got the suggestion to move the oil dispenser to a more convenient location and the idea to paint a "no parking" sign where cars continually blocked the driveway. "I'll sit and work with a technician as he works, and we bounce ideas off each other."[7]

■ At the *Consolidated Diesel Company* facility in Whitakers, North Carolina, the 1,700-employee, $250 million company attributes its success to self-directed teams based on practices such as extensive cross-training, allowing employees to design solutions to problems in the plant, and letting teams design new schedules with increased flexibility. The teams also hire, and fire, their own members. "Expectations in a team environment are much higher than at any other place where I've worked," says Larry Williams, director of human resources. The plant's turnover rate is less than 2 percent.[8]

■ According to Jeff Stark, president of *The Box Connection*, a La Habra, California moving-box supplier, "The single best way for small-business owners to get employee suggestions is to be there every day and just listen to their conversations." Stark installed a new point-of-sale computer system after listening to his employees talk about their experiences. When he schedules a staff meeting, he announces the agenda three or four days ahead so that employees have time to prepare comments and suggestions on each topic. He believes that, once employees have taken the courageous step to offer suggestions, "follow-up is crucial. Otherwise, it's demoralizing. You have twenty-four hours to respond. If you don't, the next time they won't speak up." Stark says he is convinced that "the best reward an employee can get is action on an idea."[9]

■ "You won't be successful if people aren't carrying the recognition of the problem and the solution within themselves," said Jan Carlzon, former CEO of *Scandinavian Air Service*. "The key is to let them discover the problem." During his first two years as CEO, Carlzon "demonstrated through a variety of symbolic acts . . . eliminating the pretentious executive dining room and burning thousands of pages of manuals and handbooks—the extent to which rules had come to dominate the company. . . . 'The leaders' most important role is to instill confidence in people,' said Carlzon. 'They must dare their people to take risks and responsibilities. You must back them up if they make mistakes.' "[10]

■ *Whirlpool Corporation* provides low-wage workers a voice by placing them on strategic teams with senior managers and executives. These frontline workers, some of whom earn $12 an hour, help make decisions regarding the company's facilities across the United States. They also travel abroad with executives to visit new manufacturing facilities, providing input that helps top managers gain a better perspective on production and labor issues.

■ Bob Schrader, general manager of the former *Ritz-Carlton Hotel* (now the *Fairmont*) in Kansas City, Missouri, introduced the concept of self-directed work teams by eliminating the job titles of all management staff and putting them on a participatory management task force. The managers dived into cross-functional training so that they could understand, and function in, other hotel departments.

Soon, all 430 employees were being asked to start making decisions on their own, after years of being told exactly what to do. For front-line workers, the change meant learning to work as members of a team, succeeding or failing as a group instead of as individuals. Some cafe workers worked harder than others, so peers became involved in deciding on disciplinary measures. The atmosphere in the restaurant improved. The cafe team even asked that some workers be removed from the team because they were absent too often or weren't carrying their weight.

Schrader had to adjust his managerial style as well. "My role is to be out on the floor, not sit in my office and look at paperwork," he said. "I attend team meetings and try to get people comfortable about approaching me on issues, but then a lot of my job is directing people back to their teams for solutions. A lot of what I should be doing now is asking questions instead of dictating methods."

The impact on the restaurant's staff turnover was dramatic. Whereas it had been running at well over 100 percent per year, within nine months it was reduced to "a single-digit figure," according to Schrader. Overall hotel turnover dropped from between 50 percent and 70 percent, considered fairly standard in the hotel industry, to about 35 percent.[11]

Ritz-Carlton Hotels nationwide began allowing direct service employees $2,000 to rectify a customer complaint on the spot, no questions asked, but employees first received training and guidelines in how to make those judgments.

■ Other companies, such as *Bookminders*, a Pittsburgh firm that does weekly bookkeeping for businesses, gives workers more autonomy by letting them work at home. Company founder Tom Joseph trains and equips his employees to work from home, keeping his overhead low, and his turnover as well—it is almost nil. Although workers are paid only for work completed, and there are no benefits, job seekers call him every week, and his help-wanted ads draw hundreds of responses.

■ *Nordstrom* department stores are well known for their legendary customer service based on the freedom the company gives to its sales associates to make on-the-spot decisions. The company's only rule: "Use your best judgment at all times." One employee helped press shirts a customer had bought at another store so that the customer could get to an appointment on time. Another delivered a bathrobe ordered by an expectant mother to the maternity ward of a hospital when she found out that the customer had gone into labor.

None of these success stories could have happened unless managers had let go of their need for power and control, their insistence on doing the work themselves, and their fear of trusting their people to be creative problem solvers. It all comes down to your willingness to delegate.

Check Your Delegation Practices

Use the following checklist to determine how you are doing as a delegator:

	Yes	No
1. Are you now, and have you for some time, been taking work home with you nearly every night?	____	____

2. Do you consistently average five to ten more hours work per week than those you manage? _____ _____

3. Do you have adequate time for leisure and community activities? _____ _____

4. Are you frequently interrupted by your direct reports, asking you to make minor decisions or answer simple questions? _____ _____

5. Do you feel that you are running all the time, but never catching up? _____ _____

6. Is unfinished work piling up on your desk? _____ _____

7. Do you spend more time on details than you do on planning or directing the work? _____ _____

8. Do you have trouble meeting deadlines? _____ _____

9. Do you lack confidence in the ability of your people to handle problems? _____ _____

10. Do you hesitate to admit that you need help to stay on top of the job? _____ _____

11. Do you fail to ask your direct reports for suggestions? _____ _____

12. Do you feel that you are drowning in a mass of paper and detail? _____ _____

If your answer to more than four of these questions was yes, you may need to change your delegation and work assignment practices.

You Might as Well Delegate—Your People Know More Anyway

Managers are increasingly discovering that so-called average employees know more than the managers thought they did. They may actually possess more information and wisdom that is truly vital to the company, as Figure 18-1 shows.

Guidelines for Better Delegation and Empowerment

The following suggestions will help you as you move to delegate more work to your employees and to give them freer rein in deciding how they do their work:

1. Remember—people support what they help design. Those who have the opportunity to develop the plan are more likely to buy into it.

Figure 18-1. The Iceberg of Ignorance.

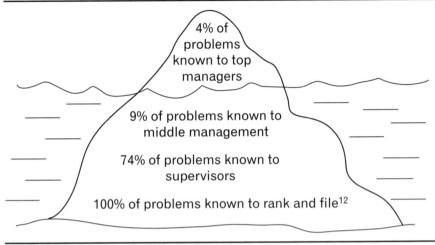

4% of
problems
known to top
managers

9% of problems known to
middle management

74% of problems known to
supervisors

100% of problems known to rank and file[12]

2. Match the person's abilities to the task or project.

3. Understand that there are degrees of delegation. You decide which degree is appropriate by considering the nature of the task, the ability of the person doing the work, the amount of top management interest, and the time available for task completion. W. W. Nesbitt of Westinghouse Electric is credited with detailing these degrees of delegation:

- *Investigate and report back.* You make the decision and take appropriate action.
- *Investigate and recommend action.* You evaluate the recommendations, make the decision, and take action.
- *Investigate and advise of action you intend to take.* You evaluate the decision made by your staff member and approve or disapprove.
- *Investigate and take action; advise of action taken.* Here you display faith in your staff's ability but want to be kept advised of what's going on.
- *Investigate and take action.* This is full delegation and displays complete faith in your staff's ability.

4. Full delegation should be your goal in the delegation process. To reach this level, you must be willing to give up a portion of your authority.[13]

5. You must support decisions after they have been made, whether or not you feel they were the best ones.

6. You must be willing to gamble that your workers can do a better job when left on their own than when closely supervised.

7. Bear in mind that you may have people on your team who will resist being given more autonomy and initiative, either because they are not mature enough or because they simply don't want to be held accountable. You will have to choose between living with these team members or replacing them with those who are comfortable with increased accountability or are willing to be trained in how to accept it.

8. The person doing the task may not do it as well as you would. You must resist the temptation to step in and take over the project.

9. Delegate by results expected, not by the method to be used in performing the task.

10. Set performance standards to measure accomplishment against results.

11. Give the employee all of the relevant information you have about the task.

12. Delegate only to those who are qualified. This means you will need to train some of your staff before delegating to them.

13. Analyze the work you are now involved in, and classify it into one of three categories:

   a. Work that can only be done by you, the manager
   b. Work that can be delegated as soon as someone is trained to do it
   c. Work that can be delegated immediately

14. As much as possible, delegate all the routine work of your job.

15. When you have identified work that is to be delegated, but that no one is trained to perform, you have identified training needs to be accomplished by you or others as appropriate. Start immediately to provide the necessary training to prepare someone to take over these duties. Then proceed to delegate by degrees until full delegation has been achieved.

16. If you find yourself not trusting an employee's ability to perform, use the degrees of delegation, begin to train that individual, or consider assigning a smaller piece of the job on a trial basis.

17. Praise employees when they do anything that shows independent judgment and initiative.

18. When you see increased delegation by any of your direct reports who manage people, praise them as well.

19. Whenever possible, share financial information about the company when delegating. When they see that their decisions and actions affect their financial rewards, your workers will be more likely to make appropriate decisions.

20. Beware of loading up the employee with too many challenges or enlarging the job without enriching it. Examples include:

- Asking the employee to crank up production in a meaningless task
- Adding another meaningless task to an existing one
- Rotating assignments of a number of unchallenging jobs
- Removing the most difficult parts of the assignment in order to free the worker to accomplish more of the less-challenging assignments

21. Empowering your people does not always require approval from the top. Simply dare to delegate! Remember, your employees are certainly empowered during the 128 hours per week they are not on the job! Empowerment happens when you reach a new agreement with the individuals on your team about how they will share responsibility, authority, and accountability for the work you all do together.

22. Keep tabs on what you delegate. As the deadline nears, make sure that everything is on target.

23. Because delegating can be risky, make sure your workers understand the kinds of activities that are off limits from an ethical standpoint. Pressures to achieve superior results may sometimes come into conflict with your organization's code of conduct.

Remember, the critical ingredient is trust—trust that a failed experiment in new ways of working will not lead to punishment from above, and trust that your team will not abuse whatever new authority you have extended them. To keep the best people you must give them your trust.

Now grade yourself and your organization on Retention Practice #18: "Give Autonomy and Reward Initiative."

How good a job is your organization doing on this practice?

Circle one: (A) Excellent   (B) Very good   (C) Good   (D) Fair   (F) Poor

How good a job are you as a manager doing on this practice?

Circle one: (A) Excellent   (B) Very good   (C) Good   (D) Fair   (F) Poor

How important do you believe this practice is to your organization's strategy to attract and retain the talent necessary to meet its business objectives?

Circle one: (A) Critical (B) Very important (C) Somewhat important
            (D) Not important

What can your organization do to improve on this practice?

What can you as a manager do to improve on this practice?

THE FOURTH KEY

Coach and Reward to Sustain Commitment

It is one thing to gain an employee's initial commitment, but it is more difficult to sustain the employee's commitment over the long haul.

Sustaining employee commitment is demanding, unglamorous work. It means paying attention to employee performance, following through to check and monitor results, correcting poor performance, scheduling progress reviews, answering employees' questions about career advancement, keeping spirits up when times are bad, giving frequent praise, disciplining when necessary, and sometimes making tough decisions about who stays and who is let go.

While this work may seem frustrating, doing it well is what makes managing people so rewarding. The point is: This work that must be done well if your organization is seriously committed to winning the war to find and keep the right talent. The heroes of this war will be those managers who thrive on this work and want to do it. Managers like you will be the front-line soldiers.

As noted in Retention Practice #11, 50 percent of work life satisfaction is determined by the employee's relationship with his or her manager. By looking back at the reasons why good performers leave, you will notice that several of them have to do with the manager's failure to:

- Establish a link between employee performance and reward.
- Help employees perceive career growth and advancement opportunities.
- Keep employee goals aligned with team and organizational goals.
- Make employees feel valued and appreciated.
- Confront nonperformance.

- Give the employee a manageable, sustainable work load.
- Allow, create, and encourage a fun and spirited environment.
- Treat all employees with respect and dignity.

The next six retention practices will provide you with tools and ideas for doing all the above. If you use these tools and ideas, you can and will sustain the commitment of your people.

Proactively Manage the Performance Agreement

> One of the worst things we do in corporate America is not tell people what we think of them. Every appraisal looks the same.
> —Lawrence A. Bossidy, former CEO, AlliedSignal

Once you have made a performance agreement (see Retention Practice #16), you must manage that agreement in a proactive way. This doesn't mean that you simply wait ninety days to check with the employee to see whether the performance objectives were achieved. It means that you are paying attention to performance results on a daily or weekly basis and giving praise or corrective instruction, as appropriate.

This is what being a performance coach is all about. It would be ridiculous to imagine a basketball or football coach waiting until the end of the season to give feedback to the players, and yet this is exactly what many managers do. They practice what Blanchard and Johnson in *The One-Minute Manager* call the "let-alone . . . zap!" management style—basically laying back, ignoring employee performance except for infrequent observations, and withholding feedback until performance review time, when they "zap" the employee with a negative evaluation, often based on hearsay and biased perceptions. Such management behavior often becomes the "push" factor that drives the employee to begin looking elsewhere.

What Great Coaches Do

The late performance technology theorist Thomas F. Gilbert was a professor of psychology at the University of Alabama during the coaching tenure of the legendary football coach Paul "Bear" Bryant. Dr. Gilbert had frequently listened to Coach Bryant's speeches, in which he extolled such coaching wisdom as "select the right players, inspire them to win, and show them you care."

But when Dr. Gilbert spent a season observing Coach Bryant at work during practices, he noticed relatively little inspiration or affection. Instead, he observed the coach doing a great deal of watching—using video cameras to record players' movements and keeping meticulous charts of their performance in every game.

In other words, Bryant's basic activity as a coach was to observe and gather data. "When he saw a player consistently making an error—say a right tackle had his feet out of position or a shoulder dropped the wrong way—Bryant told him about it, walked him through the proper movements, watched him do it right, and, yes, gave him a 'well done' for mastery when the player finally did the right thing."

Dr. Gilbert concluded that Coach Bryant was employing a simple and effective technique that is applicable to employee coaching as well:

1. Gather data.
2. Provide feedback.
3. Question.
4. Inform and instruct.
5. Reward, often with simple praise.[1]

Why Managers Fail as Performance Coaches—Fear of Giving Feedback

The number one cause of performance problems in 60 percent of companies, according to one study, was poor or insufficient job performance feedback from supervisors.[2]

A survey of 1,149 people at seventy-nine different companies found that manager feedback and coaching skills were consistently rated as mediocre.[3]

Another study found that 41 percent of employees believe their managers have no effect whatsoever on their performance, and 14 percent say their manager actually made their job harder.[4]

What these studies show, in short, is that most managers are weak coaches, and, furthermore, their employees know it.

There appear to be six main reasons that managers fear giving feedback:

1. *Reluctance to Confront.* One obstacle here is that you have to observe the behavior before you can confront it. Second, it's only human to dread

confrontation. And, finally, it is even more difficult when the employee is more technically expert than the manager.

2. *Fear of Hurting.* Again, it is only human not to want to offend. Many managers haven't been trained in how to critique the behavior without having the employee take it personally.

3. *Fear of Failure.* Until you have had practice or training in the right way to coach and give feedback, your fear of failing at it will keep you from trying.

4. *No Time for Coaching.* With continuing downsizings and consolidations, managers report they have less time for coaching, as they are expected to carry more of the workload themselves.

5. *They Never Received Feedback Themselves.* Many managers have grown up in a culture that doesn't value coaching. Having never received it themselves, they have no role models for offering feedback except negative ones.

6. *Little Incentive to Coach and Give Feedback.* In many organizations, giving feedback and coaching is not encouraged, recognized, or rewarded, yet there is a negative consequence for these organizations and their managers—they continue to experience high turnover.

How to Reward Results with Simple Praise and Appreciation

Many managers withhold praise, saving it for what they might consider "big" employee accomplishments. What they fail to realize is that the frequent individual acts of "catching someone doing something right" work most effectively in motivating and sustaining top performance.

Some managers say, "I reserve praise for truly exceptional performance. I expect people to do their jobs without having to be praised all the time." Other say, "No one ever praised me, so why should I have to do it for my workers?" While understandable, neither of these attitudes is acceptable in today's competitive environment. People perform better and stay longer when they receive consistent praise and appreciation for doing good work.

Here's how to get started:

1. Commit to "managing your people by walking around" (MBWA).
2. Tell your employees you will be observing them and giving feedback.
3. Praise people immediately when you see them do something right.
4. Be specific. Tell them exactly what they did right.

5. Tell them how much you appreciate what they did and what it means to the organization.
6. Encourage them to keep up the good work.
7. Track employee results through data and reports as well.

Praise is usually most effective when delivered in person, but a well-phrased note or letter can work wonders as well. The best of these notes are detailed enough to let the employee know you took the time to find out more about their contributions. Here is an example:

> Please pass along my appreciation for a job well done to your crew members. Their performance is a good reflection of your skills as a trainer, mentor, and motivator. One of your servers, Jim Jones, mentioned that he was impressed by your willingness to come in before the shift to make sure the point-of-sale buttons were finished before the start of the contest. Through efforts such as those by you and your staff, the company increased breakfast sales by 3 percent for the period.[5]

How to Give Prompt, Encouraging Corrective Feedback

Shouting, berating, name calling, and public humiliations have the unfortunate effect of negating, devaluing, and alienating the employee. Instead, give prompt, brief, and encouraging corrective feedback, as Coach Bryant would have given. It is important to keep in mind your goal of eliminating the behavior while keeping the person. Before you can give an effective reprimand, you must also show that you are sincerely interested in the person's welfare and success.

The process works best when you:

- Give immediate feedback.
- Are specific about what the person did wrong.
- Are specific about what you expect next time—show the person if you can.
- Reaffirm that you value the person for his or her contributions.
- Never give a reprimand based on hearsay.

This process "is tough on performance, not on the person," and is based on the principle that "goals begin behaviors while consequences maintain behaviors."[6]

Feedback—How to Say It and How Not to Say It

Feedback is always easier to accept when it describes behavior, not just your judgment about the behavior, as shown in these examples:

How Not to Say It	*How to Say It*
"You don't care."	"The contract omitted a vital section."
"You don't know enough."	"The data analysis was inaccurate according to my figures."
"You are never here when I need you."	"Six absences in two months is not acceptable."
"You really botched the semiconductor contract."	"We had a lot of trouble processing the semiconductor contract because the forms were incomplete."

As you can see, using behaviorally anchored language keeps the feedback from becoming personal while still allowing you to hold the employee accountable for his or her actions.

What Employees Value Most in Manager Coaching

36 percent ....Clear feedback
23 percent ....A new perspective
20 percent ....Advice on handling situations
7 percent ....Understanding of organizational objectives
7 percent ....General encouragement
7 percent ....Handling organizational politics[7]

Guidelines for Quarterly Progress Reviews

When you meet quarterly to discuss progress toward objectives set on your employees' quarterly performance agreements, as outlined in Retention Practice #16, here are a few guidelines for effective discussions:

- Review progress toward achievement of results in the performance agreement using the Get-Give-Merge-Go communication model outlined in Retention Practice #16 (start the discussion by getting the employee's perspective on his or her progress before giving yours).

- Give praise and corrective feedback as appropriate.
- Negotiate and sign a new performance agreement (Merge-Go).
- Use the opportunity to re-recruit valued performers; let them know how happy you are to have them on your team; ask what resources or training they need to be more successful and what other help they may need.
- During times of intense change, deliver as much good news as possible about new plans and strategies, new pay plans or incentives, marketing initiatives, new products, services, and so on to rekindle enthusiasm about being on the team.
- Communicate in no uncertain terms how much you value your employee's contributions and emphasize that you look forward to a long-term relationship.

Who's Doing It

- Quarterly re-recruiting sessions between managers and top performers have become the centerpiece of *Hyatt Hotel*'s selective retention efforts, resulting in an 8 percent per year reduction in turnover.

Mistakes Managers Make in Performance Reviews

Besides the major problem of "let-alone . . . zap!," managers are vulnerable to several other mistakes when doing traditional performance reviews with their employees:

- "Similar to Me": Rewarding those who are similar to the manager in one of several ways—gender, age or generation, race, national origin, educational background, religion or personality type.

- "Halo Effect": Rating an employee highly because of a strong positive first impression that continues to color the manager's judgment and prevent objectivity. This could be based on something as superficial as seeing an employee keeping a neat desk.

- "Recency Effect": Basing a performance review only on recent events, not on performance during the entire review period. This tends to happen most when the manager does a rush job or hasn't kept track of the employee's performance throughout the year.

- "Leniency Effect": Attempting to stay popular with one's employees by giving everyone high marks. This helps no one improve.

- "Central Tendency": Giving everyone average ratings as a way of avoiding tough choices. As with leniency, this defeats the purpose of the review, and no one benefits.[8]

Problems like these help explain why, in a survey of 745 managers, the American Management Association found that 98 percent used performance evaluations, but only 13 percent strongly agreed that they improved worker performance.[9] A major part of the problem is the use of rating systems instead of performance objectives, which leaves too much subjectivity at play in the process.

Ten Things the Best Coaches Do

Researchers Lois Frankel and Karen Otazo, of Atlantic Richfield (ARCO) in Los Angeles, asked several hundred of their employees to list the characteristics of managers for whom they had done their best work. These were their top ten characteristics. Take a moment to check the ones you think most of your people would use to describe you:

_____ Took time to listen to me.

_____ Saw me as a person, not just an employee.

_____ Cared about me personally and helped if I had personal problems.

_____ Set a good example.

_____ Let me know I could do more than I thought I was capable of—stretched me.

_____ Encouraged me.

_____ Never pulled rank; rolled up his or her sleeves and pitched in.

_____ Didn't keep me in the dark; let me know what was going on.

_____ Praised me for a job well done.

_____ Let me know in a straightforward manner when I didn't do a job well.[10]

If you found it difficult to check many of these, you may be a good candidate for training in performance management and coaching. You may also want to seek out the opportunity to receive 360-degree feedback through your organization so that you can see how you are perceived by your employees on this important retention practice.

Now grade yourself and your organization on Retention Practice #19: "Proactively Manage the Performance Agreement."

How good a job is your organization doing on this practice?

Circle one: (A) Excellent   (B) Very good   (C) Good   (D) Fair   (F) Poor

How good a job are you as a manager doing on this practice?

Circle one: (A) Excellent   (B) Very good   (C) Good   (D) Fair   (F) Poor

How important do you believe this practice is to your organization's strategy to attract and retain the talent necessary to meet its business objectives?

Circle one: (A) Critical (B) Very important (C) Somewhat important
            (D) Not important

What can your organization do to improve on this practice?

What can you as a manager do to improve on this practice?

RETENTION PRACTICE #20

Recognize Results

> The deepest craving in human nature is the craving to be appreciated.
>
> —William James

"A man at a pay phone asked to speak with the manager. 'Sir, I hear you are recruiting for a supervisor,' he began. Pause. 'You say you have already hired one a couple of months ago? I see. How is he working out?'

"He listened carefully, then ended the conversation, wishing the manager continued success with his new supervisor.

"A gentleman sitting near the pay phone overheard the conversation. 'Better luck next time, buddy. Sorry you didn't get the job,' he offered sympathetically.

"'Oh, no,' the man laughed. 'That was my manager I was speaking to. I just wanted to see how I was doing.'"[1]

We see the humor in this story because of the not-so-humorous truth that lies within it—that most workers are starved for recognition. Is it possible that some of your employees are experiencing a recognition deficit? Maybe you know what that feels like yourself.

While most managers continue to believe that pay is the most important factor in whether employees stay or go, employees consistently rank recognition for their good work as number one. Employees rated a manager's thanks as the most motivational incentive of all in a Wichita State survey, but 58 percent of respondents said they seldom if ever got a personal "thank you" from their managers. In another study, two out of three employees said they don't get enough recognition and want more of it.[2]

The great mother lode of employee motivation and job satisfaction lies in the cycle of Challenge followed by Achievement followed by Recognition—the C-A-R motivational cycle, as first presented by Frederick Herzberg, the father of modern worker motivation theory.[3]

Herzberg's study of 1,685 employees showed that the factors that produced the most instances of job satisfaction were, in order:

- Achievement
- Recognition
- The work itself
- Responsibility
- Advancement
- Growth

These factors were all related to job content.

Factors that Herzberg found could take away job satisfaction but not produce it—"demotivators," if you will—were all related to job environment. These included: company policy/administration, supervision, relationship with supervisor, work conditions, salary, relationship with peers, personal life, relationship with subordinates, and status and security, in that order.

Studies like Herzberg's and many others have long since proved the bankruptcy of what he called the old "kick-in-the-ass" theory of motivation, which remains all too prevalent today. Smart managers know they must motivate-to-retain by feeding their employees an enriched diet of challenges, starting on the employee's very first day on the job (see Retention Practice #17).

You may be measuring what counts, and what you are measuring may be getting done, but if you are not recognizing and rewarding what gets done (see Retention Practice #2), the productivity of your people will decline along with your retention rates.

Why Managers Don't Recognize What Gets Done

There seem to be a few main reasons why managers aren't getting the motivational mileage out of the C-A-R cycle that they should be getting. Check any of the following that apply to you:

1. ____ They subscribe to the management philosophy of "If you don't hear from me, that means you're doing a good job." This is a rather low-energy, low maintenance management practice, akin to the "kick-in-the-ass" and "let-alone . . . zap" practices described earlier. It is a popular practice in autocratic environments, and among managers who have worked for managers who treated them this way.

Many managers who use this style are governed by the proposition that "my people are expected to do their job, and they get paid to do it." They sometimes openly resist employee recognition practices, asking, "Why should I have to always be telling them they're simply doing what they are supposed to be doing?"

This is also a common philosophy among managers who are driven primarily by thinking and logic, who have a hard time empathizing with employees who are more governed by their feelings and who need more praise, recognition, and pats on the back than they do.

2. ＿＿ They believe that "rewards and recognition" is the responsibility of the human resources department. Many large organizations do have "rewards and recognition" departments within the human resources function, which has led to the unintended effect of letting some managers off the hook in terms of providing less formal types of recognition. The problem here is that if the manager doesn't "own" the practice, it may never get done.

3. ＿＿ They don't spend enough time observing their employees' performance to know when they are achieving results in the first place (see Retention Practice #19).

4. ＿＿ They simply don't know how to recognize and are afraid they will do it the wrong way. If you haven't been taught how to recognize results, and if you aren't used to being recognized yourself in creative and appropriate ways, how would you know how to do it? The following guidelines will help you get started:

Guidelines for Recognizing Results

Employee recognition has become a large industry, providing organizations with prizes, travel, clothing, coupons, and plaques for the sole purpose of recognizing achievement. Other staples in the employee recognition game are the always-popular cash incentives and, of course, good old-fashioned praise.

Many managers believe that only cash rewards—bonuses, raises, and promotions—are effective for motivating and keeping their good performers. While money is certainly important to all employees, it is more important to some employees than it is to others (see Retention Practice #2). Money can help to motivate and retain when it given promptly in recognition of a specific achievement and in sufficient quantity to reflect the value of the achievement to the organization. Yes, money is important, but most employees report that the factor that keeps them motivated and committed is the opportunity to be challenged, achieve results, and be recognized.

There are basically two forms of recognition:

1. Informal rewards, which are initiated at the manager's discretion to recognize and motivate individuals in a timely way
2. Formal rewards, which the organization initiates to motivate all employees

In his book *1,001 Ways To Reward Employees*,[4] Bob Nelson presents a multitude of ways to recognize employees both formally and informally, providing stimulating examples of both methods. Here is a sampling:

Informal Ways to Recognize and Reward

■ *No-Cost Recognition.* The type of reward most preferred by all employees is personalized, on-the-spot recognition that costs nothing except the caring and energy that goes into it.

Example: Handing out preprinted "Bravo" cards with a few handwritten words of specific praise.

■ *Low-Cost Rewards.* Memorable and effective rewards for less than $50. As a wise person once said, "Spending a dollar on something clever and unique is better than spending $50 on something ordinary and forgettable."

Example: Giving employees who render exceptional service "scratch-off" cards redeemable for prizes.

■ *Recognition Activities.* One-time events that celebrate a significant achievement or milestone, such as the employee's anniversary date.

Example: Having managers serve employees lunch or dinner.

■ *Public Recognition/Social Rewards.* Social reinforcers that intensify the degree of appreciation.

Example: Having white-collar manufacturing employees work on the production line one day a year.

■ *Communication.* Open-forum communication is desired by almost all employees, yet only about one fourth of managers use it.

Example: Inviting all employees to attend "50-50 forums" with management at which managers speak half the time, and employees speak during the other half.

■ *Time Off.* An increasingly popular form of recognition.

Examples: Giving people one day off for each day ahead of deadline that they meet goals, assuming high quality of results. Also, giving people the rest of a day off if they achieve specified results by a certain time or awarding time off for improvements in quality, safety, teamwork, or other behavior you value.

■ *Cash/Cash Substitutes/Gift Certificates*. Cash and cash substitutes give the employee flexibility in how to use the reward. Gift certificates can be tailored to the interests of employees.

Example: When an employee refers business that results in a sale, he or she receives a cash award of 1 percent to 5 percent of the gross sale, depending on the value of the business to the company.

■ *Merchandise/Apparel/Food*. These work best when the individual has a choice among items. These kinds of rewards have "trophy value"—they serve as a tangible reminder of past achievement and as a reminder that future performance will be rewarded. Many recipients of cash awards spend the money to pay bills or for other necessities and cannot remember later how they spent the money.

Example: One company gives both travel incentives and a piece of merchandise that can be used on the trip, such as luggage, golf clubs, or anything that is relevant to the trip.

■ *Recognition Items, Trophies, and Plaques*. Similar to general merchandise, recognition items are customized for the individual, company, or event.

Example: Giving Swiss army knives, ball caps, pens, etc., that have been imprinted with the employee's name.

■ *Fun/Celebrations*. Appropriate for any company or department trying to put more fun in the workplace while recognizing employee contributions (see Retention Practice #24).

Example: Hosting an after-hours "Margarita Happy Hour" award for the employee who did the best job that week of dealing with a tough customer.

How to Get the Most Out of Informal Rewards

1. *Match the reward to the person, that is, to the person's personal preferences*. For example, some employees are more motivated by a letter of appreciation or by one-to-one appreciation and would be embarrassed by public recognition.

2. *Match the reward to the achievement, that is, how significant the achievement is, in terms of impact and/or length of time spent on it*. Don't overdo when recognizing your people for relatively small achievements.

3. *Reward in a timely way, that is, give the reward as soon as possible after the achievement*.

4. *Explain exactly why the reward was given*. Don't just say, "Good job" or "Well done." Instead, say, "I appreciated the commitment you demonstrated by coming in three Saturdays in a row to complete that project."

5. *Recognize groups and individuals within groups.* It is important to recognize everyone on the team, but it is especially important to single out those who made the greatest contributions.

6. *Realize that what used to be a reward may come to be expected.* If that yearly bonus, for example, is now considered an entitlement, it no longer has the power to motivate. Find out what your workers value as rewards.

Awards for Specific Achievements and Activities

When you want to encourage the achievement of specific contributions by key performers on highly valued assignments, consider the following kinds of rewards:

- *Outstanding Employee Awards.*

Example: Employee of the Year or Month awards based on a variety of criteria, such as completing urgent projects, collaborating cross-functionally, generating the best money-saving ideas, fostering teamwork, and achieving high quality, to name a few. These can be given for a single achievement or an accumulation of praiseworthy results and are perceived to be more fair and more meaningful when peers are involved in the selection.

- *Productivity and Quality Awards.* About 90 percent of American workers think their companies would perform better if they were given meaningful incentives to improve quality and productivity. The key here is that effective performance should be rewarded consistently.

Example: Awards breakfasts for factory workers who have met certain quality goals.

- *Employee Suggestion Awards.* Only about four in ten employees believe that their companies listen to their ideas, and the average American worker only makes one or two suggestions per year, compared to the average Japanese worker, who submits hundreds of suggestions per year.

Example: An employee whose suggestion is implemented receives 15 percent of out-of-pocket savings achieved in the first two years of use.

- *Customer Service Awards.* It costs six times more to win a new customer than to keep an existing one. These awards reinforce and encourage the highest standards of customer service.

Example: Employees can win points toward a shopping spree if managers hear them calling customers by name.

- *Sales Goal Awards.* Sales awards are one of the most common forms of recognition in for-profit organizations, largely because sales results are more easily quantifiable than are results of other jobs.

Example: Providing a male employee with a fully paid paternity leave when he achieves ambitious sales goals.

■ *Group/Team Awards.* The way to reward a team that achieves is to reward all the members of the team, not just the manager or the star performer.

Example: Managers assess a fine to individuals who come late to company meetings and pass out the money to the people who arrive on time.

■ *Attendance and Safety Awards.* Attendance awards encourage employees to be prompt and not miss workdays. Safety awards recognize employees for following safety procedures and minimizing accidents on the job.

Example: Award bonuses every six months to anyone who was not absent or late more than three times during the preceding half year and who was not involved in a preventable accident.

Formal Ways to Recognize and Reward

You may want to work within your department and with your human resources department to encourage the creation of a more formal rewards program that will help keep your most valued employees. Formal, company-initiated reward programs, though not as motivating as less formal, more personal forms of recognition, still remain important reinforcers.

Here are some of the most effective and frequently used:

■ *Multilevel Reward Programs and Point Systems.* These are tailored to the needs of different levels and types of employees and usually recognize only a small number of employees in a dramatic way.

Example: In a program specifically designed to increase employee retention and improve service, hotel employees receive points for being on time, providing excellent customer service, improving quality in operations, reaching department, profit, and production goals, and referring new employees. Points are redeemable for gifts ranging from TVs to tuition reimbursement.

■ *Contests.* Keys to a successful contest include: limiting the contest to a short period of time, keeping contest rules uncomplicated, ensuring that prizes are desirable to employees, linking rewards directly to performance, and giving rewards and recognition promptly.

Example: To combat high turnover among its 90,000 dealers, a company developed an incentive recruiting program. Dealers who recruit at least one new dealer in September—when turnover reaches a peak—receive a special prize.

■ *Field Trips, Special Events, and Travel.* These are extremely desirable and promotable incentives, but, because of the costs involved, they must be limited. One added attraction—the "bragging value" involved.

Example: One insurance company sends top-performing agents to the Masters golf tournament each year. They are flown there on the company jet, then wined and dined at the event.

■ *Education, Personal Growth, and Self-Development.* This includes additional training and services that build needed skills while satisfying the employee's need for growth and development.

Example: A foods company replaced the annual across-the-board pay raise with a pay-for-responsibility system. As people take on new duties— budgeting, for instance, or training—they earn additional base income.

■ *Advancement, Responsibility, and Visibility.* Promoting one of your people to a position of greater responsibility is definitely a formal reward. But the reward does not always have to be a promotion to be effective. Adding responsibility in the current job, giving special assignments, or offering the opportunity to train/mentor younger employees or lead a cross-functional team can yield payoffs in visibility and job enrichment.

Example: At an instrument manufacturer, outstanding performers are "promoted" to special assistant to the president for two weeks.

■ *Stock/Ownership.* Ownership incentives, such as Employee Stock Ownership Plans (ESOPs), are one of the most powerful motivators of performance and retention, desired by 85 percent of U.S. workers, according to one survey.[5]

Example: When the founder of a hardware chain died, his will specified that his employees would have the option of buying all his stock through a profit-sharing plan and trust.

■ *Employee Anniversaries.* Many organizations now celebrate employment anniversary dates in the interest of recognizing and keeping long-term employees.

Example: A hotel chain holds an annual banquet honoring employees with more than five years' service.

■ *Benefits, Health, and Fitness.* Not all employees want the same benefits or health and fitness programs.

Example: Cafeteria benefits programs that allow employees to select the benefits that best fit their needs. Still, some benefits are best given to all employees (see Retention Practice #1).

Example: Employees of a food-service firm receive free lunches.

■ *Charity/Social Responsibility.* Employees appreciate companies that value their efforts in supporting charities and local government.

Example: A clothing manufacturer makes a donation of $500 to community organizations in which an employee actively participates for a year.

How to Make a Formal Rewards Program Work

1. Tie rewards to organization and employee needs.
2. Ensure the reward's fairness.
3. Make sure the reward is given in a timely manner.
4. Talk up the value of the rewards.
5. Don't oversell the program.[6]

If You're Not Sure What Types of Recognition to Give, Just Ask!

If you don't tailor the reward to the employee, the reward will not have the motivating effect you desire. When in doubt, just ask.

Who's Doing It

■ *Henley Healthcare*, a Sugarland, Texas, maker of noninvasive medical products, polled its office staff to determine what gifts of appreciation they would prefer for working long hours, or through weekends or lunch breaks. The results: 42 percent said days off, 22 percent said clothing, and 20 percent said tickets to theater and sporting events.[7]

■ *GeoAccess* of Kansas City set up an intranet survey site where all employees answered the question "If you had an extra $100 to spend, how would you spend it?" This gave the company a registry of tangible rewards tailored to the desires of employees.

The Ten Best Ways to Reward Good Work

Michael LeBoeuf, author of *The Greatest Management Principle in the World*, offers the following top ten list:

1. Money
2. Recognition
3. Time off
4. A piece of the action
5. Favorite work
6. Advancement
7. Increased freedom
8. Personal growth

9. Fun
10. Prizes[8]

Ask yourself which of these, in general, would have the greatest appeal to you as a way of being recognized or rewarded. Chances are good that your staff would rank them differently than you would, and that their rankings would be very different from one another. Why not simply ask your people? Give them a list of several ideas to choose from, with a space for them to write in their own ideas, and have them submit their preferences. One company asked its employees to answer the question.

For the Biggest Impact, Ask Two More Questions

To get the desired effect from your efforts to recognize and reward, there are two more questions you should ask your people:

1. *For what do you want to be recognized?* Their answers will vary depending on the employees' differing motivations and sources of pride; some are proud of dealing with difficult situations, some want to know that their dependability is acknowledged, and others will want to be recognized for their new ideas (see Motivation Inventory in Appendix D). This question is particularly important when you are giving informal recognition, as your own key objectives and the organization's strategic objectives will govern what will be recognized in formal reward programs.

2. *How would you like to receive your recognition?* Remember that not everyone wants public recognition. Some like the recognition in written form, while others prefer face-to-face communication. Some may prefer to be recognized at a luncheon, banquet, or party. If you are thinking of surprising the employee, ask one of the person's closest coworkers first to tell you what the colleague thinks the employee would prefer.

Don't Overlook the Power of Peer Recognition

Many organizations that offer incentive programs are convinced that peer recognition programs have a unique power to enhance employee commitment, cooperation, and productivity.

Who's Doing It

■ *WestAmerica Graphics,* of Santa Ana, California, knowing that its employees were starved for recognition, but also realizing that one supervisor couldn't give out as much recognition as he should each day, decided to make recognition everybody's job. The company created a peer recognition program called "COPS," for "Catching Other People Succeeding." Employees can award coworkers COPS tickets, and the number of tickets each employee receives is posted monthly and by year-to-date. An employee earns one point for receiving a ticket, one point for writing a ticket for someone else, and one point for making a suggested improvement in company procedures or service.

The recognized work is supposed to be a contribution that reduces errors, improves service, cuts costs, or makes the company run more smoothly. Each month, the top ticket recipient is honored with the "People's Choice Award" at an all-hands staff meeting. Each COPS point is worth $1. In one year, employees cashed in their points for bonuses ranging anywhere from $10 to $602.

WestAmerica president Doug Grant is pleased with the results. "I have to think that COPS adds to the bottom line because our company is growing at a time when the print industry has struggled," he says. "But the benefit we see most is camaraderie among employees."[9]

■ *Scitor*, of Sunnyvale, California, has a similar program, called "Be Our Guest," which allows employees to give coworkers bonuses ranging from $100 to $800 for doing something beyond the call of duty. The giver simply fills out a card indicating the amount of the bonus; then the recipient charges the bonus to his expense account. The company, which also gives every employee the power to make decisions without the approval of a supervisor, has had revenue growth of at least 28 percent a year for the last three years.[10]

■ Harry Griendling, CEO of *Staffing Solutions Group,* had always resented the fact that, in previous companies where he had worked, the glamorous overseas vacations went only to the sales people. "I was so annoyed," he recalls, "that I was building their product and nobody took me to Hawaii." Now that he has his own company, all employees and spouses attend yearly training sessions at locations like Key West, Florida, and Snowbird, Utah.[11]

■ At *InstallShield Software Corporation,* in Schaumburg, Illinois, innovative employees receive cash for patents—$1,000 when a patent is filed and $2,500 if it is granted.

The *Plitt Company*, a Chicago seafood business, gives bonuses to employees' kids, up to $20 for each "A" they earn in school, and throws parties to celebrate their good grades.

Resolve to Recognize Results

Starting today, make a resolution to begin recognizing your workers, not as you would like to be recognized, but as they would like to be recognized (remember the "Platinum Rule"!). The following tips may be helpful:

- "Instead of focusing on big events to recognize people, work to create a culture of appreciation. Make acknowledgment a part of the daily routine.
- "Become an obsessive observer. Notice what other people are doing and respond by acknowledging their efforts . . . a simple 'thank you' or 'awesome job'—sincerely conveyed, of course—can transform a relationship.
- "Regardless of what you do or where you are in the organization, make yourself a model of down-to-earth acknowledgment.
- "Remember that dialogue plays a key role in all of this. Instead of engaging in hit-and-run acknowledgment, take time to talk about efforts and successes with those involved."[12]

Now grade yourself and your organization on Retention Practice #20: "Recognize Results."

How good a job is your organization doing on this practice?

Circle one: (A) Excellent   (B) Very good   (C) Good   (D) Fair   (F) Poor

How good a job are you as a manager doing on this practice?

Circle one: (A) Excellent   (B) Very good   (C) Good   (D) Fair   (F) Poor

How important do you believe this practice is to your organization's strategy to attract and retain the employees necessary to meet its business objectives?

Circle one: (A) Critical (B) Very important (C) Somewhat important
            (D) Not important

What can the company do to improve on this practice?

What can you as a manager do to improve on this practice?

RETENTION PRACTICE #21

Train Managers in Career Coaching and Expect Them to Do It

> When most companies were manufacturers, equipment was the resource they bought and maintained. Today, the key resource is the knowledge and talent of people, and career development is the way we maintain that resource.
>
> —Richard Knowdell

As easy as it is for employees to move from one company to another these days, the following is an all-too-common scenario:

A valued employee comes into the manager's office to announce that he has a better offer elsewhere and gives two weeks' notice. The manager is shocked by this announcement and responds, "I'm disappointed to hear this, because I had actually been thinking of assigning you to manage a new project . . . and there would have been a promotion involved . . . I wish I had known you were thinking of leaving the company."

The issue here is, of course, a lack of communication that caused the employee to perceive that there was no opportunity for internal advancement. This was the "push factor" that made the employee receptive to the "pull factor" of an attractive outside offer.

In a competitive environment that makes employee career development a critical retention tool, managers must initiate career development discussions with their most valued employees. Yet, many managers are reluctant to spend time developing even their best people.

There are five main reasons for this:

1. They say they lack the time because of pressures to get results and to respond to day-to-day operational concerns, such as increasing production, reducing costs, improving sales, streamlining inventory/warehousing operations, and other such activities, all focused on improving the bottom line. Many have not yet been sold on the idea that spending time developing their workers—"sharpening the saw," as it has been called—produces payoffs in all the operational areas.

2. In many cases, their companies do not provide any reward for developing people or any consequence for not developing them. For example, when one production manager was willing to let two of his workers move into advanced assignments in another department, he was nonetheless required to maintain his previous level of output.

3. Employees, all too often, are not prepared to meet the manager halfway in the career development process by doing some self-assessment, then taking the initiative to schedule a meeting to discuss their careers. Employees often do not have the tools for planning their careers.

4. Many managers do not know how to talk about career development or answer employee questions. They are afraid of overpromising or encouraging unrealistic aspirations.

5. Managers resist the notion of being proactive in developing the careers of their employees because they have never received any career development assistance themselves. "Who looks out for my career?" is a common response. Often, managers are dissatisfied with their own careers and are not disposed to helping others with theirs.

These are obstacles that should not be taken lightly. Any company that is looking to reduce turnover by addressing the career development needs of its employees must overcome these objections. Until companies take this step, many managers will never understand what's in it for them in learning and practicing new career coaching skills.

Why do it? Among the payoffs to managers for developing their people are these:

- Increased communication will keep employees from leaving the organization before they realize what plans their managers have for them.
- Regular discussions can help detect and revitalize any employees who may be plateaued, restless, or disengaged.
- Succession planning will be made easier, which is especially important to the manager who must develop a successor before becoming promotion-eligible. It is also vital in anticipating the possibility that the employee may resign unexpectedly.

- Employees who discuss their development frequently with their managers usually have more realistic career goals and are less likely to become disillusioned and leave.
- Frequent talent reassessment of all employees enables managers to respond quickly and flexibly, matching employees' talents to emerging organizational needs and challenges.
- Managers who become known in the organization as good developers of people will attract new talented employees to their team.

Who's Responsible for What?

Before managers can be expected to embrace their responsibilities for employee career development, those responsibilities need to be made clear, and differentiated from career development responsibilities that belong to the organization and to the employee. These responsibilities need to be clearly communicated to all employees as well.

Here is how one organization delineated the three levels of responsibilities:

Employee's Responsibilities

- Make on-the-job performance your number-one priority.
- Make your career aspirations known to your manager.
- Assess your own abilities and get frequent feedback on your performance and abilities as your manager perceives them.
- Continually seek new learning and on-the-job growth opportunities and enlist the help of your manager in taking advantage of them.
- Learn how to uncover "hidden needs" within the organization that match your talents and can be turned into promotional or new job opportunities.
- Understand that not all internal growth opportunities are upward movements.
- Learn how jobs are filled inside the organization, both formally and informally, and how to compete effectively for these opportunities.
- Seek information on how to prepare for internal positions to which you aspire, then make a plan for reaching your job objective.
- Accept the reality that you, not the organization, have primary responsibility for managing your career.

Organization's Responsibilities

- Commit organizational resources to creating internal systems and policies that facilitate the growth and development of all employees.

- Provide training and resources to managers to enhance their effectiveness in coaching and developing their people.
- Recognize and reward those managers who excel at career coaching and people development while also meeting performance objectives.
- Establish and make known long-range strategies and staffing needs to guide managers' employee development activities and decisions.
- Create and maintain a system for posting internal job opportunities and filling those positions in a fair and timely manner.
- Provide formal training opportunities to all employees that will enhance performance and enable career growth.

Manager's Responsibilities

- Identify work to be done by anticipating future needs, understanding company and unit objectives, and forecasting staffing requirements.
- Assess employee strengths, motivations, and developmental needs, and match them to the work to be done.
- Coach and communicate frequently with employees to maintain the best possible fit between individual and organizational goals.
- Assist employees with the implementation of their developmental goals and action plans to the mutual benefit of the employee and the company.

How Can Managers Be Expected to Help Develop the Careers of Their Workers?

There are four basic roles that managers can reasonably be expected to master if they are to retain valued employees. These roles are:

1. Human resources planner
2. Performance appraiser/talent scout
3. Career coach
4. Sponsor/mentor

Within each of these roles are specific activities for which the manager can be held accountable. As you scan these activities, check those you typically perform:

Role: Human Resources Planner

_____ Seeks information about organization's future needs and goals.

—————— Links organization's needs and goals to unit objectives.

—————— Anticipates staffing needs to meet objectives.

—————— Conducts succession planning for all positions.

Role: Performance Appraiser/Talent Scout

—————— Assesses employee performance against goals and objectives.

—————— Identifies employee strengths, motivations, and developmental needs.

Role: Career Coach

—————— Provides feedback to employees regarding performance and talents.

—————— Teaches specific job-related or technical skills.

—————— Holds formal and informal, ongoing, uninterrupted career discussions with employee.

—————— Helps employee achieve greater self-awareness of talents, interests, values, and motivations.

—————— Helps employee identify and evaluate various internal career options.

—————— Advises employee on how best to prepare for various options, including appropriate training and development opportunities.

—————— Makes employee aware of the informal and formal realities of progression within the organization.

—————— Assists employee in preparing a yearly career development plan that aligns with performance objectives and organizational needs.

Role: Sponsor/Mentor

—————— Helps employee plan strategy to achieve career goals.

—————— Refers employee to best sources of information about internal career options.

—————— Arranges for employee to take part in high-visibility activity either inside or outside the organization.

—————— Allows employee to participate in short-term work assignments, task forces, action learning teams, or ad hoc committees that provide job enrichment, skill development, and visibility enhancement.

_____ Allows valued employees to move inside the organization when it serves the interests of the larger organization and the individual, instead of acting to block such moves.

_____ Recommends employees as appropriate to other managers within the organization.

_____ Serves as role model by undertaking successful professional development activities.

The manager's career development activities must be tailored to the needs of his or her staff, which vary based on the stage of the workers' careers and the level of their performance, as shown in Figure 21-1.

It is also important to recognize the changing needs of employees as they grow, develop, and mature in their organizational careers. The vocational psychologist Donald Super identified the following stages of career growth, each involving its own rites of passage and gains (or possible losses) in organizational status:

Phase 1: Career Establishment

Stage 1: Exploration

Individuals research alternative career choices and try on several jobs until they find a career niche that fits their personal needs

Stage 2: Trial

Individuals settle in an organization where they are comfortable and apply themselves to learning the business, hopeful that they will rise to the higher levels.

Stage 3: Acclimation

Individuals earn a reputation, make a contribution, and become valued assets in the organization.

Phase 2: Career Development

Stage 1: Growth

Individuals earn promotions and move upward in the organization, becoming key candidates for top positions and new spin-off ventures as they arise.

Stage 2: Family Building

Those who become parents must satisfactorily balance work and child-rearing responsibilities and will critically reassess job satisfaction levels on the basis of how "family-friendly" the organization's policies and practices are.

Stage 3: Plateauing

Individuals have attained the long-sought position of their dreams, or they experience diminished hope of ever attaining it. Productivity may be high, but entrepreneurial drive can atrophy if not redirected.

Figure 21-1. Who gets developed . . . and how.

NEW HIRES and NEWLY PROMOTED	POOR and MARGINAL PERFORMERS	STEADY PERFORMERS	HIGH and STAR PERFORMERS
⇩	⇩	⇩	⇩
NEEDS	NEEDS	NEEDS	NEEDS
▪ Orientation and Integration ▪ Realistic Expectations ▪ Matching Skills and Needs ▪ Realistic, Challenging, and Specific Performance Objectives ▪ Significant Amount of Manager's Time ▪ Praise and Validation ▪ Training for Current and Future Performance Objectives	▪ Training to Meet Current Objectives ▪ Coaching to Correct Poor Performance ▪ Realistic Expectations ▪ Correcting Job Skills Mismatch or Reassignment ▪ Performance Planning	▪ Performance Planning ▪ "Stretch" Assignments ▪ Feedback and Recognition ▪ Frequent Progress Reviews and Appraisals ▪ Attention to Job Enrichment ▪ Assistance Identifying Growth Options ▪ Training for Current and Future Options	▪ Same as for Steady Performers, plus: ▪ Constant Challenge ▪ Increasing Responsibility ▪ Cross-Functional Assignments ▪ Increasing Visibility ▪ Special Recognition ▪ Regular Meetings to Recruit
⇩	⇩	⇩	⇩
EMPHASIS ON:	EMPHASIS ON:	EMPHASIS ON:	EMPHASIS ON:
Integration and Performance Planning	Improved Performance	Performance/ Developmental Planning	Challenge, Growth, and Recognition

Phase 3: Redirection or Retirement

Stage 1: Renewal

Individuals reassess their priorities. If the organization appears to be underutilizing their experience, then they will focus their energy on redirecting their career paths or planning for postretirement ventures.

Stage 2: Closure

Those looking forward to retirement become more conscious of their legacy and try to leave on a high note by mentoring younger workers and solidifying their reputation with peers. Given advanced longevity, part-time or consultative work may have great appeal.[1]

Although you may recognize intuitively these different stages among your employees, identifying which of these stages they are in can help you to better understand and anticipate their needs.

Let's take a look now at some of the tools and some tips you can use in appraising and coaching your workers.

Tools and Tips for Appraising and Career Coaching

The most frequent first step you may need to take with your employees will be to appraise their most pressing career-related concerns. Often, the people you manage will not be able to verbalize their own concerns. They may know only that they are not satisfied with the way things are going. In these situations it may be helpful to have them complete the inventory of concerns in Figure 21-2 to provide focus for a career discussion.

The Talent Inventory as a Career Coaching and Feedback Tool

As we have said, a job is a talent that meets a need. The most important part of your job as a manager and as a career coach is to make sure that the talents of your workers are matched to the work that needs doing. This obviously impacts both performance and employee satisfaction.

One of the key factors in employee job satisfaction among all levels of employees is whether the job allows them to use their natural talents. For many of your workers, the source of dissatisfaction will have to do with the fact that they are not using their talents, as discussed in Retention Practices #6 and 7. Here are a few other possibilities:

- They may have a talent they do not get to use on the job as much as they would like.

Figure 21-2. Sample inventory of concerns.

Rank your top five career concerns (1–5) on the list below in order of importance:

CAREER CONCERN	PRIORITY
Improving performance in current job	_____
Getting more training in current job	_____
Increasing satisfaction in current job	_____
Reaching educational goals	_____
Learning more about career options	_____
Taking stock of abilities, interests, and values	_____
Learning more about possible career paths	_____
Exploring different jobs or assignments	_____
Preparing for promotion or advancement	_____
Balancing work and personal life	_____
Other:	
_____	_____
_____	_____
_____	_____

- They may have an inflated view of their own talent in a certain area.
- They may underestimate talents they take for granted.
- They may aspire to a job or assignment for which they are not competent.
- They may have no idea what they want to do and may benefit from taking inventory of their talents, knowledge, traits, and motivations.

In all these cases it would be appropriate for both you and your employee to separately complete a different version of the Talent Inventory in Appendix D. This different version—the Manager-Employee Talent Inventory (see Appendix H)—features the same talents and categories of talent as the original, but allows the employee to rate the strength of his or her talents on a 1–5 scale, and to rate the importance of each talent in the current job on a 1–5 scale as well. You may also make copies of the same inventory and rate the employee's talents from your perspective and your view of their importance in the employee's job.

By comparing the separately completed inventories, you will create an opportunity to share with your staff the abilities you think they have, and they can benefit by understanding how you perceive them. Be sure to discuss rating gaps of two or more on both the importance and the talent factors. This will help your workers develop more realistic and appropriate career objectives. Here's another possibility: You may also learn that they have hidden talents that could be of use to you now.

As you complete the inventory, circle words that you feel are particularly descriptive, and write in abilities you have observed if you feel they belong in that category. Also, write any appropriate comments in the right-hand column that will help employees better understand the thoughts behind your ratings.

The differences may be surprising to one or both of you and will provide grist for an insightful and productive discussion.

Revisiting the Job Enrichment Rating

If the employee is unhappy in his or her current job, remember the Job Enrichment Rating form presented in Appendix C. Have the employee complete the form while you do the same, then compare your ratings, as you did with the Talent Inventory. This is another situation where the difference in perception may surprise both you and the employee and lead to some productive goal setting.

Be prepared for the possibility that there may be organizational obstacles to increasing some of the five factors (skill variety, task completion, task significance, autonomy, and feedback), but if you and the individual make a good-faith effort and use your imaginations, resolving the individual's dissatisfaction will be easier than you thought.

Managing Different Personalities Differently

Any manager looking to retain key talent also needs to be sensitive to personality differences and to realize that different temperaments bring different gifts and approaches to their work and have differing communication styles. The table in Appendix G shows the sixteen different temperament types by which individuals can be classified on the Myers-Briggs Temperament Indicator (MBTI) and will remind you of the diversity of personalities for whom you are challenged daily to coach and keep on board.[2]

You may recognize your own temperament type among these. The talent required to coach different types of employees does not come naturally to all managers, but managerial skill can be improved by interactive training that allows the practice of new behavior. Many companies train managers in these skills, with emphasis on initiating and facilitating "developmental discussions" with employees.

Using a Developmental Planning Worksheet

Before meeting with an employee for a career discussion, it is a good idea to collect your thoughts and to consider career options and actions that you may want to bring to the table. Use the Developmental Planning Worksheet in Appendix I for this purpose.

As you meet with your staff to discuss career options, keep in mind that they have six legitimate options at any given moment as depicted in Figures 21-3 through 21-8.

Retention-focused organizations often require managers and employees to jointly create a career development action plan on a yearly basis. Figure 21-9 presents an example of a career planning form.

How to Respond When an Employee Asks . . .

Employees' career-related questions can come at any time of the day, catching you totally off guard. You and the employee will both be better

Figure 21-3. Stay in current job and find ways to be more satisfied and successful.

Figure 21-4. Change to a different job or assignment in the same department of organization.

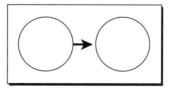

Figure 21-5. Change to a different job or assignment in a different department of organization.

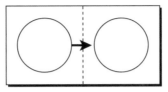

Figure 21-6. Change careers within the same organization.

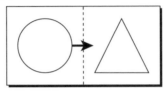

Figure 21-7. Find another job outside the organization.

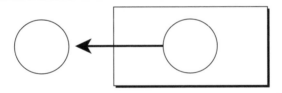

Figure 21-8. Change careers outside the organization.

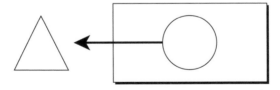

served if you do not try to field questions on the spot. It is usually best to set a mutually agreeable time to thoroughly discuss the issue. This will allow time for both of you to do some thoughtful preparation that will result in a more productive discussion.

Certain career-related questions come up frequently, and you must learn how to field them. It is impossible to advise you exactly how to ad-

Figure 21-9. Career development action plan.

Employee _____ Position _____

Manager _____ Date _____

Directions: Write a "SMART" objective for each action below—one that is **S**pecific, **M**easurable, **A**ctionable, **R**ealistic, and **T**ime-bound. All actions will be the responsibility of the employee except those initialed by the manager, indicating the manager's responsibility to take that action on the employee's behalf.

Actions for Development in Current Job

Consider on-the-job training, formal training, computer-assisted training, new work assignments, task forces, committees, self-study, and other possible actions.

-
-
-

Future Internal Position Options Being Considered

1. _____
2. _____
3. _____
4. _____

Actions to Prepare for Possible Future Assignments

-
-
-

dress these concerns in cookbook fashion. The person and the context always combine to create a unique situation that tests your empathy and problem-solving skills. The intent here is to help you develop a workable strategy for addressing these concerns as they come up.

1. *"Where can I go from here?"* Related or underlying concerns may be:

"Tell me what you think of my potential."
"I'm ready for a new challenge."
"What else is available?"
"What career paths are available to me?"
"How do I get promoted?"
"Should I continue my schooling?"
"How can I make better use of my training?"
"Should I go the technical or managerial route?"
"Where is the company going?"

How to respond:

■ Find out what is motivating the employee to approach you with this concern at this particular time.

■ Review the employee's performance and career history, then use the Developmental Planning Worksheet to think on paper about possible future options.

■ Evaluate your own willingness to let the employee rise to a higher level or even move to a different area with your blessing and assistance.

■ Have the employee complete the Talent, Knowledge, Self-Management Trait, and Motivation Inventories (Appendix D), then have a meeting to discuss the ratings, compare them with your own, and discuss appropriate options.

■ Thoroughly explore job enrichment options using the rating form in Appendix C. Consider lateral moves or the possibility of "taking one step backward in order to take two steps forward," such as taking a lower-level position or returning to school in order to get into a different area where the employee can pursue what he or she really wants to do.

■ Give honest feedback about how realistic the employee's goals are, based on performance. For poor and marginal performers who want to discuss advancement, address the performance issue first, reclarify your performance expectations, and redirect their attention to skills improvement. Evaluate whether the poor performer is simply mismatched with the job and consider reassigning the person to other tasks, or even to another department.

2. *"How do I get the job I want?"* Related or underlying concerns:

"I've seen a job posting I want to apply for."
"I know the job I want; can you help me get it?"
"Can I get there from here?"

How to respond:

■ Find out what the employee thinks he or she would like about the job. Assess the realistic potential of the employee's answer.

■ Help the employee evaluate the real probability of reaching the position goal by discussing the demands, working conditions, and qualifications needed for the desired job. Suggest the employee explore other specific positions that you believe to be suitable.

■ Stress the importance of maintaining high performance in the current job.

■ Suggest that the employee find out more about the desired position, then report back to you.

■ If the employee is qualified and still interested in the position after exploring it, come to terms with your own willingness to let the employee move on with your support or sponsorship.

3. *"Can't I just stay in the job I have?"* Related or underlying concerns:

"I'd rather not be transferred."
"I really enjoy what I'm doing now, and I don't want to be promoted."

How to respond:

■ Ask what the employee likes about the current job.

■ Help the employee consider the consequences of staying put, such as becoming stagnant or burned-out.

■ Challenge the employee to consider how he or she will stretch and grow in the current position.

■ Respect the employee's right to restrict his or her options. You also have a right to expect and to suggest that the employee explore a broad range of developmental steps, including job enrichment, continuing job mastery, new assignments, or training. The four competency inventories and job enrichment rating form may both be useful here.

4. *"Why didn't I get the promotion?"*

How to respond:

■ If you are not prepared to respond, set a time for serious discussion, then gather your facts. Review the relative importance of factors you considered in making your decision, such as attendance, quality of work, quantity of work, education/skill level, people skills, time on the job, time since last promotion, competition, attitude, and willingness to do more than required.

■ Question the employee about what he or she understands the facts to be, and what meaning the person has attached to the decision. Does the worker feel undervalued? Does he or she feel that contributions made to the company have gone unacknowledged? Does the person believe that future chances for advancement have been harmed? Is he or she angry at perceived unfair treatment?

■ Review the facts, the factors you considered, and how you balanced them in making your best decision.

■ Focus on the skills your employee needs to develop, while acknowledging the person's demonstrated strengths. Discuss performance improvement options and potential rewards, but don't make promises you can't keep.

General Guidelines for Development Discussions

The following guidelines apply to any discussion of an employee's development, regardless of whether you or the employee has initiated it. They are organized into three phases—Preparation, Discussion, and Follow-through. The Get-Give-Merge-Go process remains at the heart of career-related discussions as much as it does with performance discussions.

1. *Preparation.*

■ Clarify the purpose of the discussion. Avoid confusion by asking the employee to submit a written agenda when appropriate, or preparing one yourself when you are initiating the discussion.

■ Schedule the right time and the right place. Development discussions are often emotionally charged. Help to diffuse the emotion and engage the reasoning process by setting a mutually convenient time to discuss the issue when possible. Allow just enough lead time for preparation. Schedule a mutually convenient time, perhaps at the end of the day.

Hold the discussion in a quiet, private setting with no interruptions. Allow enough time to have a meaningful discussion.

■ Complete a developmental planning worksheet when possible. Collect your thoughts about the employee beforehand, using this worksheet, as previously discussed.

2. *Discussion.*

■ Listen and understand the employee's viewpoint. Restate what you heard, and ask the employee if you understood correctly. Listen more than you talk. Observe the employee's nonverbal behavior (facial expression, gestures, eye contact, voice tone, loudness, posture).

■ Communicate your viewpoint openly, directly, honestly and clearly. Ask the employee what he or she understands you to be saying and, if it is not what you intended to say, restate it in a different way. Consider the employee's feelings, but not to the point of softening or diluting your message.

■ Communicate your sincere interest in the employee's growth and development.

■ Keep the discussion on track. You have a limited time, and digressions can happen. Stay focused on the real purpose of the discussion.

■ Focus on growth in the current assignment. The possibility of enriching the employee's current job is usually more realistic than the possibility of promoting the employee. Do a thorough job of evaluating various ways you can better match your employee's abilities to the work to be done in your unit. Solicit and listen to the employee's ideas for redesigning the job.

■ Keep the discussion focused on real behavior—what the employee has done in the past—as evidence of strengths or limitations; on what the person is doing now as proof of performance or evidence of natural interest; and on what the employee sees as specific options for the future. This keeps the discussion in the real world of facts and away from the arguable realm of biased perceptions, idealized self-image, imposed judgments, and unrealistic goals.

3. *Follow-Through.*

■ Keep your word. Do what you told your employee you would do. Don't procrastinate; set target dates as you would expect employees to do for themselves.

■ Keep confidences. Mutually agree about what is and is not to be repeated, then keep your word.

■ Set a date for the next discussion. Set a date by which you and the employee will complete agreed-upon actions.

Development Discussion Do's and Don'ts

Don't . . .	*Do . . .*
■ Discourage a stated ambition.	■ Seek evidence that the stated ambition is realistic or not, and encourage the employee to seek more information to test how realistic the ambition is.
■ Give your evaluation of how ready your employee is for a stated career path	■ Get the employee's evaluation before offering yours.
■ Display a negative, uninterested attitude.	■ Exhibit a positive, encouraging attitude. If the employee is at least a steady performer, you will want to be his or her champion.
■ Solve the employee's problems.	■ Provide information and alternatives while letting the employee manage his or her own career.
■ Limit your discussion to only promotional options.	■ Consider a variety of directions, including technical paths, assignment changes, and development in place.
■ Impose your personal values on the employee.	■ Help the employee more clearly understand his/her own values and how they impact future choices.
■ Take control of the discussion.	■ Let the employee keep control of the discussion, to reinforce that she/he has responsibility for her/his own development.
■ End with judgmental statements.	■ Ask the employee to translate ideas into specific action plans.

Answers to Managers' Questions about Employee Development

Question: "If I encourage my good people to think about career development, won't I just lose them that much sooner?"

Answer: Realistic career planning generally results in employees making a stronger commitment to an action plan for their own development. As often as not, this means that employees who had been thinking about leaving the organization now decide to stay after discovering that the opportunities they want do exist internally. These opportunities may exist right under their noses or in another department, in which case the employee is kept within the organization as a whole.

You may lose a valued employee, but one who would probably not have been as happy and productive if kept in your area without seeing a viable growth opportunity. Yes, you may lose an employee to another manager or unit, and this will create a temporary inconvenience as you try to find a replacement. But, if you focus on hiring the right new person for the job, the replacement may well be someone from inside the company who is moving up with enthusiasm and commitment.

High-performing employees will always seek new challenges, and you will often reach a limit to the challenges you can keep offering them. But, by encouraging their growth and movement, you will achieve a reputation as a manager for whom other high performers will want to work.

Question: "Won't all this emphasis on career development just raise the expectations of my workers and make them even more unhappy if we can't meet their expectations?"

Answer: The key to avoiding this situation lies in helping your employees to reach more realistic, not raised, expectations. A realistic employee development process keeps the focus on the three key realities of organizational career development:

1. In any organization, all employees eventually reach limits to their upward movement. Promotions are limited, not just by the pyramid structure of most organizations, but by the competition for available jobs, the level of one's performance, and the availability of openings at any given time resulting from factors such as budgetary/headcount restrictions or the cyclical nature of the business.

To encourage realistic views of promotion possibilities, you must remind your employees of these facts and help them keep focused on continuously revitalizing their current jobs through competency development, formal training, negotiating changes in tasks/assignments, and continuing job mastery.

2. Career development is the shared responsibility of the employee, the manager, and the organization. Some employees still have the unrealistic, outdated expectation that the organization will take charge of their development and that they can passively "be developed." This can lead to a "victim mentality" when these expectations don't pan out. Managers, and the organization as a whole, must send the message loud and clear to all employees that they are responsible for taking the initiative (see Retention Practice #22). What the organization and managers can do, however, is provide the tools, the coaching, and the know-how to allow employees to grow their careers within the organization.

3. Even the best-executed development plans are sometimes frustrated by unanticipated events outside one's control. There is no guarantee that the employee's best plans and efforts will cause things to turn out according to plan. You must help employees understand that career success usually comes from staying focused on current performance and "organizing one's luck" by being prepared when opportunity happens.

Expecting Managers to Do Career Coaching Means Measuring Whether and How Well They Do It

Organizations that are serious about employee retention have two ways to make sure their managers are doing career coaching besides providing the training and the tools. One is to require all managers to complete a career development action plan in partnership with their employees every year. The other is to institute a way of measuring how well managers are doing as career coaches, such as an employee survey.

Who's Doing It

■ Since 1995, *the Security Benefit Group of Companies* in Topeka, Kansas, has been doing surveys of managers' people management performance every two years. Employees rate their managers on a variety of people management skills, including career coaching. The surveys are sent directly to the managers' managers so that they can be incorporated into performance appraisal discussions. Security Benefit has noticed that most managers' ratings have steadily improved on these surveys over the years. The company believes this is attributable to the managers' desire to improve their ratings.

To find out directly from your direct reports whether you are meeting their career developmental needs, take a risk and give them the checklist in Figure 21-10 to fill out on you. Then, for comparison purposes, fill one

Figure 21-10. Survey of manager as employee developer.

Directions: Read each statement below and indicate the degree to which you feel the statement is typically true of your manager's behavior.

5 = Highly 4 = Very 3 = Moderately 2 = Somewhat 1 = Not at all

1. Provides a thorough orientation to new employees.	5	4	3	2	1
2. Teaches specific job-related or technical skills.	5	4	3	2	1
3. Makes sure I understand developmental priorities and objectives.	5	4	3	2	1
4. Makes sure I have specific goals in key performance areas.	5	4	3	2	1
5. Assigns work so that I am able to use my skills.	5	4	3	2	1
6. Communicates to me the formal and informal realities of progression in the organization.	5	4	3	2	1
7. Makes sure I have opportunities to develop.	5	4	3	2	1
8. Gives me feedback about my performance.	5	4	3	2	1
9. Provides me with guidance to improve my performance.	5	4	3	2	1
10. Encourages, supports, and counsels me in my pursuit of job-related training.	5	4	3	2	1
11. Provides opportunities to discuss performance problems.	5	4	3	2	1
12. Solicits input and concerns in relation to proposals and pending decisions.	5	4	3	2	1
13. Promotes my participation in "high visibility" activities.	5	4	3	2	1
14. Represents my interests and concerns to higher management.	5	4	3	2	1
15. Holds informal career development discussions.	5	4	3	2	1

out on yourself. If there is a sizable gap between your ratings and theirs, this may motivate you to improve your skills in this area.

Now it's time for you to give your organization and yourself as a manager a grade on Retention Practice #21: "Train Managers in Career Coaching and Expect Them to Do It."

How good a job is your organization doing on this practice?

Circle one: (A) Excellent   (B) Very good   (C) Good   (D) Fair   (F) Poor

How good a job are you as a manager doing on this practice?

Circle one: (A) Excellent   (B) Very good   (C) Good   (D) Fair   (F) Poor

How important do you believe this practice is to your organization's strategy to attract and retain the talent necessary to meet its business objectives?

Circle one: (A) Critical (B) Very important (C) Somewhat important
            (D) Not important

What can your organization do to improve on this practice?

What can you as a manager do to improve on this practice?

Give Employees the Tools for Taking Charge of Their Careers

> The switch from career dependence to career resilience is not only imperative, but also inevitable. The company that recognizes this sea change and rides the waves has a huge strategic advantage.
>
> —Robert H. Waterman

In Retention Practice #8 we looked at the "psychological contract" each employee makes with the organization and with the manager. A big part of this unwritten contract has to do with the employee's and the employer's assumptions about career growth and development. Those assumptions have changed dramatically since the early 1980s, as the following comparison shows:

Old Career Contract	*New Career Contract*
■ Long-term employment is expected.	■ Shorter-term expectations, affected by changing business needs; no guarantees.
■ Reward for performance is promotion.	■ Reward for performance is growth, recognition, and self-satisfaction.
■ Management controls career progress.	■ Employees are in charge of own careers.
■ Lifetime career is offered.	■ Employee and organization bond is based on fulfillment of mutual needs.

■ Has definite career paths and ladders.	■ Offers nontraditional, undefined career paths.

Resulting in:	*Resulting in:*
■ Fixed job descriptions	■ Changing jobs, projects, task forces
■ Compensation & benefits that reward tenure	■ Tenure-free recognition systems
■ Long-term career planning by organization	■ Short-term career planning by employee
■ Plateaued workers	■ Flexible, task-invested workers
■ Dependent workers	■ Empowered, responsible workers[1]

Having witnessed so many friends, relatives, neighbors, and colleagues downsized out of their jobs, employees today are less likely to believe that long-range opportunities will be there for them. They have seen rungs eliminated from the "career ladder" and have come to believe that the whole notion of a career path is an antiquated idea.

Employees have lost a sense of security, permanence, and loyalty. Yet many have awakened to the realization that, by taking charge of their own careers, they are less likely to become powerless victims if they should lose their jobs.

As the contract between employer and employee has changed with the times, so has the way employees must manage their careers and find internal opportunities. Because you, as the manager, are your employees' primary resource for guidance and information about career advancement and professional development, you must make sure they understand the new rules for remaining "career-resilient."

The New Ground Rules for Corporate Career Resilience:

Rule #1: *The company is not in charge of your career—you are.* Your people can no longer wait for you to come to them with a new assignment or opportunity; they must seek out such opportunities themselves. Your relationship with them is no longer one of parent-to-child, but adult-to-adult. They share the responsibility for initiating career discussions. Even being designated as a "high potential" or a valued employee may not guarantee they will keep their place in the succession plan, as these plans have become less relevant as the pace of change has picked up. You will meet your employees more than halfway by giving them the tools and counsel they need to take charge of their careers.

Rule #2: *Instead of ladders and paths, there are now webs and mazes.* Your employees must learn, if they haven't already, to think of a career less as a ladder and more as a web. Webs have a center but no top and a lot of paths that connect. Unlike ladders, webs often dissolve when their purpose is fulfilled. Smart workers will move along the webs, picking up new skills that meet the organization's needs, looking for problems to solve, and working on team projects. And if a web breaks or dissolves, it can always be rewoven in a similar or different pattern.

Rule #3: *Every job is now subject to a "make or buy" decision.* Because of the flexibility and cost savings involved in using contract employees, vendors, and temporary employees to do the work previously done by downsized employees, your workers must understand that they may now be competing with these outside resources. This means they have to continually prove their value. Their only security lies in their ability to continually retool themselves to remain valuable to their employer. This is why continuous learning is so important to all workers today. All employees should also consider that their next opportunity may lie in becoming an outside resource themselves.

Rule #4: *Hidden needs in the organization's internal job market are more promising sources of advancement than the formal job postings.* There has always been, and will always be, a "hidden job market" in every company. Only now the inside job market contains more hidden jobs than ever. New needs appear so fast that there is little time to wait for the slow wheels of the formal hiring process to start rolling. These days, about a third of all jobs filled are newly created ones. And, of course, with the loss of rungs on career ladders, there are fewer formal job slots in the first place.

All employees—you included—must be on the lookout for unmet needs, then make proposals to the person who "owns the problem" to help meet the need. Getting your employees to accept this proposition is a part of helping them learn to take more initiative in every aspect of their jobs. Many times, by looking to meet the organization's needs, they will carve out their next career move.

Rule #5. *The most "vendor-minded" employees will find or create the most opportunity.* The employees who think of themselves as "intrapreneurs" will see the organization as a market for their skills. They will understand the truest, most empowering definition of a job—"a talent that meets a need." With your help, they will come to see themselves as vendors, and they will perceive more opportunity as a result. Vendor-minded employees realize that the purpose of the organization is to provide goods and services that customers value and that, if the organization's employees do not do that, eventually they may all be out of a job.

Of course, many employees and organizations still have one foot in the old contract and have not yet accepted these new rules. But the ones who are now living by these new rules are serving as role models to others in the art of career self-management in the new millennium. The following profiles illustrate this art of reinventing one's career in the organization.

Four Employees Who Took Charge of Their Own Careers by Finding a Need and Filling It

Drew Melton started working as a copy machine operator for Prospect Associates, Ltd., a Maryland health-communications-policy consulting firm. "Within two weeks, he had met with the company president and explained how he could produce better documents faster. The president gave him a "green light," and in the next three weeks, Melton completely recreated his role at the company. Now he runs a highly complex printing operation, partners with Prospect's consultants to prepare more effective and professional-looking proposals, and earns almost half again as much as he did when he began."[2]

Joe Demeyer felt underutilized at Keithley Instruments after eleven years as an engineer. He wanted to move from developing software to directing the development of software overall. While exploring jobs in manufacturing, he noticed a number of independent software development projects that could be consolidated into one job. He presented his ideas to the department head, who challenged Joe to draw up a job description and a ten-year work plan. Six months later, Joe was happily working at his new software development position in manufacturing, with more autonomy to make decisions and choose his work and the potential of someday running his own department.[3]

Betsy Blair saw a job that wasn't being done at Dell Computer. As a sales manager who had worked on manufacturing-related projects, she observed that sales reps promised deliveries with little knowledge about manufacturing's ability to keep those promises. Manufacturing, in turn, knew little about customers' requirements. She felt she could bridge the gap and successfully sold the idea to several senior managers, persuading Dell to create a communications liaison job.[4]

David Morrison sought to free himself from his desk-bound training manager's job at Toronto Dominion Bank. What he liked was public speaking, a skill he had developed to overcome a stammer. While speaking at business conferences, he started picking up on significant trends. His reports to bank management about growing customer demand for better product delivery, for example, helped push efforts to expand and improve the bank's customer services. This led to his modest proposal: Instead of managing trainers, he would become the corporate trend-spotter. He was offered a year to prove the position's value. Nearly a decade later, he's been promoted twice, ultimately to vice president, human resources development.[5]

The "Find-a-Need-and-Fill-It" Grid

To help employees begin to see new ways to find growth opportunities, William Bridges created the "Find-a-Need-and-Fill It" grid[6] (Appendix K). This grid helps employees consider the variety of unmet organizational needs that may be appropriate to their talents. It can give them the impetus to create a new job or project, as did the four employees just described.

Consider sitting down with your key employees and helping them complete this grid. Combining your perspectives will result in greater awareness of unmet needs and opportunities across the organization, and will help stimulate your plateaued top performers to think of new ways to grow. This is an especially effective technique to introduce right after the employee has completed the Talent Inventory (Appendix D).

From Dependence to Resilience

The problem is that there are still not enough employees who take charge of their careers and actively seek out new internal opportunities. Many employees remain stuck in a dependent mindset, waiting for their managers to take the initiative. Even some of your steady and good performers may feel disempowered and victimized, needing a new challenge but burned out from doing more with less for too long.

There is much to discourage workers, especially in companies that are not growing as fast as they once were or that have been merged, acquired, or restructured. Besides the generalized feelings of fear, uncertainty, and doubt, there may be fewer opportunities for upward mobility, fewer salary increases, and limited resources of all kinds.

Your challenge as a career coach is to transform the "Powerless and Victimized" into the "Empowered and Resilient" even in the face of these circumstances. This is no easy task. We are talking about changing the way people think, even if the company itself does not change.

James Swails has proposed asking questions designed to determine where an employee falls on the victim vs. self-empowered continuum:

Question #1: "Are your earnings limited by the provisions of the company's pay plan?

Victim's response: Yes.

Empowered response: No, my earnings are limited only by the value I bring to the organization. If I'd like to earn more, all I need to do is bring more value.

Question #2: Is change a necessary evil?

Victim's response: Yes.

Empowered response: No, any entrepreneur knows change creates opportunity, and the bigger the change, the bigger the opportunity. I embrace change for the opportunities it creates."[7]

These questions, or variations on them, may open a dialogue through which you may help the employee begin to realize that a victim mentality is limiting his or her ability to see and seize opportunities.

Tools for Helping Your Workers to Take Charge

The Personal Power Worksheet

Think of an employee who needs to be challenged to take charge of his or her career. It may be someone who seems to be hopelessly and passively coasting, someone who complains bitterly about being stuck in the same job, or someone who seethes quietly with resentment about the lack of opportunity.

Ask the employee to sit down with you and complete the Personal Power Worksheet presented in Figure 22-1. The first step is to identify and describe the source of dissatisfaction, or the change, or the choice to be made. Next, have the employee write what he or she is doing or not doing in each of the four quadrants. Keep in mind that that the employee may be operating in all four of these areas at the same time.

For example, if your employee is "taking action" by complaining about being in a situation he or she cannot control (Quadrant 2), such as having been passed over for a promotion, you need to challenge the person to either let go of the resentment (Quadrant 4) or begin to master the situation (Quadrant 1) by doing what he or she must do to become ready for the next opportunity.

If the employee is giving up (Quadrant 3), for example, by not expressing interests or desires, but is merely passively coping from day to day, you will need to challenge him or her to take some kind of developmental action.

Figure 22-1. The Personal Power Worksheet.

Describe the dilemma you are facing:

_____

_____

_____

_____

	CAN CONTROL	CANNOT CONTROL
TAKE ACTION	MASTERY 1	CEASELESS STRIVING 2
NO ACTION	GIVING UP 3	LETTING GO 4

Focus your people on either quadrant 1 or quadrant 4. If they are investing their mental energy into quadrants 2 or 3, they are limiting their effectiveness and potentially endangering their health.

Six Options Worksheet

Employees with disempowered attitudes need to be reminded that at any given time, they can take any of the six basic paths to professional growth and development mentioned in Retention Practice #21. You can challenge them to list the actions they might take to explore each of these options, using the following worksheet.

Option #1. Stay in your current job but change it to meet an unmet need, change your attitude or approach to the job, improve a key relationship, find ways to be more successful, take on a new challenge, or redesign the way the job gets done.
Ideas or possible actions:

_____

_____

Option #2. Seek or take on a different job/assignment in the same area or department.
Ideas or possible actions:

_____

_____

Option #3. Seek or take on a different job/assignment in a different area or department.
Ideas or possible actions:

_____

_____

Option #4. Change careers within the same organization.
Ideas or possible actions:

_____

_____

Option #5. Find another job outside the organization.
Ideas or possible actions:

_____

_____

Option #6. Change careers outside the organization.
Ideas and possible actions:

_____

_____

You may feel hesitant about having employees consider options 5 and 6, or even options 3 and 4, but experience has shown that employees who choose any of these options with an awareness of the full range of other options feel more free in their choices and bring more commitment to their work.

Questions to Stimulate Career Self-Reliance

Another effective technique for helping employees come to terms with their seeming "stuckness" is to simply ask them questions that create insight and move them along the continuum toward taking charge of their situations. Here are some you may want to use to open or maintain a dialogue:

- What talents or abilities would you most like to use at work?
- What abilities are most needed in your job, and in the organization?
- What have you done lately to develop or improve the abilities needed by the organization?
- What kind of new challenge would you like to take on?
- What is the best next professional development step you can take?
- What is stopping you from taking the next step?
- What actions have you taken to reach the objectives you set in your last performance review?
- Do you know what others think of your performance and attitude? If not, how can you find out?
- Do you know whether you are satisfying your internal and external customers? If not, how can you find out?
- How does your work increase internal and external customer satisfaction? How do you know for sure?
- What more could you do to increase internal and external customer satisfaction?
- What ideas do you have for attracting new customers?
- Have you asked others for their feedback or taken part in a company-sponsored 360-degree feedback process? Why or why not? What were the results?
- Have you sought out a mentor elsewhere in the organization? Why or why not? What happened as a result?
- Have you built relationships with other parts of the organization? Why or why not? With what results?
- When was the last time you approached me with a proposal about a new way to address a problem or volunteered for a new assignment?
- Are you doing everything you can to master new technologies needed by the organization?
- Have you read a new business book or attended a professional seminar in the past six months? If so, what did you learn? If not, why not?

- Do you read business periodicals and stay on top of business trends? Which ones? What are you learning about this business and your profession?
- If appropriate, have you considered joining professional associations to increase your professional growth and visibility? (Be prepared to provide the names of those that are appropriate and information on how to contact them.)
- What other jobs or areas of the company interest you? What have you done to learn more about these other areas?
- If our department were eliminated tomorrow and you were without a job, what would you do?
- Would you say you have responded positively to changes in the work environment in the past year? In what ways?
- Who do you think has the greatest impact on your career progress—you, me, or the organization as a whole? What more can you do?

Those who feel victimized and powerless need to be engaged and challenged. Questions like these can help move them off dead center so that you can partner with them to create a new plan that helps them take charge of their own professional development.

Work/Life Preferences Checklist

Many employees have difficulty expressing what it is they want. When they are dissatisfied, they may not know exactly why. Until they do know why, they cannot engage in a meaningful conversation with anyone, other than themselves, who can help them get what they want. You, the manager and career coach, can be the major influence here by helping them sharpen the focus on what they want at work and in life. The checklist in Appendix L can help them prepare for a career conversation with you.

Words of wisdom from the management expert Peter Drucker seem applicable here: "Successful careers are not planned. They develop when people are prepared for opportunities because they know their strengths, their method of work, and their values. Knowing where one belongs can transform an ordinary person—hardworking and competent but otherwise mediocre—into an outstanding performer."[8]

Your main job is to help your workers become outstanding performers by helping increase their self-awareness, encouraging their ambitions—even if it means they move on—helping them set realistic, achievable goals and coaching their career success. Your counsel should include the following:

Cardinal Rules of Career Advancement

1. Perform well in the present job, first and foremost. Remember—fortune favors those who do a brilliant job today.
2. If you are in the wrong job, change to the right one—love what you do, which means first figuring out who you are.
3. Support the organization as a team player.
4. Seek assignments that meet real company needs and make use of your talents.
5. Develop an understanding of all areas of the company.
6. Seek continual training, both formally and informally.
7. Be open to horizontal moves, projects, and assignments that will result in new skill acquisition and greater versatility, thus increasing your value and making mobility more likely.
8. Familiarize yourself with career paths of those in positions to which you aspire, gain their advice, and seek their mentorship, if appropriate.
9. Act on the understanding that *all* people in the organization, not just your manager, are valuable sources of information about growth opportunities.
10. If a desired position is not presently available, seek mini-assignments that will help prepare you and allow you to try out pieces of the desired job.
11. Exhaust all options for seeking new challenge and more satisfaction in the present job before pursuing other alternatives.
12. At the right time, communicate your growth desires, abilities, ideas, or proposals to your manager or to whomever has the power to approve or hire internally.
13. Kick-start your career by acting like an entrepreneur, either by starting a new line of business or by providing the company with some new service.

Obstacles to Employee Career Development

1. Poor performance
2. Lack of clear goal
3. Lack of self-knowledge
4. Passivity/dependence
5. Unrealistic expectations
6. Reluctance to talk with manager
7. Not prepared to talk with manager
8. Manager reluctant/unprepared to talk
9. Manager won't invest time in process
10. Employee mismatched with job

What You as Career Coach Can Do to Facilitate Employee Career Growth

■ Don't wait for the employee to ask, "Where can I go from here?" Start the discussion yourself during the interviewing process or on the employee's first day.

■ In career discussions, as in performance discussions, get employees' input—their aspirations, frustrations, and so on—before giving your input.

■ Give them honest feedback on their strengths and limitations, always citing examples of actual instances when they demonstrated both. If you don't believe they have the abilities, assets, or attitude to succeed in a desired position, tell them so, then discuss how they might change or prepare themselves better.

■ Instead of focusing on career paths and ladders, help them envision scenarios based on forecasts and projections of where the company is going and the needs that will arise that could capitalize on their talents and ideas.

■ If they don't know their abilities, have them complete the Talent Inventory (Appendix D), or have them get 360-degree feedback from the coworkers with whom they most frequently interact. They can also benefit greatly from a self-analysis of their life/work achievements, as shown in Richard Bolles's perennial best-seller, *What Color Is Your Parachute?* Your company may also want to consider acquiring computer software by which all employees can assess their talents, interests, and values at their own workstations, then develop internal career growth plans.

■ Focus on growth in the present assignment and how it can be made more satisfying. Refer to the five-point job enrichment rating in Appendix C to determine how the present job can be made more rewarding. Solicit and listen to the employee's ideas for job redesign.

■ When no opportunities are apparent for movement into desired jobs, have employees prepare a list of unmet needs in your area and in the organization as a whole. Give them thirty days to research these needs with the appropriate people, then come to you to discuss it. You may be able to help them make the transition, assuming you believe it is a realistic and achievable one.

■ Be willing to let the employee move on to another desired assignment, project, or position within the organization, if the employee and the organization will both be better served. This is a hard one to do, especially if a top performer is involved, but if you try to block the move, you increase the risk that the employee will leave the organization and speak poorly of you and your company in the future.

■ Before any employee begins a college-degree or formal training program that is to be reimbursed by the organization, have the employee complete a thorough assessment of abilities, interests, personality, and values, if they have not already done so, to determine whether their aspirations are compatible with those called for by the program. Also, let the employee know that when he or she does finish the program, there are no guarantees of promotion.

■ Don't impose your personal values on the employee. For example, don't assume the person might want to pursue a managerial track, as you did. Help the person more clearly examine his or her own values and priorities and how they could impact future choices.

■ Encourage your organization to develop and maintain on-line access to current internal opportunities—not just traditional openings, but emerging needs throughout the organization—even before they become official openings.

■ When you have posted a job in human resources, remember that this is probably one of the busiest departments in the organization. Go to HR yourself and talk with the people there. Agree on how you can get involved with the search for good internal candidates.

How Retention-Focused Companies Are Helping Employees Take Charge of Their Careers

During the 1990s, many companies entered into new covenants with their employees. As their part of the covenant, employees, however reluctantly, agreed to take responsibility for managing their careers. Many employers, for their part, agreed to provide employees with the tools to assess and plan their careers and the internal systems, services, training, and opportunities to help employees take charge of their career progress and enhance their future employability. The result of these efforts has been a more "career-resilient" workforce that can adapt to change. It should come as no surprise that many of these companies are located in California's Silicon Valley, where the pace of business change is unparalleled.

Here are some of their more effective practices:

■ *Providing Employee Assessment and Career Planning Workshops.* Companies such as Raychem, Apple Computer, and Sun Microsystems hold on-site workshops where employees learn to take charge of their careers, beginning with assessing their abilities, interests, and values. They then engage in a planning process where they explore the organization's needs to determine possible future options and how to prepare for them. Then they are ready for productive career discussions with their managers.

▪ *Conducting Career Coaching Workshops for Managers.* While employees are learning to take charge of their careers, managers are learning how to support their efforts by becoming familiar with the career assessment and planning process, practicing career coaching techniques, preparing for various types of employee-initiated career discussions, and giving honest feedback.

▪ *Establishing Employee Career Centers.* Companies such as Raychem, TRW, Fel-Pro, Advanced Micro Devices, IBM, and Motorola, to name a few, have set up internal career centers where employees can come for self-assessment. Services may include computerized programs that incorporate 360-degree feedback, competency assessment, confidential counseling, career management and resilience training, lunch-and-learn seminars, and information, sometimes through an intranet system, about internal opportunities. Some of these centers were started for the purpose of internal redeployment, also known as "inplacement." Successful centers were never used as transition centers for outplacement of downsized employees, however, because many employees would never want to be seen there for fear that coworkers would think they were "on their way out." Career centers are often staffed by outside career consultants on a contract basis. Most companies with career centers urge managers to encourage their employees to make use of them but let employees decide whether to tell their managers they have gone there or what services they received.

Fel-Pro's center is staffed three days a week by two local outside career consultants, to ensure confidentiality. Arlis McLean, vice president of human resources, says, "Some employees may decide to build their careers elsewhere and need help to do it; others—the majority—want to stay with us and need to know the mechanisms for moving ahead."[9]

▪ *Giving Open Business Briefings.* To meet employees halfway in planning their careers inside the organization, companies such as Sun Microsystems, 3Com, Advanced Micro Devices, Intel, and Microsoft openly discuss strategic decisions and plans that may impact jobs or skills that will be required in the future. At 3Com, most departments hold weekly discussion sessions on the status of the business and what it may mean to employees.

IBM has a national website for employees that provides information about the strategic direction of the company. Managers are also expected to provide strategic information to their people. Sun's management has promised workers that it will make employees aware of a strategic decision that will affect staffing, such as plans to outsource a function. "As soon as we've decided something, you'll know," Sun says. Then it follows through on its promise.

Sharing such information would be frowned upon by many companies. But the companies that practice such openness believe they are simply treating their employees as respect-worthy adults rather than perpetuating the outdated parent-child relationship.

Andy Grove, chairman of Intel, is a strong believer in giving employees the information they need to stay resilient, or, as he calls it, "owning your own employability. "Every quarter," he says to his employees, "I give you a two-hour dump of what's happening to us. You have to figure out what that means to you."[10]

- *Creating an Internal Network of Information Providers.* Raychem, for example, has set up a network of more than 400 people throughout the organization who are willing to take the time to talk with employees who want to learn about the nature of their work and job qualifications. Called "I.I.I.N.siders" (for Insiders Information Interview Network), the computerized database houses the names and backgrounds of volunteers.

Chase Manhattan Bank maintains a list of employees who are willing to be shadowed by those interested in moving into their line of work. An employee who wants to be a derivatives trader, for example, can spend the day with an actual trader, learning about the challenges of the job, and come away with a realistic understanding of the work.

Raychem and Apple Computers also ask all employees to volunteer to give information interviews to other employees. When someone signs up, he or she agrees to do a certain number. After a set period of time, the person can either drop out or sign up to do more of these interviews. Apple goes so far as to let people "sample" jobs by filling in for those taking the sabbatical that is available to all employees.

- *Maintaining Internal Job and Talent Banks.* Microsoft has created an on-line service where employees can learn about open positions and the skills required for them. Microsoft also places large amounts of career information on what it calls its "electronic campus," including a "resource and referral" section with lists of books, professional associations, conferences, courses, articles, and other information recommended by coworkers.

In its Career Partnership Center, Advanced Micro Devices maintains a data bank of employee skills that can be accessed by managers looking for internal talent. The company also integrates the career development plans of all employees into its long-range workforce planning process.

Many other companies are moving to implement virtual career centers that feature on-line computer platforms that show various career paths and allow employees to benchmark their skill levels against those required for desired jobs so that they can make plans to close the gaps.

- *Establishing Individual Learning Accounts.* As more and more employees seek opportunities for customized and self-directed development, some progressive companies have created individual learning accounts, providing designated amounts of time and money that employees may "spend" on classes, internships, or other learning opportunities of their choice. While giving employees more freedom to select personalized learning experience, this concept also helps companies save money previously spent on large-scale, "one-size-fits-all" training programs.

■ *Starting a Mentoring Program.* Formal mentoring programs have grown in popularity in recent years. The list of companies who have launched mentoring programs includes Hewlett-Packard, Texas Instruments, Charles Schwab, Ford Motor Company, Ernst & Young, Quaker Oats Company, IBM, Georgia-Pacific, Ceridian, J. C. Penney, PriceWaterhouse-Coopers, 3M, and General Mills.

In one study, mentoring programs were found to be effective in increasing employee retention by 77 percent within companies that implemented them.[11] There are three main goals for most mentoring programs—to increase opportunities for women and minorities, to develop leaders, and, increasingly, to enhance performance and increase the retention of employees at all levels.

Companies with successful mentoring programs report that having the CEO and senior managers actively involved in mentoring and supporting the programs is important. When the practice of mentoring cascades through the organization from the top, it becomes a prestigious thing for managers to take part. Some companies expect all managers to become mentors, to the point that they include mentoring as an item to be reviewed on performance appraisal.

Current mentoring programs have become highly structured. Hewlett-Packard maintains an on-line mentor database that mentees can use to search for mentors with specific areas of expertise. They can even interview potential mentors and submit their choices in order of preference. Hewlett-Packard's program uses written mentoring agreements that establish the ground rules for the partnership, and the company conducts half-day training sessions for mentors and mentees. Other companies have appointed internal human resources staff as "retention managers" or "career management representatives" to act as consultants to all employees, especially the difficult-to-replace talent, such as software engineers.

Many companies now encourage mentoring relationships that are mentee-driven to reinforce employee career self-management. Mentees take the initiative in approaching potential mentors and making sure meetings happen.

Because of travel demands and the general shortage of senior mentors, many companies have begun providing group mentoring where one executive may be matched up with four to eight mentees. Another way to overcome the shortage of available mentors is to match mentors and mentees for short periods of time.

Some organizations have begun using peers as mentors as a way to increase employee awareness of cross-functional opportunities. It is not unheard of to even see younger employees mentoring older ones, particularly as it relates to the transfer of technical know-how.

As a creative alternative to mentors, the Toronto technology consulting firm LGS Group, Inc., assigns one "Career Manager" for every twenty-five to forty employees to help reduce turnover (typically 25 percent to 35 percent) among IT staff. The Career Managers are set apart from human resources. They manage employees' performance reviews, create career development plans, research market salaries to ensure that the company stays competitive, and listen to and resolve issues that interfere with daily performance. The Career Managers are the voice of employees to management and help to manage employee expectations from a management perspective. They do not become involved in such issues as corrective action, terminations, and payroll. They represent "a safe place to go" when employees have issues that need to be addressed. LGS, with 2,500 employees in offices across Canada, in the United States, and in Europe, reduced turnover from 30 percent to 15 percent in its first year using Career Managers in its Toronto office. The company now feels it has a competitive edge in the industrywide war for talent.

Keys to Creating a Successful Career Development Initiative in Your Organization

1. *Define the need.* To "hit the bull's-eye," you need to talk with employees to find out what's missing. Is it lack of perceived opportunity, not enough training, too little communication, diversity issues? Exit interview analysis, employee surveys, and focus groups can help you become clearer about employees' views on these issues.

2. *Identify target groups.* Focus on the employees you most want to keep. This helps you to get buy-in from all levels of management, which is important in building enthusiasm and gaining acceptance for the initiative.

3. *Tie the initiative to human resources systems and policies.* Company policies and practices regarding application procedures for posted jobs, managers' ability to block internal movement, hiring from within, use of computer job/talent banks, training, tuition reimbursement, use of pay systems that reward flexibility rather than hierarchy, and performance management all impact the career development initiative and should be in synch with it.

4. *Tailor the initiative to fit the culture.* Not every company is ready for all of the practices described in this chapter. Start with the pieces that the current culture will accept. If you are trying to change your culture to cre-

ate more employee initiative, giving workers the tools to take charge is an important way to do it.

One company, Komatsu, took an initiative to develop a web of relationships across the company. It included an innovative new career path concept—"a 'return ticket' policy to encourage the transfer of young employees to subsidiaries and affiliate companies that had previously been viewed as 'banishment'; and the Strategic Employee Exchange Program, which allows employees to work on projects in other parts of the company on a short-term basis."[12]

5. *Select from within.* See Retention Practice #12.

6. *Take a long-term approach with short-term payoffs.* To build momentum, develop the program in stages. Begin by conducting a needs evaluation with a manager task force, then design and pilot a program, measure the results, spread the good word, and gradually include more managers and employees. If the gradual approach is solidly designed and well executed, the long-term results in keeping the right people will take care of themselves.

7. *Redesign performance management system to make the process easier, if necessary.* Some companies require managers to have career discussions with their employees at least twice a year, or to jointly create career development action plans once a year. Others incorporate manager ratings as career coaches on the performance review.

8. *Use multiple approaches.* Pull from the various approaches covered earlier in this chapter.

9. *Codesign with line management.* The career development system, like the performance management system, should be owned by line management, not by human resources, if it is to be successful. Getting line management to help design this system from the outset will go a long way toward making this happen.

10. *Separate career management from performance appraisal.* Keeping the two apart helps assure employees that the purpose of the program is to help them manage their careers and not to help their superiors manage them. Career discussions between manager and employee should be scheduled between performance appraisal discussions.

11. *Ensure top management support.* This is the key to success with almost all initiatives. Sometimes successful programs can be created gradually from the bottom up (or from the middle up), but the way to more immediate success starts at the top.

12. *Build managers' career coaching skills.* See Retention Practice #21.

13. *Measure results.* Collecting manager and employee comments from career management workshops and disseminating them to other managers

and employees works quite well. So does documenting the success stories of employees who decided to stay within the company or whose performance improved because they attended the workshops and initiated career discussions with their managers

14. *Publicize results.* Making presentations to managers that include the results and success stories collected in #13 is the key.

Now it's time for you to give your organization and yourself as a manager a grade on Retention Practice #22: "Give Employees the Tools for Taking Charge of their Careers."

How good a job is your organization doing on this practice?

Circle one: (A) Excellent   (B) Very good   (C) Good   (D) Fair   (F) Poor

How good a job are you as a manager doing on this practice?

Circle one: (A) Excellent   (B) Very good   (C) Good   (D) Fair   (F) Poor

How important do you believe this practice is to your organization's strategy to attract and retain the talent necessary to meet its business objectives?

Circle one: (A) Critical (B) Very important (C) Somewhat important
            (D) Not important

What can your organization do to improve on this practice?

What can you as a manager do to improve on this practice?

RETENTION PRACTICE #23

Know When to Keep and When to Let Go

> Falsely telling a manager he's doing fine for twenty years, then firing him at age 53 when he's got two kids in college—that's the definition of cruelty.
> —Jack Welch, Chairman, General Electric

Up to now, we have focused on doing everything in your power to attract, select, integrate, and retain the right people. But what about the bad fits and the marginal or poor performers? These are the people who make the most mistakes, drive away the most customers, and create resentment and morale problems for your most productive employees. High-growth companies especially cannot afford subpar performers; they can change team chemistry for the worse, leave a poor impression with potential customers and business partners, and have a negative multiplier effect on the company's overall productivity. You know when you need to take action to correct the situation.

And yet, many managers cannot bring themselves to confront nonperformance, as the following story illustrates: One manager worked hard to recruit a key information systems specialist from a larger, out-of-state company. The new employee dived into his job with great enthusiasm but promptly fell on his face. The manager tried coaching and counseling the employee, but his performance did not improve.

The new worker's peers approached the manager, asking him to do something about the situation, but he hesitated. He knew by now that he had made a hiring mistake, but he was paralyzed by guilt. He told the employee he would give him some time to find another job. But the employee's performance declined even further. Finally, when a valued client was lost and the rest of the staff became demoralized, the manager let the employee go.

The manager learned a costly lesson: "Next time, I won't agonize. I will take action. I wasn't doing the company or the employee any favors by delaying the decision."

Why Managers Are So Reluctant to Terminate Even When It's Necessary

You should begin to question your hiring decision when an employee keeps making the same mistakes despite your best coaching efforts, or when you begin to decrease your job expectations and standards when the new employee fails to meet those expectations (we will assume that you have explored whether the poor performance may be a temporary downturn brought on by a personal or family problem and the possibility that the employee has not received the right kind of training, resources, or supervision from you or a previous supervisor).

Most managers know within three weeks, or often sooner, when they have made a hiring mistake, but it generally takes three months before they finally decide to correct the mistake. There are plenty of reasons managers hesitate to step up and do what needs to be done. Can you identify with any of these?

- They are embarrassed to admit they made a bad hiring decision.
- They feel guilty about making the bad hire and can't bring themselves to terminate the person they brought in with such high hopes.
- They feel guilty that they didn't make their performance expectations clear when they first hired the employee (see Retention Practices #8 and 16).
- They fear and/or dislike confrontation (see Retention Practice #19).
- They know they haven't done a good job of giving performance feedback and coaching to give the employee a chance to improve performance (see Retention Practice #19).
- They have failed to document coaching efforts and fear that the employee will take legal action against the organization.
- They dread the prospect of having to go through the costly and time-consuming process of replacing the terminated employee.
- They are afraid they will mishandle the termination meeting.

It becomes clear after reviewing these reasons that if managers were doing a good job of hiring the right people in the first place and managing performance with frequent coaching and feedback, they wouldn't need to terminate as often as they do. Of course, the situation is different if you have inherited a team you did not hire or have not coached. In these cases your reluctance to terminate may be lessened, but you will need to be open-minded enough to coach the nonperformers on the team if they have not been coached or given frank feedback in the past.

New managers who now have to supervise their former peers can be faced with an altogether different problem. They may be unable to maintain the tough-minded objectivity needed to terminate those with whom they have such empathy and companionship. Carried to an extreme, some managers become so dependent on their employees for friendship and attention that they unknowingly put the employees in a controlling role. This makes the employee "less dependent on the manager for professional support than the manager is dependent on him or her for psychic support. A dependent relationship like this virtually precludes termination."[1]

You must be honest with yourself about this—are you tolerating nonperformance because of emotional ties that are hindering your objectivity?

Confronting Nonperformance

Before going forward with any plans to terminate an employee, you need to ask yourself in fairness to the employee, "Have I confronted the employee with the fact of his or her nonperformance and given the employee every chance to improve?" Have you taken these steps?

■ *Set clear performance expectations for the employee (see S-M-A-R-T Objectives, Retention Practice #16)?*

■ *Confronted the employee with specific feedback regarding exactly how the employee's performance has fallen short of objectives?*

■ *Documented the employee's nonperformance by keeping a detailed log of performance data, incidents, conversations, and/or progress reviews and performance appraisals in which you confronted the employee with problems and agreed on how the employee would resolve them?* During performance discussions, have employees evaluate their own performance (remember the "Get-Give-Merge-Go" process?). If the employee acknowledges the problem, then you'll be that much closer to solving it. If the employee denies the problem, you will have a stronger case that the employee did not respond to constructive coaching.

■ *Put the employee on probation, or give the employee a deadline for performance improvement as a last resort to termination?* While putting an employee on probation or issuing a written warning prior to dismissal is not a legal requirement, it may be effective in improving performance when all else has failed. One manager told an employee the company would have to let him go if his project wasn't done in the next thirty days. The employee met the deadline. Make sure the employee is given sufficient time to improve.

■ *Looked for other alternatives to termination?* If you have made a hiring mistake, that doesn't mean the employee cannot be effective in another job or assignment. A bad fit of the person with the job may be the true cause of the nonperformance. Can the employee be trained to become more effective in the job? What about retraining for a different position in the organization?

Consider reassessing the employee's talents, motivations, and vocational interests. Perhaps the job can be redesigned, or perhaps there are other needs in your area for which the employee's talents would be a better fit. Have you explored redeployment options elsewhere in your organization? Is a transfer possible? If you accept some of the blame for hiring or promoting the person into the wrong job, then consider every possible option for making a "compassionate reassignment" within the organization.

Have you considered confronting the employee with 360-degree feedback from coworkers as a "wake-up call" that will motivate the employee to receive third-party coaching by a consulting firm that is skilled in this process? You may first need to evaluate whether the employee's performance is correctable and the degree to which the employee wants to improve.

Another form of "wake-up call" is a practice IBM has used to discipline those who have violated one of its corporate norms, such as handling a subordinate too harshly. The company temporarily assigns the offending employee to "penalty box" assignment—a less important job at the same level, sometimes at a less desirable location. To the outsider, these may look like job rotations, but they take the individual out of the game temporarily while hard feelings are gradually forgotten. The penalty box assignment gives the employee time to reflect on his or her behavior and to open up to the idea of being coached. This practice also sends the message that the company is interested in retaining its talent and will not fire anyone capriciously.

■ *Considered whether your evaluation of this employee's performance has been colored by your feelings about the person's race, national origin, religion, age, pregnancy, marital status, or disability—categories covered by discrimination laws?* With one out of every five lawsuits in the United States being brought by a worker, you need to arm yourself and your company against the possibility of a costly jury verdict. This is one more reason that you must carefully document nonperformance. If you and an employee cannot get along for personality or other differences that you consider irreconcilable, consider the option of transferring that employee to another manager with whom they may be more compatible.

Stepping Up and Taking Action

Let's say you have confronted the nonperforming employee with frank and frequent feedback, coached to improve performance, set specific performance objectives along the way, documented the employee's failure to improve performance, and looked at alternatives to termination. None of these actions have brought resolution to the problem, and your last remaining option is to terminate the employee. You have decided to take action. Before you do, consider these thoughts:

First of all, get comfortable with the decision you have made. The employee has not met your expectations, and, even though you may be partially responsible for the employee's being in the wrong job or feel guilty for letting the situation go on so long, you know you must make the change for the sake of the company, the other key people you want to retain, and, yes, for the sake of the employee, too.

You must have a "tough-love" mind-set, which means you are maintaining an uncompromising focus on standards of excellence while also showing that you genuinely care about the employee as a person. Most likely, the employee's talents have not been well suited to the challenges of the role. If this is the case, then it is uncaring of you to allow the employee to continue to struggle to succeed in a job that doesn't fit. You are taking action to correct a mistake in casting. As you do, you must speak the truth and still maintain a caring relationship with the individual.

This "tough-love" mind-set is captured well in Buckingham and Coffman's *First, Break All The Rules*. The authors recount the words of a factory owner who let one of his managers go by saying, "Come in, sit down, I love you; you're fired; I still love you. Now, get a drink and let's talk this through." The authors go on to describe the phenomenon they call "manager-assisted career suicide," when the poor performer deliberately, if perhaps not quite consciously, "puts himself in situations where his weaknesses are exposed. . . . If you suspect that this is happening, the best thing you can do," the authors say, "is help put him out of his misery."[2]

Even when you are comfortable with your decision, that doesn't mean you will look forward to it. Terminating an employee, regardless of the reason, remains one of the most dreaded and distasteful acts a manager must perform. Some managers report that they can't sleep or get physically ill prior to conducting a termination meeting. There is plenty to be nervous about; not only are you taking away the source of this person's livelihood, but the way you do it will make an impression on those remaining in the organization, including the ones you most want to keep. Here are a few practical guidelines that can help make these necessary meetings less dreadful and more humane and successful:

- Follow your company's procedures for employee terminations as laid out in your employee handbook if you have one.
- Review the termination with an employment attorney to discuss possible legal ramifications.
- Think about costs of termination, such as possible loss of talent, investment, morale, and commitment among surviving employees.
- Look beyond the problem at hand. You will not want to create a problem by solving one. For example, how will this person's work continue to get done? To whom will you distribute it? Is the person scheduled to represent the company at an important meeting?
- Schedule the termination early in the week so that the employee can begin to take action toward finding another job or register with unemployment. Friday terminations only result in the employee's stewing helplessly over the weekend.
- Always deliver the news in a face-to-face meeting with a witness present (usually a human resources representative so that details of the separation agreement can be discussed).
- Terminate in a place where you will not be interrupted (no phone calls).
- Meet right before lunch or at the end of the day so that the person can clear his or her own workplace in privacy.
- Keep the meeting brief. State the business and/or performance reasons, as appropriate. In a calm, factual, and serious way, let the employee know in no uncertain terms that the decision is final and not subject to change. Express your concern and desire to help the employee move on successfully. If you have engaged a career transition (outplacement) firm, explain how it will assist. Never say, "I know how you feel"; all employees experience job loss in their own way. Acknowledge the employee's contributions. Never apologize, argue, or advise.
- Meet with remaining employees as soon as possible and explain to them what has happened.

There are many other details to arrange and questions you will need to have answered. You can receive expert advice on how to plan for and conduct a successful termination meeting from a local career transition consulting firm. It can have a consultant on-site to meet with the departing employee to explain the available services and to help the employee vent his or her feelings immediately after the termination. Having career transition services available can "soften the blow" for the terminated employee and make for a smoother transition from the organization into a new job or career.

Another suggestion that many companies don't follow is to make sure to conduct an exit interview with the terminated employee. Many companies hire a third party to conduct these interviews several days or weeks after the employee's departure, when the person will be more likely to be objective about what happened. Regardless of the circumstances, the departed employee can provide excellent feedback that you can use to take constructive action to make your work environment a better one. The third party will need to assure the employee that what he or she says will not cause you to withhold a good reference or other benefits you have already agreed upon.

Finally, do a postmortem. Every time you terminate someone, you should critique the way you handled it so that you don't repeat the same mistakes. Over time, you may also learn how to hire better. Alegent Health of Omaha, Nebraska, conducts impromptu focus groups with peers of the terminated employee to get their take on what may have gone wrong.

Letting Them Move On
vs. Making Heroic Efforts to Save

Knowing when to let go doesn't just mean knowing when to terminate. It also means knowing when you can afford to let certain workers, or categories of workers, move on without making special efforts to keep them. By now, you may have already read one company's guidelines (in Appendix A) for convincing highly valued workers to change their minds when they resign. One survey revealed that 56 percent of corporate CFOs would be willing to make counteroffers to keep a "good employee."[3]

On the other hand, managers and companies must also be clear about which employees they will allow to move on, whatever the reason. Targeted, selective talent retention by definition requires that you know where to invest limited time and money. Many companies, of course, have made the decision not to retain employees at all but instead to outsource entire functions.

Some companies—for example, those that employ large numbers of entry-level engineers—may consciously decide not to go to great lengths to retain them. Such a strategy might be based partly on the existence of a large and continuous pool of recent university graduates, partly on the company's recognition that the new recruits will continually infuse the organization with the most up-to-date skills, and partly on the fact that such a practice can keep a lid on compensation levels, since the new hires have lower salaries than longer-term employees.

Other project-driven companies focus on keeping contract employees only as long as they need them to complete a key project. In such cases, short-term commitment is desired, even though long-term loyalty is not required. This will continue to be a fact of life in a U.S. economy that is increasingly dependent on a vast contingency workforce. "Get their commitment while they are here" will be the ongoing watchword, meaning that the use of all talent retention practices at your command will remain relevant.

Letting Talent Go in Order to Keep It— Cooperating with Your Competitors

Who's Doing It

- As the challenge of finding and keeping good workers has become more difficult over recent years, several large companies have banded together in what they call the *Talent Alliance*. Member companies, now numbering about thirty, have agreed that when any company among them has to lay off workers, the other companies will make every attempt to hire them. The group now even provides standardized surveys for prehire screening and evaluation for job matching.

- In a less formal collaboration in Grand Rapids, Michigan, the local *Burger King* has joined forces with *Cascade Engineering*, a plastic parts manufacturer, in an agreement to hire any job applicants that the other does not hire. Cascade applicants who seem like good workers but who may lack the technical skills required for the company's production jobs may be hired by Burger King. When Burger King employees are ready to look for more skilled positions, they are referred to Cascade for vocational counseling.

The Down Side of Downsizing

Most of the postmortems on the massive downsizings of the 1990s have concluded that much was lost in pursuit of the "holy grail" of cost-cutting:

- The concept of "employee loyalty" was forever altered.
- Business was lost and customer relationships were damaged when veteran salespeople were severed and major customers were transferred to new sales divisions. Buyers felt abandoned.
- Strategies of downsizing companies to become the low-cost supplier backfired with high-end customers.
- More valuable senior employees were let go and less expensive em-

ployees were brought in. Customers noticed the drop-off in service and took their business elsewhere.

- Many companies realized their mistakes in letting experienced people go and began hiring them back as contractors at even higher pay rates. *The Wall Street Journal* ran a front-page article on May 14, 1996, calling this practice "dumbsizing."
- Many companies reported that they were worse off financially than they had been prior to downsizing.
- Employees who survived the downsizings felt less secure, less committed, demoralized by lost relationships, and betrayed by having to take on the extra work, which didn't go away, even though their colleagues did.
- Heightened cynicism about corporate intentions and higher-than-ever burnout and stress levels were created among many workers.
- Many managers were left with smaller staffs and had to do the detail work themselves, making it even more difficult for them to do the challenging work of managing and retaining their workers.
- Companies with high concentrations of creative technical workers experienced negative impacts on the productivity of these workers.

Does this mean that all downsizing has been bad? Not at all. Even Aaron Feuerstein, the much-admired owner of Malden Mills, who spent millions of dollars keeping 1,000 employees on the payroll after a fire destroyed his factory, advocates downsizing under the right conditions. "Legitimate downsizing as the result of technological advances or as a result of good industrial engineering? Absolutely, I'm in favor of it," Feuerstein said. "We try to do it in such a way as to minimize human suffering, but downsizing must be done."[4]

Companies that are enlightened enough to know that committed workers are the key to their long-term success don't "dumbsize." Some companies, such as those mentioned in Retention Practice #1, have actual no-layoff policies. Others, like Nucor, of Charlotte, North Carolina, have tried their best to offer "continuous employment." Nucor realized that skilled labor was in short supply, and, when business was down, rather than letting its hourly workers go, offered them the option of taking non-production maintenance jobs at their base pay of $9 per hour. When demand picked up, Nucor paid the workers $23 per hour for seven days a week—the bonus rate. Another example is FedEx, which managed to find jobs for 1,300 employees within the company when it shut down its Zap-Mail program.

The good news about downsizing is that it has taught workers that they can survive the loss of a job and that they need to start taking more control over their careers, albeit reluctantly, and it has motivated many displaced workers to start new businesses, thereby creating new jobs for other displaced workers.

The overall lesson for senior managers who realize the importance of retaining the right talent is to understand the true value of the key people in your overall business strategy and the cost-benefit trade-off involved before you commit your company to a downsizing effort.

Now it's time for you to give your organization and yourself as a manager a grade on Retention Practice #23: "Know When to Keep and When to Let Go."

How good a job is your organization doing on this practice?

Circle one: (A) Excellent   (B) Very good   (C) Good   (D) Fair   (F) Poor

How good a job are you as a manager doing on this practice?

Circle one: (A) Excellent   (B) Very good   (C) Good   (D) Fair   (F) Poor

How important do you believe this practice is to your organization's strategy to attract and retain the talent necessary to meet its business objectives?

Circle one: (A) Critical (B) Very important (C) Somewhat important
             (D) Not important

What can your organization do to improve on this practice?

What can you as a manager do to improve on this practice?

Retention Practice #24

Have More Fun!

There's no reason that work has to be suffused with seriousness. . . . Professionalism can be worn lightly. Fun is a stimulant to people. They enjoy their work more and work more productively.

—Herb Kelleher, CEO, Southwest Airlines

As noted in the first key to keeping the right people, "Be a Company That People Want to Work For," U.S. companies are suffering a burnout crisis, fueled by too much change and not enough fun in the workplace.

You can see it in your absenteeism rates, which serve as an early warning sign of turnover to come. You can see the tightness and stress on the faces of your employees. You can see it when your employees become short-tempered and argumentative with one another. You can see them not smiling when they interact with your customers. You know it when you see it. You may be feeling it yourself.

What Smart Companies Know about Fun and Keeping Good People

Managers and organizations who are focused on winning the war for talent understand that good people will move on when work stops being fun. They also understand the following truths:

- Working in high-commitment, nonabusive workplaces is much more fun!
- The more high-stress the work environment, the more need for fun to keep it in balance.

- Stress reduction through efforts to increase fun can translate into lower health care costs, higher productivity, and improved morale, which means less absenteeism and lower turnover.
- Employees with good senses of humor tend to be more flexible. Flexible people make organizations more creative and innovative.
- An enhanced sense of fun helps employees deliver service with a smile. It also helps rekindle a feeling of team spirit.
- Senior executives must approve of fun activities and understand that they can be a source of competitive advantage. The humor and motivational consultant Barbara Glanz says that "the most productive workplaces have at least ten minutes of laughter every hour."[1]

Some Serious Tips about Fun in the Workplace

Before attempting to increase the "fun factor" in your workplace, consider these points:

- What is fun for one person may not be for another. What is fun for one organizational culture may not be appropriate in another, as well. Know your people—and your culture—well enough to introduce the type of fun that all can enjoy.
- Before expecting your employees to lighten up, you will need to do so yourself. Find a comfort level that fits your style.
- If your work isn't providing personal satisfaction, you need to change it. Otherwise, you won't be much fun to be around, and it will be that much harder to build a more fun environment for your employees.
- Workplace fun doesn't need to be planned. In fact, most of the fun that happens in the workplace is spontaneous. Some organizations encourage impromptu celebrations and "spontaneous disruptions." As the manager, you don't have to make the fun happen, but you should let it happen. Squelching laughter in the workplace because you believe it takes away from decorum and professionalism will only serve to create a repressive atmosphere. The "law of reasonability" pertains here—there is such a thing as having too much fun if it distracts from getting things done.
- Remember that it can take time to change your corporate culture from one in which only seriousness and professionalism are rewarded to one in which fun is encouraged as well.

Who's Doing It

- *Wilson Learning Company* gives each employee a Mickey Mouse watch after three months of employment as a reminder to always have fun while working for the company. On their tenth anniversary, employees are given a gold watch.

- *Linda Miles*, president of her own seminar planning firm, treated her six-woman staff to pedicures, an award that has come to be known as Happy Feet Day.

- *The Chase Group* rents a stretch limousine between Christmas and New Year's to pick up employees' children and bring them to a pizza party at the office.

- *Merle Norman Cosmetics* sponsors an Employee Night every other Saturday at its container manufacturing facility. First-run movies are shown, and employees may bring up to six friends. After the movie, employees and friends can make their own free ice cream sundaes.

- *Odetics, Inc.*, has its own Fun Committee, which has launched "Project Girth." For every pound an employee loses, a dollar is sent to his or her favorite charity. Odetics also sponsors a Guess-the-Stock-Price contest each March 31 in which the winner gets free lunch. The morning after a product passed a crucial test at Odetics, a mariachi band paraded through the plant, followed by clerks from the local Baskin-Robbins offering ice cream.

- On April 1 each year, *Sprint* holds "Fun at Work Day" parties. The company sponsors a parking lot beach party between 11 A.M. and 1 P.M.

- At *Eastman Kodak,* an executive formed a Humor Task Force to gather comedy videos, humor books, plastic chattering teeth, and other props into a "Humor Room."

- Ken Hawk, founder of *1-800-Batteries Inc. (now iGo),* has given himself the title of Chief Energizing Officer, whose mission is to make the company a fun, creative place to work, a place that buzzes with energy. The company provides those who make their livings on the road with the power they need to keep their gears charged up. "Our customers are demanding," he says. "They're always staying at hotels, dealing with airlines. So when they call our company, they're often not in the best of moods." That's why Hawk provides his staff with snacks every morning, holds monthly barbecues where his managers cook for the team, and organizes fun group activities such as bowling, snow-tubing, and clay-painting.[2]

- *Southwest Airlines*, famous for encouraging fun among its staff, runs contests for the fun of it, such as a Halloween costume contest, a newsletter design contest, and an annual chili cook-off.

- *Bank of America* sponsors a one-month Laugh-A-Day challenge in which each employee tries to make coworkers laugh daily with cartoons and jokes. Winners receive T-shirts and books in which the best jokes and cartoons have been compiled.

- At a humor seminar, *Digital Equipment Corporation* customer service employees learned to juggle bean bags. If employees felt uptight after a call, they were encouraged to juggle to break the tension and prepare for the next call.

- *Digital Equipment* also instituted a "Grouch Patrol," which was empowered to tell grouchy people to take a break.

- *First Chicago Bank* gives out "Felix-and-Oscar" awards to the employees with the neatest and messiest work areas.

- *Liebert Corporation* offers free popcorn to employees all day long.

- *Central Bank of the South* plans a lunch outing for each employee's birthday. The person whose birthday it is gets to select the restaurant, and the manager personally picks up the tab. All other staffers are invited to attend on a "Dutch treat" basis.

- *Children's Hospital* hosts a stress relief fair for employees, with booths, dunk tank, Velcro dartboards, massages, and food.

- At a quarterly meeting, *Apple Computer* executives used kazoos instead of applause to indicate approval of speakers.

- The *Brookstar Corporation* keeps a large, inflatable punching bag with a sand-filled bottom—its "stress reduction dummy," which employees can punch to release stress and frustration.

- Store managers at *Crate and Barrel* give sales associates a "surprise hour off" to go for a walk, go shopping, or whatever they want to do so that they will come back refreshed.

- *General Motors* headquarters sponsored an ugly tie contest for men and an ugly shoe contest for women. After the winner of the ugly tie contest was selected and awarded a gold tie pin, all the ties were cut up and used to make a wall hanging, which is now a part of the decor and commemorates the fun had by all.

- *Dun and Bradstreet* created "Stress Support Kits" for customer service consultants, consisting of chewing gum, aspirin, a comedy cassette, wind-up toys for the desktop, and a rubber head for squeezing during tense moments on the phone.

More fun ideas:

- Have a party or picnic for no reason at all.
- Thank people by giving chocolate kisses, balloons, or other small items.
- Staple Kleenex to potentially stressful memos.

- Give employees a casual dress day such as Hawaiian Day or Suspender Friday.
- Make campaign buttons out of employees' baby pictures. Have employees wear one another's buttons and try to figure out who's who.
- Designate days when anyone who makes a negative comment forks over a small sum of money, which is used to start a Fun Committee fund.
- Have a Chinese bakery make special-order fortune cookies for your staff that include personalized fortunes you design yourself. Serve at coffee breaks, during long meetings, or for dessert after a meal.
- Hold fun contests on occasion—Nerf basketball, bubble blowing (bring some to your next staff meeting)—or play cooperative games such as charades or treasure hunts.
- Order pizza or a huge submarine sandwich for a communal lunch.
- Attach cartoons or humorous anecdotes to the more mundane memos that need to be circulated.
- On Friday before the Super Bowl, suggest that employees dress in the colors of their favorite team.
- Schedule a staff meeting off site in a congenial atmosphere.
- Take a daily humor break; designate someone to share a joke or funny story with the rest of the staff.
- Order a bouquet of flowers and give it to a coworker to enjoy with the stipulation that he or she must pass it on to another colleague after enjoying it for a half hour.
- Bring a Polaroid camera to work. Take candid shots of employees, and post throughout the office.
- Make it a point to always smile and say hello to your workers.
- Give everyone an opportunity to arrive an hour late or leave an hour early one day a week.
- If you're still not sure what to do next, simply ask your employees what would make work more fun for them, or form a "fun committee' " to come up with some ways to build in more fun and de-stress your workplace. Some companies even have "fun budgets."
- Never take anything too seriously. Keep reminding yourself, "This isn't brain surgery" (unless, of course, it is brain surgery).[3]

Now it's time for you to give your organization and yourself as a manager a grade on Retention Practice #24: "Have More Fun."

How good a job is your organization doing on this practice?

Circle one: (A) Excellent   (B) Very good   (C) Good   (D) Fair   (F) Poor

How good a job are you as a manager doing on this practice?

Circle one: (A) Excellent   (B) Very good   (C) Good   (D) Fair   (F) Poor

How important do you believe this practice is to your organization's strategy to attract and retain the talent necessary to meet its business objectives?

Circle one: (A) Critical (B) Very important (C) Somewhat important
(D) Not important

What can your organization do to improve on this practice?

What can you as a manager do to improve on this practice?

Selective Retention: Planning to Keep the Right People

So now you have reviewed the twenty-four retention practices, you have evaluated your performance as a manager, and/or the performance of your organization on each of these practices, and you have reflected on the special retention management needs of key populations and situations. The logical next step is to put together an action plan that identifies by name those you can least afford to lose and how you will retain them.

You probably thought about your most valuable employees as you considered each practice. You already have a good idea of who they are. But sometimes your initial views can change after looking at things in a different light. Before creating your Selective Retention Action Plan, consider the following questions:

—————— Am I clear about the business objectives of my unit and the organization as a whole (see Retention Practices #3 and 16)?

—————— Have I reflected on the competencies that will be needed to achieve these objectives (see Retention Practice #6)?

—————— Have I taken a fresh look lately at each player on my team to determine who has which of those competencies and what challenges each is seeking (see Retention Practices #21 and 22)?

—————— Have I identified the people whose departure would have the most damaging impact on my unit?

_____ Have I estimated the probability of losing my key people so that I can take preemptive action to keep them?

Before you complete your Selective Retention Action Plan, we will deal with these last two questions. First, who are the people whose loss would hurt the most? Are they in the categories we identified earlier when discussing "Who Are the Right People?," those who are:

- Most loyal?
- Top producers?
- Most experienced?
- Good people managers?
- Women and minority workers?
- Those who best fit the culture?
- Hard-to-find technical specialists?
- Those who can best manage conflict?
- Those who might go to work for a competitor?
- Those who could take customers and revenues with them?
- Those who could take secrets or valuable knowledge with them?

Another way of putting the question is to ask, "Who creates the most value for the organization?" Try to set aside your personal feelings and answer this question objectively. These key "value creators" may not be the highest-paid, highest-level, or longest-tenured people in your area. They may not even be full-time employees but may be key contractors, part-timers, or project staff. Also consider how difficult they would be to replace.

In the spaces provided, classify your available talent in one of three groupings—high, medium, or low—on the basis of how much value they create for your organization as a whole and toward the achievement of your unit's objectives:

High	*Medium*	*Low*
_____	_____	_____
_____	_____	_____
_____	_____	_____
_____	_____	_____

Now consider which of your highest-valued people may be "at risk"—that is, are more likely than others to leave. How can you estimate the risk of their leaving?

Criteria for Identifying "At-Risk" Talent

- Length of service. In general, higher numbers of employees leave either during the first year or after three to five years with the organization.
- Whether their skills are considered "hot" in the job market.
- Whether they are paid "below market."
- The frequency with which they have changed employers in the past.
- The people management ability of the manager to whom they report and the quality of that relationship.
- The availability of new challenges and learning or advancement opportunities.
- The possibility that they may be experiencing a personal crisis.
- The degree to which they appear to be engaged and committed.

There may well be other factors to consider. The worker may have experienced a recent disappointment, or may have shown signs of overwork or burnout; perhaps the person lost a well-liked manager or has been promoted to a management position and is not sure he or she likes managing others.

On the basis of all such factors, and your own intuition, who among your most valued contributors do you consider "at risk" of leaving? Use the following matrix for listing the names or initials of your direct reports, relying on both your previous ratings of their value and your estimates (again, high, medium, or low) of how great you believe is the risk of losing them.

Risk of Losing Employee

	HIGH	MEDIUM	LOW
HIGH VALUE TO ORGANIZATION			
MEDIUM VALUE			
LOW VALUE			

Naturally, you will want to focus your greatest energy and attention on retaining those individuals whose names appear in the "High-High" box in the upper left corner, if there are any. If you have managers reporting to you who may be vulnerable to losing key people, you may want to have them complete the matrix as well and discuss it with you.

What Will You Do to Retain These Key At-Risk People?

In addition to weighing how you might use the twenty-four retention practices as precision tools you can use with high-risk people, consider having a one-on-one conversation with each of them along the lines of the "development discussion" outlined in Retention Practice #21. Make it absolutely clear to them how important they are to you and to the organization. Let them know that you are willing to do everything within your power to keep them challenged and satisfied. Then agree on a plan for making it happen. Be prepared to go to bat for them, and keep your end of the deal.

As you prepare for these meetings, you may want to complete the following Selective Retention Action Plan to help you prepare for it. Here's how to get started:

1. First, copy both pages of the blank planning form. In the "Key At-Risk Person" column, list in order the names of your key at-risk people.
2. In the "Impact of Loss" column, describe the probable impact of their loss, for example—loss of key clients, loss of skills that are difficult to replace and critical to your business objectives, loss of knowledge of a core product or service, loss of momentum on a key project, or loss of morale among remaining employees in the same group or team.
3. In the "Key Motivators" column, list what you believe to be the key motivators and/or preferences of these key people—the talents they most want to use, the types of challenge they enjoy, their pay/benefits priorities (keeping in mind that pay is the easiest factor for competitive companies to match), geographic preference, and such values as career advancement, autonomy, and feedback/recognition. If you are not sure, then you need to ask these key employees about what is important to them when you meet with them.
4. In the "Preventive Actions" column (second page of the planning form), list the actions you are prepared to take to increase your chances of retaining these key people and the date by which you will take these actions.
5. In the "Possible Obstacles" column, list the obstacles you will need to overcome, including company culture, resistance of top management, company management practices, HR policies, lack of funding, organizational stress/change/crisis, your own lack of clarity about company mission/strategy/objectives or results expected, lack of time, lack of people management skills or training, and your own lack of commitment. You may think of others.

(text continues on page 260)

Selective Retention Action Plan

Key "At-Risk" Person	Impact of the Loss	Key Motivators
1.		
2.		
3.		
4.		
5.		
6.		

Preventive Actions	Possible Obstacles	How to Overcome
1.		
2.		
3.		
4.		
5.		
6.		

6. In the "How to Overcome" column, describe what additional action steps you will take to overcome these obstacles, and the date by which you will have taken them.
7. Meet with the key employees to discuss your commitment to retaining them, and how you are prepared to make that happen.
8. Complete new Selective Retention Action Plans for key people as needed.

An Organizationwide Selective Retention Initiative

Entex Information Services, a Rye Brook, New York–based computer services company, decided, in 1998, that it needed to take action to stem the loss of key technical staff. With fast growth, high turnover, and more than 600 technical positions open nationwide, the senior human resources executive believed that the answer lay not in simply beefing up the staffing department but in figuring out how to keep the good people the company already had. Patti Hanson, director of field human resources at the time, was asked to put together a multilevel, cross-functional task force to explore the causes of turnover and to develop a plan to keep key people.

The task force made a highly conservative estimate that the company was spending about 30 percent of each departing employee's annual salary on recruitment and retraining costs. With annualized turnover running at 33 percent, the 6,000-employee company was losing 2,000 employees per year at a cost of $18 million.

The task force decided to first gain a better understanding of the root causes of the turnover, not just the superficial reasons given during exit interviews. Exit surveys had indicated that lack of opportunity for advancement was the main reason employees were leaving. But the task force felt that beneath that reason were buried "push" factors that were causing employees to begin looking outside in the first place, or to be receptive to recruiters' calls.

The company conducted two surveys, one among current employees, asking them about the factors with which they were most and least satisfied, and another among employees who had resigned within the previous four to six months. The internal survey revealed areas of dissatisfaction; workers complained about not feeling recognized, not having a thorough orientation, not being informed of company goals and performance, feeling undercompensated, and not understanding how bonuses were earned.

Data from the exit surveys showed the following real reasons for leaving: Employees didn't think the company valued their work, they perceived a lack of training and technological growth, they felt they were accorded insufficient pay or status, or they had a bad relationship with a supervisor.

The task force recommended a seven-step initiative that it hoped would reduce turnover by 5 percent per year and result in a first-year savings of $2.7 million.

Step 1. *Standardize the selection system.* The company decided to expand the computerized interview process it had tried the previous year because it had found turnover among those screened in from it to be 10 percent less than the national average. The process was expanded to all locations. A technical assessment, behavioral questions, and generic job history questions were also instituted. The company found that the response to the simple question "How many jobs have you held in the past five years?" could be highly predictive of the outlook for long-term employment. The company also required peer interviews, at least two business reference checks, and a thorough background check.

Step 2. *Implement a new orientation process.* The highest percentage of all turnover was occurring within employees' first nine months on the job. The company created a new welcome package, including a video sent to each new hire's home, an interactive CD and mentor assignment on day one, a first-month orientation schedule, and ninety-day feedback.

Step 3. *Improve communications.* Managers began holding formal quarterly meetings with technical staff as well as informal meetings that had no preset agendas. The company offered free food, invited customers and vendors to participate, and sponsored recognition events. The main goal was to listen to employees.

Step 4. *Improve job content.* The task force recommended that all managers have quarterly one-on-one discussions with staff to discuss job performance, training needs, career development, and job enrichment. Job rotations were also begun.

Step 5. *Train management.* In a one-month blitz, the company trained 500 managers in selection and interviewing techniques, career development, performance management, communications, and rewards/recognition.

Step 6. *Measure for continuous improvement.* The company decided to continue doing the internal and external surveys twice a year. The company also overhauled the standard exit survey that was handed to employees upon resignation to make it more effective in uncovering push factors.

Step 7. *Keep management attention on turnover.* To get and keep management's attention on this key issue, the company incorporated a component that Hanson believes had the greatest impact of all the steps: It announced that 20 percent of all managers' bonus opportunities would be determined by whether they overachieved in one of two key areas—maintaining low turnover within a given market or department and improving retention in an area with previously high turnover.

After one year, the company had realized savings of $3 million from reduced turnover. In the meantime, Hanson led a second task force to further address compensation and career growth issues. Hanson's advice: "Take action now. You may be asking whether you can afford the time, energy, and money it takes to find out why employees are leaving and to take the necessary steps to fix the problem. But the question you must ask yourself is, "Can we afford not to take these steps?"[1]

Keeping *All* the People Who Keep You in Business: Special Groups and Situations

Before finalizing your Selective Retention Action Plan for retaining key individuals (see preceding section), you will find it helpful to think about the diversity of people and situations that may exist in your organization.

A cardinal rule of retention is that different people have different needs and desires and must be treated differently. In the next several pages you will review the special needs of several different groups of employees. As you do, consider the key people on your team who fall into these categories and how you can better meet their needs so that they will continue to stay and contribute.

Because many readers are currently, or may eventually, experience the turbulence brought on by a major downsizing, merger, or acquisition, we also include a section with guidelines on how to retain your key people during these challenging situations.

Retaining a Diverse Workforce

> We need every human gift and cannot afford to neglect any
> gift because of artificial barriers of sex or race or class or
> national origin.
>
> —Margaret Mead

If you know you are in a war for talent, then you and your organization must value and be open to all talent, regardless of the size, shape, or color in which it may come packaged. Because of the shortage of talent that affects all industries now and for the foreseeable future, no company can afford to overlook, disregard, discount, or devalue any talent source. The companies that prevail in the war for talent, in fact, will make sure that all their managers understand that managing and retaining a diverse workforce is a key measure of their performance and a condition of their advancement and continuing employment.

Diversity is about managing all issues of difference as they present themselves in your team. This means providing equal opportunity for promotions and challenging, high-visibility, and high-responsibility assignments to women, members of racial and cultural minorities, and younger and older workers.

It also means not just tolerating but encouraging diversity of opinion, perspective, and personality, which can be the most difficult kind of diversity for many managers to accept. As the CEO of Bell Atlantic, Ivan Seidenberg, put it: "What we need most is more diversity of thinking. If everybody in the room is the same, you'll have a lot fewer arguments and a lot worse answers." (Refer to the Myers-Briggs temperament types, described in Appendix G). You may recognize your own temperament type among these. The ability required to coach these different types of employees does not come naturally to all managers, but can be improved by interactive training requiring the practice of new behavior. Many companies train managers in these skills, with emphasis on initiating and facilitating "developmental discussions" with employees (see Retention Practice #21). Diversity means cultivating difference, puncturing conformity, and encouraging different perspectives. Research shows that teams with the greatest diversity generally achieve superior performance, incur fewer lawsuits, retain a wider range of customers, draw from the largest possible talent pool, and are more likely to become employers of choice.[1] Retaining a diverse workforce will give you and your company a distinct competitive advantage.

General Guidelines for Building and Retaining a Diverse Workforce

1. Understand that the dynamics of diversity demand a new definition of fairness—not treating all employees the same but treating each appropriately according to his or her needs.

2. Resist the "principle of social similarity"—the all-too-human temptation to hire, promote, associate with, and reward only those who are most like you.

3. Balance the organization's need to hire people who fit the culture with the need to maintain a rich diversity of viewpoints. Hiring based on fitting people into the culture works fine unless the culture you are comfortable with doesn't open the way for minorities and women.

4. Admit your own prejudices to yourself. This is the first step toward change.

5. Make a conscious effort to spend time developing those who are different from you and from others on the team. Look for opportunities to give them challenging assignments and increasing responsibility.

6. Provide job rotations to prepare as many women and other minorities as possible for higher-level positions.

7. When in doubt about how any minority population feels about its experience working in your organization, or what would make it a better experience, get together with these minority employees and ask them. Then, and most important, follow up with action.

8. Remember—true diversity is about creating an environment that maximizes the contributions of all available talent.

Retention and the Nine Dimensions of Diversity

In addition to personality differences, there are nine dimensions of diversity that make for visible and invisible differences in the workplace that retention-focused managers must manage:[2]

- Gender
- Race
- Age
- Religion
- Ethnicity
- Hierarchy/class
- Sexual orientation
- Family situation
- Disability

Here are some retention guidelines for each of these dimensions:

Gender

- Meet with women in your organization and ask them what would make their working lives more livable (see Retention Practice #1), then provide what you can as an investment in keeping all employees.

- Provide a clear policy and training in sexual harassment, do not tolerate offensive language or behavior, and monitor, through surveys, the degree to which the work environment is friendly to women.
- Train all those who interview not to ask such illegal and discriminatory questions as "Do you have children" or "Do you intend to start a family?"
- When hiring at all levels, make sure that at least one woman is on your shortlist of candidates.

Race

- Widen your pool of candidates (see Retention Practice #13) by recruiting through a broader selection of high schools, colleges, community associations, and publications.
- Start a buddy or mentoring program (see Retention Practice #14) to make sure that members of racial minorities know they are valued and to encourage socializing and communication across racial lines.
- Ask the company to provide training on racism and the business benefits of diversity for your work unit.
- Hold regular career discussions with members of racial minorities (see Retention Practice #21). Partner with them in helping them prepare for higher-level positions.
- Do not tolerate racial slurs and inappropriate jokes.
- Don't withhold negative job performance feedback with people of color; it is the only way they will know how to improve.
- Don't assume that one person of color speaks for all members of that group or that all members of a group share the same perspective. Treat each person as an individual.

Age

- Meet regularly with older workers to let them know how much you value them.
- Invest in their training and development as you would with other employers. Encourage them to pursue whatever training they may need to keep their skills up-to-date.
- Have ongoing career discussions with your older employees.
- Look for opportunities to recruit semiretired workers who may be interested in part-time, contract, project, or flextime work arrangements (see Retention Practice #13).
- Instead of assuming that older workers will want to pursue full-

time retirement, offer them the opportunity to reduce their working hours on a gradual "phase-down" basis.
- Provide training for all employees on intergenerational differences, teamwork, and communication.
- Confront performance problems just as you would with other employees.

Religion

- Show respect for religious differences by asking those in your work unit to let you know about any special needs they have with regard to religious practices or holiday celebrations. Make a calendar of religious holidays for the coming year to avoid work conflicts.
- Consider moving to a total paid time-off program instead of having traditional distinctions such as sick days, vacation days, holidays, and personal days.
- Do not tolerate offensive or disparaging remarks against any religion or beliefs that may be creating a hostile environment. Likewise, do not tolerate unwelcome proselytizing.
- Train all who interview about the impropriety of asking questions about a candidate's religious affiliation.

Ethnicity

- Consider providing language training to those who want to improve their English skills (see Retention Practice #1).
- Survey foreign-born workers to find out whether they are being treated with respect and what they may need to assist with their acculturation and development.
- Consider taking a class in languages spoken by foreign-born workers in your work group.
- Do not tolerate stereotyping or put-downs of those from minority ethnic groups.
- Do not insist on English fluency unless it is truly critical to job performance.
- Encourage social interaction among all workers regardless of ethnic background.

Hierarchy/Class

- Break down class barriers in your organization by including all employees at social events whenever possible. Create opportunities for socializing via sports teams, investment clubs, fun committees, and "lunch and learn"–type events.

- Solicit suggestions from those lower in the company hierarchy about how to make the workplace and the work processes better.
- Review all perks and privileges in your work unit and explore ways they might be expanded to all workers or eliminated entirely if they create resentment.
- Open up your recruiting to a wide range of schools and colleges, not just an exclusive few.
- Assume that all workers want a career, not just a job. Meet regularly to discuss their career aspirations.

Sexual Orientation

- Announce to your work group that you value talent and diversity of all kinds in building and retaining a strong team.
- Confront discrimination and inappropriate slurs and jokes that you observe in the workplace.
- Be aware of the wide range of views that all people in your work group may hold regarding sexual orientation.
- Find out whether your human resources department has a policy that prohibits discrimination based on sexual orientation.
- Focus only on the individual's ability to do the job when hiring, promoting, rewarding, and selecting for special assignments and training.

Family Situation

- Conduct regular exit and stay interviews and focus groups to find out what family-friendly services may help to retain workers with child or elder care responsibilities (see Retention Practices #1 and 4).
- Meet with the entire work group to discuss what is fair and practical for all.
- Familiarize yourself with the Family and Medical Leave Act and its implications.
- Be willing to experiment with work-at-home and job-sharing arrangements.
- Measure performance and make promotion and pay decisions on the basis of results, not of time spent at work.
- Encourage men as well as women to use family-friendly services.

Disability

- Express your interest in hiring people with disabilities to your human resources department and/or senior managers.

- Give careful consideration and the benefit of the doubt to those with disabilities in hiring situations.
- Make a special effort to prepare the workplace to accommodate disabled workers prior to their first day on the job. Pay regular attention to their needs and progress, especially during the first several months on the job.
- If you are not sure how to deal with an individual's disability, contact a professional with extensive experience working with those who have disabilities.
- Don't hesitate to confront performance problems because of a person's disability.
- Don't isolate those with disabilities by avoiding normal contact.
- Finally, don't forget to consider the situation of white males in the workplace. Many white men are concerned about quotas or designated affirmative action positions. When they express resistance to diversity initiatives, listen carefully. White men also need assurance that they will be evaluated on the basis of their performance and given every opportunity to participate in career development programs and to advance within the organization.

Retaining All Generations

This section presents information on techniques for retaining people of different ages as part of your workforce.[3]

Retaining "Nexters"

Generational Profile

There are 73 million Americans born between 1980 and 2000 who are now entering the workforce in significant numbers.

Emerging Values and Beliefs

- Optimistic
- Have a sense of civic duty
- Are confident
- Are achievement-oriented
- Are resilient
- Are sociable
- Are street-smart
- Are accepting of diversity

Emerging Talents

- Are techno-literate.
- Are goal-oriented.
- Are willing to follow strong leader.
- Are team players.
- Have a strong sense of fairness and ethics.

Managing and Retaining "Nexters"

- Put energy and time into getting them off to a good start.
- Appeal to their desire to be team players.
- Give them a strong team leader.
- Expand your training capabilities to feed their desire for learning.
- Match them up with seasoned workers for mentoring.
- See all Retention Practices, but especially #1, 3, 8, 10, 11, 13–18, and 24.

Retaining Generation X[4]

Generational Profile

There are about 52 million Americans born between 1960 and 1979, and they constitute about 35 percent of the workforce and almost 40 percent of computer workers.

Key Common Values and Beliefs

- Dues paying is obsolete.
- Satisfying work should offer short-term dividends.
- People should "work to live," not "live to work."
- Large companies and institutions will not look out for their employees' best interests.
- Workers must keep investing in themselves because they cannot count on others to do it.
- Workers must look at themselves as free agents and sole proprietors of their careers.

Common Talents among This Generation

- Have computer skills.
- Are independent and self-reliant.
- Are not intimidated by authority.
- Are career-resilient. Are capable of multitasking.
- Are focused on immediate results.

- Enjoy independent problem solving.
- Are flexible.

Effective Motivators

- Acquiring new skill or knowledge
- Having an objective, the freedom to achieve in their own way
- Having available the newest hardware and software
- Having relatively few rules
- Working in a fun and relaxed workplace
- Meeting challenges to their creativity
- Being responsible for achieving tangible results
- Receiving immediate feedback

How to Manage and Retain Gen X'ers

- Tell them you look forward to having a win-win relationship no matter how long they may stay.
- Let them know that you are committed to helping them achieve their goals within the context of the company's goals. Don't mention climbing the corporate ladder or paying their dues. Too many X'ers have seen their parents lose their jobs after years of ladder climbing and dues paying.
- Let them know that you will provide as much training as possible to help them develop new skills and knowledge while they are there. Allow them some input into what training they will receive.
- Tell them you will challenge their creativity, then keep your promise by giving them a challenging assignment or problem to solve.
- Provide opportunities for them to work in spirited team situations, but with opportunities for individual achievement and recognition.
- Make the work environment fun and informal. Introduce them to others and encourage the development of workplace friendships.
- Without hovering, allow them to experience a daily sense of tangible achievement.
- Give them opportunities to reinvent themselves within the organization by learning new skills, moving cross-functionally, redesigning their jobs, finding a new mentor, working flexible hours, or from a different location.
- Open a dialogue with them on day one about how you want to keep them and how you are willing to work with them to make that happen. Create a "personal retention plan" with them, outlining the types of roles and responsibilities they may be able to take on in the future.
- Look for opportunities to engage them in short-term, goal-oriented

projects that will bring about fast-track development and give them opportunities for tangible achievement.

- When X'ers say they want to leave, give them the option of continuing to contribute as a part-timer, flex-timer, telecommuter, periodic temp, or consultant. Consider offering them sabbaticals, then welcome them back (see Retention Practice #4).[5,6]
- See Retention Practices #14 through 24, and especially #5, 8, 16, 17, 18, 22, and 24.

Retaining Boomers

Generational Profile

There are 72 million Americans born between 1943 and 1960, and they make up 53 percent of the workforce.

Key Common Values and Beliefs

- Question authority.
- Believe in growth and expansion—and the promise of the future.
- Believe that the traditional hierarchy no longer works.
- Expect participative management.
- Support equal rights for women and minorities.
- Foster self-understanding and fulfillment.

Common Talents

- Are service-oriented, eager to please.
- Are good team players.
- Want to get along well with others.
- Accept diversity.
- Are idealistic.
- Are driven.

Effective Motivators

- Opportunity to use satisfying abilities
- Sense of being important to organization's success
- Opportunities for growth and learning
- Recognition and praise
- Managers who care about them personally
- Pay in proportion to contribution
- Doing work they believe in

Managing and Retaining Boomers

- Challenge them to be change agents.
- Make the workplace warm and humane.
- Show them how your company is on the leading edge.
- Explain the larger meaning of their work.
- Treat them as unique individuals.
- Provide learning and growth opportunities.
- Recognize their accomplishments.
- Ask, don't tell.
- See especially Retention Practices #3, 5, 11, 15, 20, 21, and 22.

Retaining Traditionalists

Generational Profile

Traditionalists, born between 1922 and 1943, constitute about 25 percent of the workforce and hold 75 percent of all the financial assets in the United States.

Common Values and Beliefs

- Hard work and self-discipline
- Dedication and sacrifice
- Respect for authority
- Patience and delayed gratification
- Adherence to rules and order
- Consistency and uniformity

Common Talents

- Strong work ethic
- Respect for authority
- Strong leadership style
- Loyaly as followers
- Perseverance in getting the job done
- Endurance through hard times

Effective Motivators

- Sense of duty
- Clear understanding of results expected
- Support of company's long-term goals
- Opportunities to mentor younger workers

- Personal, face-to-face communication
- Traditional perks, visual symbols of status

Managing and Retaining Traditionalists

- Take plenty of time to orient them.
- Let them know you see their age and experience as assets, not liabilities.
- Train them in technology; many are more comfortable with it and curious about it than you may think.
- Find them a strong leader whose experience they will respect.
- Coach them tactfully and with respect.
- Consider approaching them with the idea of staying on past normal retirement age in a part-time or consulting role. "Phased retirement" has become an increasingly popular choice among this generation.
- See Retention Practices #3, 12, 14, 15, 16, 19, and 20 in particular.

Managing and Retaining Creative Talent and Technical Professionals

- Allow them to be themselves at work; casual dress is important.
- Let them individualize and decorate their own work areas.
- Allow them flexible hours.
- Give them a sense of mission and describe expected results, then let them find their own best way to achieve those results.
- Understand that their primary loyalty is to their profession or craft, not to the organization.
- Provide cutting-edge technologies and tools.
- Focus on giving them a sense of career momentum and challenge, not just through promotions, but laterally; give them "plum assignments," give them "fascinating challenges," and put them on "coveted project teams" whenever possible.
- Give them regular briefings on the business imperatives of the organization and how customers benefit directly from their contributions. Keep providing them with the "big picture," updating it on a frequent basis.
- Offer tenure-based bonuses payable after one or two years on the job instead of up-front signing bonuses.
- Provide plenty of acknowledgment and recognition. Acclaim from their respected peers is particularly motivating. Consider incorporating peer reviews into your performance management process.

- Allow them to work in a highly collaborative way with small, close-knit teams.
- Provide food breaks and other amenities to boost morale when long hours are required.
- Appoint managers with technical or creative backgrounds to manage them, but make sure they have the necessary people management talent and the ability to refrain from micromanaging the technical details. Manager should be adept at providing administrative support, running interference, and sheltering the technical types from bureaucratic obstacles.
- Consider allowing them a small percentage of time to work on a creative project of their choosing.
- Stage lots of celebrations.
- Be honest with your feedback.
- Increase research and development spending when possible.
- Tolerate, even celebrate, intelligent failure.
- Allow, even encourage, "contrarian" thinking.
- Conduct "focus groups" with these workers to find out about their hobbies and personal interests, then adapt your recruiting efforts to source other workers like them (see Retention Practice #13, Cisco Systems).

Retaining Entry-Level Workers

- Focus first of all on creating a workforce-friendly and family-friendly work environment, and benefits that demonstrate your commitment to keeping good people (see Retention Practice #1, Wilton Conner and SAS Institute). If you are not sure what benefits or employee services would be most valued by your people, ask them!
- Resolve to keep wages competitive with what others in your industry pay entry-level workers. If you implement other key retention practices, you should not have to pay more than your competitors.
- Consider offering cash bonuses or additional benefits, such as tuition reimbursement (Hereford House) or health benefits for part-timers (Starbucks) for those who stay for six months or a year, or signing bonuses where payment is withheld for three months (Burger King) or longer.
- Consider implementing performance bonuses or gainsharing programs that allow employees to share in the rewards that come from meeting group productivity or quality goals or objectives related to satisfaction of customers, guests, or patients.

- Conduct exit interviews religiously and comprehensively to uncover the real reasons (usually different from the stated reasons) why good employees are leaving so that you can correct the situation.
- Conduct regular "morale audit" surveys (Springfield Remanufacturing) to keep your finger on the pulse of employees' attitudes. Many of their concerns will be "little problems," but if you show you are paying enough attention and are willing to resolve them, you will purchase a higher degree of commitment from your employees.
- Practice a "weed and feed" approach to manager selection and development. If your managers are driving away your entry-level workers, you need to either terminate them, move them into non-management roles, or provide them with the feedback and coaching necessary to help them change the way they manage people. Consider making a certain percentage of each manager's bonus contingent on the yearly avoidable, voluntary turnover rate on his or her team (Entex).
- Look for opportunities to redesign entry-level jobs to provide more skill variety, task completion, task significance, autonomy, or feedback (see Retention Practice #5, especially UPS example of redesigning drivers' job duties).
- Conduct in-depth interviews with entry-level high performers who stay in their jobs and display a high degree of commitment. Ask what keeps them there, then use this information to source and select more like them.
- Start an employee referral program that rewards current employees for referring people who become new hires and stay for a set period (see Retention Practice #10). Be sure to ask them about good people with whom they may have worked at their former employers.
- Expand your universe of possible employee sources (see Retention Practice #13). Be sure to consider the mentally or physically handicapped, welfare-to-work candidates, and nontraditional workers, such as teenagers, homemakers, or older people who may want to take on a part-time job.
- Think about offering cash for those who show up to interview. Offer discount days exclusively for employees of competing stores. Provide a van pool or bus service to bring people to interviews and to work after they are employed. Develop relationships with high school counselors and officials at the state job service, community centers, and welfare centers so that they will become good referral sources.
- Require all applicants to complete a thorough screening, interviewing and testing process. The 11,000-employee Cessna Aircraft plant in Wichita has reduced turnover significantly by implementing what is called "integrity testing," a written survey that asks employees to

respond to direct questions about past behavior such as drug use and criminal acts. Remarkably, many employees do respond honestly when asked such questions in a written format.

- Make sure each new employee receives a realistic job preview (see Retention Practice #8), in which the manager fully describes the upside as well as the downside of the work and the environment. Alternatively, allow applicants to become "interns" before committing to full-time employment (Jiffy Lube), give them an extended tour, or allow them to spend a day on the job as an observer prior to hire.
- Assign each new hire a "buddy" to watch over the newcomer, and pay attention to their needs and progress during the first few weeks and months.
- On their first day of employment, be sure to let them know they are an important part of the team, and ask them to promise they will come and speak with you first before they ever decide to quit.
- Make sure all managers are thoroughly trained in effective techniques for coaching front-line employees, including giving frequent praise and offering corrective feedback. Monitor their performance to make sure they are providing positive coaching and supervision techniques, including giving employees freedom to take the initiative and make customer service decisions wherever possible.
- Reward and praise your managers for thinking up new ways to recognize and reward their people, and for coming up with new ideas to bring more fun and humor into the workplace (Southwest Airlines).

Retaining During Downsizings and Mergers & Acquisitions

A few facts to consider:

- Almost half of all mergers that took place in the 1990s failed to achieve their financial objectives.[7]
- More than 70 percent of employees who remained in downsized organizations were reported as feeling insecure in their jobs.[8]
- The best performers—those who are most marketable and have the most career options—are the ones most likely to leave during an organizational transition.[9]
- Almost 75 percent of sixty-five merged companies admitted that they had failed to put employees in the right jobs within the first six months of their merged operations.[10]

Guidelines for Retaining Employees during Times of Transition

- Develop a process to identify key individuals and positions needed in the transition and in the new organization.
- Focus on retaining the true "value creators" in the organization, not just top management players.
- Determine how long you need to keep various people on the basis of business needs, and offer them stay bonuses as appropriate.
- Assess employees against key competencies required for key positions. Use these to objectively assess talents you will retain to meet important business needs.
- Remember—when you dictate objectives, people show less commitment, but when the process is collaborative, there is visibly more commitment. Involve key talent in a "retention task force" where they can have input into workforce planning and participate in discussions to help determine what it will take to keep key talent in the new organization.
- Determine which individuals will need to be relocated, if any, as early as possible in the transition process.
- Tell people what you know as quickly as you know it, and tell them what you do not know.
- Try to minimize the time that employees must endure a period of uncertainty about whether they will be staying or leaving.
- Consider developing a retention bonus plan for those considered absolutely critical to the organization's success during and after the transition.
- Understand up-front that retention bonuses can have unintended consequences and limited success. Those who get stay bonuses may be seen as "the anointed ones" by those who don't receive such bonuses. Be prepared to risk losing these people. Those who receive the bonuses will also have a date by which they can voluntarily leave the organization and still receive a bonus.
- Approach all those you want to retain one-on-one and let them know they are important to the organization's success. The simple phrase "I need your help" has a kind of magic in it. "Re-recruit" these people by letting them know what is in it for them if they choose to stay on.
- Try to retain all star performers and high performers even though their jobs may have been eliminated in the reorganization. This is the same principle by which professional sports teams draft "the best available athlete." However, be mindful of the fact that if you cannot find a challenge that fits their talent, you will not be able to keep them.

- Don't be too desperate to retain any one person. Design a "redeployment" plan by which individuals may explore reassignment, temporary assignment, relocation, and new job creation within the organization as a whole.
- Bear in mind that a merger is an involuntary career move for virtually every employee. Consider providing internal self-assessment and career decision workshops or counseling sessions for all employees to help them begin to take charge of their careers and get a better fix on where they might fit either inside or outside the new organization.
- Improve the flow of information to employees and listen to their concerns.
- Be clear, specific, and vivid in describing the mission, vision, and objectives of the new organization so that employees can see a light at the end of the tunnel.
- Invest in coaching and support to develop employees who are critical to the new organization.
- Recruit severed employees to come back and do temporary work to supplement their incomes. These temporary assignments sometimes lead to permanent positions, though this is a promise you must be careful not to make.
- Avoid waves of downsizings if at all possible—they only serve to diminish productivity and morale while heightening uncertainty for extended periods. "Do it all at once" is generally the best advice.

Try to Win Back Top Performers When They Resign

The following article, reprinted from "Across the Board," a publication of The Conference Board (1993), describes one company's determined and innovative approach to reducing turnover of top-performing employees after they have already announced their resignations:

> A top-notch employee quits. No, you don't have to accept it. T. J. Rodgers, a CEO who knows what to do when it happens, shares his secrets on how to keep it from happening:
>
> With people, as with most things in business, the best defense is a good offense. A company keeps its most valuable people by treating them fairly, rewarding their performance, and creating opportunities for them to do important work. But there comes a time when every company simply must play defense: A start-up is determined to steal one of your top salesmen, or a big company is launching a new product and wants three of your best young engineers. When it's time to play defense, and you have a good case to make, systems can improve your chances of winning.
>
> Two major systems help Cypress Semiconductor Corporation guard against raids from the outside. One is designed to seal off the company from headhunters. The other is designed to win reversals when a valued employee decides to leave Cypress. Without these systems there's no question our company would have lost some of its best people.

In any company, the first line of defense against headhunters is the support staff. That's because the first "barrier to entry" for headhunters trying to steal good people is finding out who they are. The names and titles of our vice presidents are public information; they're listed in our annual reports. The names and titles of all other people are confidential.

Headhunters cleverly manipulate the good intentions of support staff to obtain this valuable information. Their job is to say whatever it takes to obtain the roster of a department or the names of the members of a new-product team. Our job is to make their job as tough as possible.

Our defenses against headhunters begin with something as simple as the telephone book. We treat the Cypress telephone directory as a highly proprietary document. On every page of every company phone book, stamped in bright red, is the following warning:

CONFIDENTIAL. Not to be reproduced. Not to be taken off Cypress premises. This information is proprietary to Cypress. This stamp is in red. If it is in black, return it to your departmental secretary immediately!

Then "headhunter control" takes over. We like to test how good we are at protecting our borders. Twice in the last few years I've asked a "friendly" headhunter to penetrate Cypress. Both times the firm reported back that we were one of the toughest companies it had come up against.

Of course, it's impossible to completely seal off any company from raids by the competition. Top-quality employees are always receiving job offers. How you react to these offers—how quickly and effectively you make the case for staying with the company—determines how many people you keep or lose.

Five years ago, after a frustrating week in which I was called in at the very last minute to save two key people, I wrote a memo that articulated how our managers should fight to retain valued employees who quit. Intel Corp. inspired much of our approach; for many its system for retaining key people was a model for doing it right. We modified and added to the Intel principles and developed a system whose batting average has been about .500. This is an excellent turnaround figure that makes our rivals' recruitment jobs exactly twice as hard as they expected—a great reason to recruit elsewhere.

Here's the memo. It speaks for itself. Our biggest headache is getting people to follow the procedures. Every year or so we make another set of copies of the memo, distribute them to our vice presidents and top managers, and remind them how we are supposed to do things.

Cypress Semiconductor Corp. Internal Correspondence
DATE: Feb. 24, 1988
TITLE: What to Do When a Valued Employee Quits

I have not been called upon to save a valued employee for quite some time. Last week, I became involved in two such instances, both successful, but my job was made much more difficult by our not following the fundamental principles of what to do when an employee quits.

I realized that I never have stated formally what our policy is concerning resignations. Here it is:

- 1. *React immediately (within five minutes).* There is nothing more important to do than to react immediately to an employee who has quit (presuming the employee is one whom we are intent upon keeping). The next activity you have scheduled should be canceled; any delay (such as, "I'll talk to you after our staff meeting") is unacceptable. There are two purposes for reacting with a sense of urgency. First, it demonstrates to the employee that he does take precedence over daily activities, and second, it gives you the greatest chance of changing the employee's mind before an irreversible decision has been made.

- 2. *Keep the resignation secret.* To the greatest extent possible, you should prevent the knowledge of a resignation from being publicly disclosed. Keeping the resignation absolutely under wraps is important for both parties. For the employee, it removes a major barrier to changing his mind and staying with the company, that of appearing to vacillate on a major decision. Once the employee's ego gets attached to a decision, right or wrong, he is very unlikely to change course. If other employees are unaware that a resignation has occurred, the employee who has resigned does not face the embarrassment of a public reversal. The company also is given more latitude when a public announcement has not been made. When I managed to convince one employee to remain at Cypress, there were multiple rumors (all untrue) that the company changed his mind by "buying him back." The company does not negotiate the salaries of employees who have resigned.

In addition to the obvious conclusion that management should never disseminate information about a resignation, management should also do everything possible to prevent the employee from doing so. Usually, the best way to convince an employee not to disseminate resignation information is to state the arguments given above: that the employee limits his own flexibility for the future and may unwittingly damage his reputation if he decides to stay.

- 3. *Tell your boss immediately.* When an employee resigns, I expect instantaneous communication all the way up through the chain of command to me. I expect that communication to happen within an hour of the time a resignation is received. I will consider management to have done a poor job if any resignation takes more than that time to get to my attention. I can be interrupted in meetings, called out of meetings in outside locations, or called at home (I am listed in the telephone directory). There is no excuse for not informing me (and everyone in the chain of command between the individual and me) immediately when a resignation occurs.

- 4. *Listen carefully to the employee.* Once a resignation has occurred and the proper people have been informed, the manager of the individual and his VP should sit down and talk to the employee, listening very carefully to ascertain the exact reasons for the resignation. Any attempt to rescue the employee will be impaired severely unless management listens to exactly what the employee has to say and accepts it.

The message from the employee should be transmitted up through the chain of command without any changes, even if it is unflattering to the manager involved. (For example, "I quit because I do not like working for you." Perhaps the company can find useful employment for a valued employee working in another group). An exact determination must be made of what the employee's options are at the other company. Is the employee looking at a better job, more money, slower pace, faster pace, or a fundamental change in career? These issues obviously will be key in formulating an argument to change the employee's mind.

■ 5. *Construct your arguments.* Once accurate data have been gathered, you and your VP should sit down and put together a plan to convince the employee to stay, if that is possible. In some cases, a realistic assessment of the situation will dictate that you not try to keep the employee. When Russ Winslow quit Cypress to start his own company, the only reaction that made sense was to wish him good luck. Ninety percent of the time, however, a good argument can be made that it is in the employee's best interest to stay at Cypress. The only possible effective argument to retain an employee is one that validly claims that the employee's best interests are served by staying at Cypress.

Typically, an employee will have quit for two simultaneous reasons: a "push" of some sort having to do with long-standing frustrations at Cypress, and a "pull" from another company at which the "grass appears to be greener." A successful retention argument will expose the advantages perceived for the other company as unrealistic, as well as offer a real solution to some of the problems that caused the employee to consider leaving in the first place. Once you and your VP have formulated your first-cut employee-retention arguments, I should become involved to help set the overall strategy. This strategy should be defined and refined the very day the employee resigns.

■ 6. *Use all the horsepower at your disposal to win.* With a carefully constructed strategy in place, we can then proceed to win back the employee. The employee first got the message that quitting was a big deal because of your rapid reaction to his resignation. We then reminded the employee that the company truly was interested in him because we listened to what was wrong for as long as it took to hear out the problem.

On the second day, the employee should be given the message that his quitting was a mistake, that the company knows it was a mistake, and that the company will single-mindedly try to rectify that mistake. (Cypress will accept only two answers to our proposal that you stay: "Yes" and "We'll talk about it some more.") On the second or third days, during which our position is being presented, the employee should be given the firm impression that we are not continuing business as usual. Schedules are interrupted. If appropriate, we may meet over meals outside the plant during off-hours.

If the employee's spouse is a major factor in the resignation, the spouse is involved in the discussions. Any level of management required to get the job done is brought in. If it takes the president to get the job done (and it does in half the cases), then the president has nothing more important to do than to sit down with the employee. One of the greatest mistakes middle managers make when an employee quits is to assume that I am too busy to interrupt my schedule to keep a good person in the company.

■ 7. *Win back the employee by solving his problems.* If our arguments are constructed in a timely manner and really do correct the problems that caused the employee to start looking around, we will be successful more than 80 percent of the time in causing the employee to change his mind. Most often, resigning employees like Cypress, its benefits, and the people with whom they work. They usually are threatening to leave because they do not like some of the particulars of their job or their direct supervisor.

Their resolve to leave is strengthened further because they have found a job (typically) at a company that is a poor second to Cypress, but which at a first glance appears to offer some relative benefits. By eliminating the root problem at Cypress and stressing the fundamental differences between us and the other company, the employee usually can be made to agree that staying is best.

■ 8. *Wipe out the competitor.* The next step in the process is to shut down the other company. Two objectives are important here: to shut down the competitor so firmly that no further negotiations occur with our employee, and to make the competitor believe that it has wasted its time in trying to hire Cypress employees.

Get the employee to agree to call up the competitor and shut down its offer himself. He should firmly state that counter-offers and continuing negotiation are not desired, that he is going to stay at Cypress, and that his decision is absolutely final. Ask the employee to present the data to the competitor in such a manner as to discourage the company from continuing to hire other Cypress employees. For example: "There was no counteroffer; I just want to stay at Cypress. I think my long-term best interests are served by being here. The same hour that I told my boss at Cypress I was thinking about leaving, I had meetings with my boss, his VP, and T. J. Rodgers. When they made comparisons between my career at Cypress and at your company, it was clear to me that I had made a mistake in thinking about leaving Cypress. I really do not want to take any time to come over to your company to talk to you; my mind is made up. It would not be helpful to change your offer monetarily; I am fairly paid and have a good stock option. The issue is not money."

APPENDIX B

Exit Survey

Name: _____

Hire Date: _____ Resignation Date: _____

Department: _____ Manager: _____

Briefly indicate what factors first caused you to consider leaving the company. _____
_____

Briefly indicate what factors triggered your leaving the company at this time. _____
_____

What is your overall opinion of the company?
   Please rate the following using this scale:
   1 = excellent, 2 = good, 3 = fair, 4 = poor

_____ Benefits

_____ Pay

_____ Recruiting Process

_____ Orientation Process

_____ Initial Training

_____ Interest in Employees

_____ Growth Opportunities

_____ Ongoing Training

_____ Physical Working Conditions

_____ Keeping Employees Informed

_____   Treating Employees Fairly

_____   Upholding Company Values

_____   Morale Overall

_____   Open-Door Policy

_____   Morale in Your Area

_____   Performance Review Process

_____   Helpfulness/Knowledge of Human Resources

_____   Medical/Health Benefits

_____   Other Benefits

_____   Cooperation among All Employees and Management

_____   Equipment/Resources to Do Job Properly

_____   Recognition for Job Well Done

_____   Incentive/Bonus Program

_____   Communication of Internal Opportunities

_____   Company's Concern with Quality and Excellence

_____   Overall Company Image

Please comment on any 1 or 2 scores in the space below:

_____

_____

_____

_____

Please rate your manager using this scale:
   1 = always 2 = usually 3 = seldom 4 = never

_____   Resolved complaints and concerns promptly.

_____   Listened to suggestions.

_____   Encouraged cooperation.

_____   Treated you fairly.

_____   Provided leadership.

_____   Clearly communicated expectations.

_____   Was honest.

_____   Gave performance feedback.

—————————   Coached, trained, and developed you.

—————————   Recognized accomplishments.

—————————   Provided appropriate and challenging assignments.

—————————   Built teamwork.

Please comment on any 1 or 2 scores in the space below:

_____

_____

_____

_____

_____

Do you have another job? If so, how does it compare with your last job
here? _____

_____

What did you like most about your last job? _____

_____

What did you like least about your last job? _____

_____

What could have been done to encourage you not to leave? _____

_____

Was this made known to your manager? _____

Why did you originally join the company? _____

_____

What did you like most about the company? _____

_____

What did you like least about the company? _____

_____

Would you be open to the idea of returning to our company? _____

_____

Why/Why not? _____

_____

Do you have any objection to our sharing your responses with management? _____

_____

Do you think the company lives up to its values? _____ Yes _____ No

If no, which values did we not live up to, and how can we change for the better? _____

_____

What other suggestions do you have that will help the company improve?

_____

_____

_____

_____

What suggestions do you have that will help the company keep good people? _____

_____

_____

_____

Any other comments you would like to add at this time:

_____

_____

_____

_____

Appendix C

Job Enrichment Rating

Employee Name: _____

Job Title: _____

Instructions: Circle "High," "Moderate," or "Low," depending on the degree of each factor that you believe is regularly provided in this employee's job.

1. Skill Variety: A desired mix of skills and activities is required to carry out the work.

    High   Moderate   Low

    Ideas to increase skill variety:

2. Task Completion: The job is undertaken as a whole, allowing the employee to complete an identifiable piece of work from beginning to end with a visible outcome.

    High   Moderate   Low

    Ideas to increase task completion:

3. Task Significance: The job has a recognizable impact on the overall mission or on other people inside or outside the organization.

    High   Moderate   Low

    Ideas to increase task significance:

4. Autonomy: The job offers substantial freedom, independence, and discretion in scheduling the work and in choosing the procedures to be used in carrying it out.

    High   Moderate   Low

    Ideas to increase autonomy:

5. Feedback: The job provides feedback—by the observable progress and results of the job itself, and from customers, co-workers and manager.

    High   Moderate   Low

Ideas to increase feedback:

Appendix D

Competency Inventories

A. LEARNING

____ Learn quickly	____ Learn by reading/study
____ Grasp concepts	____ Learn by hearing
____ Learn by example	____ Willingness to seek feedback
____ Learn by doing	____ Willingness to develop self
____ Other: _____	

B. RESEARCH/ANALYSIS

____ Sense/notice/investigate	____ Identify problem/source
____ Research/gather data	____ Troubleshoot/test solutions
____ Compare/distinguish	____ Persist to find solution
____ Question/interview	____ Evaluate/learn from process
____ Organize/classify data	
____ Other: _____	

C. INNOVATION

____ See new relationships	____ Visualize/design
____ Synthesize data	____ Develop new products, pro-
____ Conceive new ideas	cesses, programs, systems,
____ Invent/create	etc.
____ Improvise resourcefully	
____ Other: _____	

D. HUMAN RELATIONS

____ Show empathy/sensitivity	____ Show tact/diplomacy
____ Be team player/cooperate	____ Help/serve others
____ Display warmth/sociability	____ Counsel/guide others
____ Build trust	
____ Other: _____	

E. SPOKEN COMMUNICATION

____ Listen well	____ Keep others informed
____ Express thoughts clearly	____ Contribute to group discus-
____ Express feelings assertively	sions
____ Give frequent feedback	____ Communicate in positive way
____ Make group presentation	____ Use language well
____ Other: _____	

F. WRITTEN COMMUNICATION

____ Write clearly	____ Proofread/edit
____ Write concisely	____ Take good notes
____ Write persuasively	____ Illustrate graphically
____ Other: _____	

G. TRAINING

____ Prepare sufficiently	____ Control time/process
____ Train interactively	____ Convey enthusiasm
____ Speak with authority	____ Illustrate concepts
____ Explain clearly	____ Maintain interest
____ Other: _____	

H. INFLUENCING OTHERS

____ Build rapport/trust   ____ Promote/advertise

____ Find others' self-interest/   ____ Recruit
needs
                                        ____ Mediate/arbitrate
____ See need to sell others
                                        ____ Negotiate
____ Overcome objections

____ Other: _____

I. LEADERSHIP

____ Take charge   ____ Focus on results

____ Build compelling vision   ____ Confront tough issues

____ Initiate change/take risk   ____ Use power appropriately

____ Build followership for vision   ____ Maintain motivation

____ Other: _____

J. PLANNING

____ Anticipate problems   ____ Prioritize tasks

____ Set realistic goals   ____ Set realistic schedule

____ Develop plan for attainment   ____ Establish controls

____ Other: _____

K. ORGANIZING

____ Establish logical systems   ____ Organize information and/or
                                        things
____ Organize people and tasks
                                        ____ Bring order out of chaos

____ Other: _____

L. PEOPLE MANAGEMENT

____ Communicate expectations   ____ Recognize/reward

____ Delegate tasks   ____ Correct/reprimand

____ Track progress   ____ Coach/develop others

____ Appraise performance   ____ Treat individuals fairly

                                        ____ Build teamwork

____ Other: _____

M. NUMERICAL/FINANCIAL

____ Calculate/figure   ____ Operate computers

____ Manage money/budgets   ____ Conduct audits

____ Do accounting/bookkeeping   ____ Handle purchasing

____ Do cost analysis/projections   ____ Find ways to minimize costs

____ Other: _____

N. EXECUTING/FOLLOWING THROUGH

____ Implement decisions   ____ Attend to details

____ Arrange/coordinate   ____ Deal with the unexpected

____ Expedite   ____ Get things done on time

____ Check/monitor   ____ Balance details with big picture

____ Other: _____

O. MANUAL/PHYSICAL

____ Eye/hand/foot coordination   ____ Fix/repair machines

____ Hand/finger dexterity   ____ Build/assemble

____ Operate/maintain machines   ____ Physical strength/agility

____ Other: _____

KNOWLEDGE INVENTORY

- _____   ▪ _____

- _____   ▪ _____

- _____   ▪ _____

- _____   ▪ _____

- _____   ▪ _____

- _____   ▪ _____

- _____   ▪ _____

SELF-MANAGEMENT TRAIT INVENTORY

___ Adaptable	___ Intuitive	___ Risk-taker
___ Ambitious	___ Kind	___ Self-accepting
___ Assertive	___ Logical	___ Self-aware
___ Bold	___ Loyal	___ Self-controlled
___ Careful	___ Mature	___ Self-motivated
___ Competitive	___ Methodical	___ Sense of humor
___ Confident	___ Open-minded	___ Sensitive
___ Conscientious	___ Optimistic	___ Shrewd
___ Cooperative	___ Orderly	___ Sincere
___ Courageous	___ Patient	___ Sociable
___ Curious	___ Perceptive	___ Spontaneous
___ Dedicated	___ Perfectionistic	___ Steady
___ Dependable	___ Pleasant	___ Strong-willed
___ Determined	___ Polished	___ Tactful
___ Direct	___ Practical	___ Team-oriented
___ Disciplined	___ Precise	___ Tenacious
___ Easygoing	___ Principled	___ Tender
___ Efficient	___ Progressive	___ Thoughtful
___ Empathetic	___ Punctual	___ Thrifty
___ Energetic	___ Questioning	___ Tolerant
___ Enthusiastic	___ Realistic	___ Tough-minded
___ Expressive	___ Reasonable	___ Trustworthy
___ Fair	___ Relaxed	___ Unassuming
___ Friendly	___ Reserved	___ Uncomplaining
___ Hardworking	___ Resourceful	___ Unpretentious
___ Honest	___ Respectful	___ Unselfish
___ Imaginative	___ Responsible	___ Wise
___ Independent	___ Results-oriented	___ Witty
___ Intelligent		

MOTIVATION INVENTORY

____ To advance or be promoted	____ To earn financial payoffs
____ To gain control or authority	____ To create a product or process
____ To realize a vision	____ To build an enterprise
____ To achieve measurable results	____ To have an impact
____ To make specific improvements	____ To be a change agent
____ To master a craft or process	____ To compete and win
____ To gain recognition	____ To achieve distinction
____ To gain and impart expertise	____ To exploit hidden opportunities
____ To pioneer or discover	____ To achieve elite status
____ To respond to a challenge	____ To overcome adversity
____ To meet high expectations	____ To contribute to society

APPENDIX E

Candidate Profile/ Evaluation

Candidate's Name: _____

Position Applying for: _____

Key Talents Desired

	High				Low
	1	2	3	4	5
	1	2	3	4	5
	1	2	3	4	5
	1	2	3	4	5
	1	2	3	4	5

Key Knowledge Desired:

	1	2	3	4	5
	1	2	3	4	5

	1	2	3	4	5

	1	2	3	4	5

	1	2	3	4	5

Key Self-Management Traits Desired:

	1	2	3	4	5

	1	2	3	4	5

	1	2	3	4	5

	1	2	3	4	5

	1	2	3	4	5

Key Motivations Desired:

	1	2	3	4	5

	1	2	3	4	5

Interview conducted and evaluated by: _____ Date: _____

APPENDIX F

Performance Agreement

Date: _____

To: _____

From: _____

Within the period: _____ the following will be accomplished:

I. Key Result Area: _____

_____

_____

OBJECTIVES: DATE

_____   _____

_____   _____

_____   _____

_____   _____

II. Key Result Area: _____

_____

_____

OBJECTIVES: DATE

_____   _____

_____   _____

_____   _____

_____   _____

III. Key Result Area: _____

_____

_____

OBJECTIVES: DATE

_____   _____

_____   _____

_____   _____

_____   _____

Progress toward these objectives will be reviewed at weekly meetings.

I understand that meeting these objectives will be the most significant factor in my performance evaluation and compensation.

Employee's Signature _____

Manager's Signature _____

APPENDIX G

Characteristics Frequently Associated with Different Temperament Types*

ISTJ	ISFJ	INFJ	INTJ
Quiet, serious, earn success by thoroughness and dependability. Practical, matter-of-fact, realistic, and responsible. Decide logically what should be done and work toward it steadily, regardless of distractions. Take pleasure in making everything orderly and organized—their work, their home, their life. Value traditions and loyalty.	Quiet, friendly, responsible, and conscientious. Committed and steady in meeting their obligations. Thorough, painstaking, and accurate. Loyal, considerate, notice, and remember specifics about people who are important to them, concerned with how others feel. Strive to create an orderly and harmonious environment at work and at home.	Seek meaning and connection in ideas, relationships, and material possessions. Want to understand what motivates people. Are insightful about others. Conscientious and committed to their firm values. Develop a clear vision about how best to serve the common good. Organized and decisive in implementing their vision.	Have original minds and great drive for implementing their ideas and achieving their goals. Quickly see patterns in external events and develop long-range explanatory perspectives. When committed, organize a job and carry it through. Skeptical and independent, have high standards of competence and performance—for themselves and others.
ISTP	**ISFP**	**INFP**	**INTP**
Tolerant and flexible, quiet observers until a problem appears, then act quickly to find workable solutions. Analyze what makes things work and readily get through large amounts of data to isolate the core of practical problems. Interested in cause and effect. Organize facts using logical principles. Value efficiency.	Quiet, friendly, sensitive, and kind. Enjoy the present moment, what's going on around them. Like to have their own space and to work within their own time frame. Loyal and committed to their values and to people who are important to them. Dislike disagreements and conflicts, do not force their opinions or values on others.	Idealistic, loyal to their values and to people who are important to them. Want an external life that is congruent with their values. Curious, quick to see possibilities; can be catalysts for implementing ideas. Seek to understand people and to help them fulfill their potential. Adaptable, flexible, and accepting unless a value is threatened.	Seek to develop logical explanations for everything that interests them. Theoretical and abstract, interested more in ideas than in social interaction. Quiet, contained, flexible, and adaptable. Have unusual ability to focus in depth to solve problems in their area of interest. Skeptical, sometimes critical; always analytical.

(*continues*)

(continued)

ESTP	ESFP	ENFP	ENTP
Flexible and tolerant, they take a pragmatic approach focused on immediate results. Theories and conceptual explanations bore them—they want to act energetically to solve the problem. Focus on the here-and-now, spontaneous, enjoy each moment that they can be active with others. Enjoy material comfort and style. Learn best through doing.	Outgoing, friendly, and accepting. Exuberant lovers of life, people, and material comforts. Enjoy working with others to make things happen. Bring common sense and a realistic approach to their work, and make work fun. Flexible and spontaneous, adapt readily to new people and environments. Learn best by trying a new skill with other people.	Warmly enthusiastic and imaginative. See life as full of possibilities. Make connections between events and information very quickly, and confidently proceed based on the patterns they see. Want a lot of affirmation from others, and readily give appreciation and support. Spontaneous and flexible; often rely on their ability to improvise and their verbal fluency.	Quick, ingenious, stimulating, alert, and outspoken. Resourceful in solving new and challenging problems. Adept at generating conceptual possibilities and then analyzing them strategically. Good at reading other people. Bored by routine, will seldom do the same thing the same way, apt to turn to one new interest after another.

ESTJ	ESFJ	ENFJ	ENTJ
Practical, realistic, matter-of-fact. Decisive, quickly move to implement decisions. Organize projects and people to get things done, focus on getting results in the most efficient way possible. Take care of routine details. Have a clear set of logical standards, systematically follow them and want others to also. Forceful in implementing their plans.	Warmhearted, conscientious, and cooperative. Want harmony in their environment, work with determination to establish it. Like to work with others to complete tasks accurately and on time. Loyal, follow through even in small matters. Notice what others need in their day-by-day lives and try to provide it. Want to be appreciated for who they are and for what they contribute.	Warm, empathetic, responsive, and responsible. Highly attuned to the emotions, needs, and motivations of others. Find potential in everyone, want to help others fulfill their potential. May act as catalysts for individual and group growth. Loyal, responsive to praise and criticism. Sociable, facilitate others in a group, and provide inspiring leadership.	Frank, decisive, assume leadership readily. Quickly see illogical and inefficient procedures and policies, develop and implement comprehensive systems to solve organizational problems. Enjoy long-term planning and goal setting. Usually well informed, well read; enjoy expanding their knowledge and passing it on to others. Forceful in presenting ideas.

* I = Introverted; E = Extroverted; S = Sensing; N = Intuitive; T = Thinking; F = Feeling; J = Judging; P = Perceiving.

Manager-Employee Talent Inventory

	Importance	Ability	Comments:
A. LEARNING ABILITY Learn quickly, learn by reading/ study, grasp concepts, learn by hearing, learn by examples, willingness to seek feedback, learn by doing, willingness to develop self. Other:	5 4 3 2 1	5 4 3 2 1	
B. RESEARCH/ ANALYSIS Sense/notice/ investigate, identify problem/source, research/gather data, troubleshoot/test solutions, compare/distinguish, persist to find solution, question/interview, evaluate/learn from process, organize/ classify data. Other:	5 4 3 2 1	5 4 3 2 1	

	Importance	Ability	Comments:
C. INNOVATION See new relationships, improvise resourcefully, synthesize data, visualize/design, conceive new ideas, develop new products/processes, invent/create programs, systems, etc. Other:	5 4 3 2 1	5 4 3 2 1	
D. HUMAN RELATIONS Show empathy/sensitivity, show tact/diplomacy, be team player, cooperate, help/serve others, display warmth/sociability, counsel/guide others, build trust. Other:	5 4 3 2 1	5 4 3 2 1	
E. SPOKEN COMMUNICATION Listen well, keep others informed, express thoughts clearly, contribute to group discussions, express feelings assertively, communicate in positive way, give frequent feedback, use language well, make group presentations. Other:	5 4 3 2 1	5 4 3 2 1	
F. WRITTEN COMMUNICATION Write clearly and concisely, write persuasively, take good notes, proofread/edit, illustrate graphically. Other:	5 4 3 2 1	5 4 3 2 1	

	Importance	Ability	Comments:
G. TRAINING Prepare sufficiently, control time/process, train interactively, convey enthusiasm, speak with authority, illustrate concepts, explain clearly, maintain interest. Other:	5 4 3 2 1	5 4 3 2 1	
H. INFLUENCING OTHERS Build rapport/trust, promote/advertise, find others' self-interest/needs, recruit, see need to sell others, mediate/arbitrate, overcome discouragement, negotiate. Other:	5 4 3 2 1	5 4 3 2 1	
I. LEADERSHIP Take charge, focus on results, build compelling vision, confront tough issues, initiate change/take risks, use power appropriately, build followership for vision, maintain motivation. Other:	5 4 3 2 1	5 4 3 2 1	
J. PLANNING Anticipate problems, prioritize tasks, set realistic goals, set realistic schedule, develop plan for attainment, establish controls. Other:	5 4 3 2 1	5 4 3 2 1	

	Importance	Ability	Comments:
K. ORGANIZING Establish logical systems, organize information and/or things, organize people and tasks, bring order out of chaos. Other:	5 4 3 2 1	5 4 3 2 1	
L. PEOPLE MANAGEMENT Communicate expectations, correct/reprimand, delegate tasks, coach/develop others, track/appraise performance, build teamwork, recognize/reward. Other:	5 4 3 2 1	5 4 3 2 1	
M. NUMERICAL/FINANCIAL Calculate/figure, operate computers, manage money/budgets, conduct audits, do accounting/bookkeeping, handle purchasing, do cost analysis/projections, find ways to minimize costs. Other:	5 4 3 2 1	5 4 3 2 1	
N. EXECUTION/FOLLOW-THROUGH Implement decisions, attend to details, arrange/coordinate, deal with the unexpected, expedite, get things done on time, check/monitor, balance details with big picture. Other:	5 4 3 2 1	5 4 3 2 1	

	Importance	Ability	Comments:
O. MANUAL/ PHYSICAL	5	5	
Eye/hand/foot coordination, fix/repair machines, hand/finger dexterity, build/assemble, operate/maintain machines, physical agility. Other:	4 3 2 1	4 3 2 1	

Appendix I

Manager's Employee Development Planning Worksheet

Employee's Name: _____ Date: _____

Directions:

In preparation for a "development discussion" with the employee, write your answers to the following questions:

1. What are your primary performance expectations of the employee over the next six months?

2. What specific actions can the employee take now to improve skills and performance in the current assignment? (Consider on-the-job training, formal classroom training, action learning, rotational, shadow or project team assignments, committees, task forces, seminars, short courses, readings, self study, or the like.)

3. What specific action steps can you take to better match the employee's abilities to the needs and objectives of your team?

4. What positions, assignments, needs, or challenges can you anticipate that may provide appropriate opportunities for this employee over the next year and beyond?

5. What specific actions can you and the employee take now to prepare the employee for these opportunities and for longer-term professional growth?

APPENDIX J

Survey of Manager as Employee Developer

Directions: Read each statement and indicate the degree to which you feel the statement is typically true of your manager's behavior.

5 = Highly   4 = Very   3 = Moderately   2 = Somewhat   1 = Not at all

1. Provides a thorough orientation to new employees.	5	4	3	2	1
2. Teaches specific job-related or technical skills.	5	4	3	2	1
3. Makes sure I understand developmental priorities and objectives.	5	4	3	2	1
4. Makes sure I have specific goals in key performance areas.	5	4	3	2	1
5. Assigns work so that I am able to use my skills.	5	4	3	2	1
6. Communicates to me the formal and informal realities of progression in the organization.	5	4	3	2	1
7. Makes sure I have opportunities to develop.	5	4	3	2	1
8. Gives me feedback about my performance.	5	4	3	2	1
9. Provides me with guidance to improve my performance.	5	4	3	2	1
10. Encourages, supports, and counsels me in my pursuit of job-related training.	5	4	3	2	1
11. Provides opportunities to discuss performance problems.	5	4	3	2	1

12. Solicits input and concerns in relation
    to proposals and pending decisions.   5   4   3   2   1
13. Promotes my participation in "high-vis-
    ibility" activities.   5   4   3   2   1
14. Represents my interests and concerns to
    higher management.   5   4   3   2   1
15. Holds informal career development dis-
    cussions.   5   4   3   2   1

APPENDIX K

"Find-a-Need-and-Fill-It" Career Option Grid

	Your Current Work Group	Another Department	Another Division	The Organiza-tion as a Whole
An unrecog-nized opportu-nity				
An "impossi-ble" situation				
A nonexistent but needed service				
A new or emerging problem				
A roadblock, bottleneck, chronic short-age, weakness, or limitation				
A challenge in the interface between dif-ferent groups				
A missing piece in a pattern or sequence				
An underuti-lized resource				
An unexpected failure or suc-cess				

Appendix L

Work/Life Preference Checklist

Work/Life Preference

Place a check next to each item on the following checklist that you feel is important to your satisfaction at work. Circle the five items in each category that are most important to you.

Work Environment

_____ Growing/Successful

_____ Ethical

_____ Family-oriented

_____ Good Benefits

_____ Pays Well/Fairly

_____ Physically Clean/Safe

_____ Open/Participative

_____ Rewards Risk/Innovation

_____ Access to Recreation

_____ Adequate Parking

_____ Advancement Opportunity

_____ Entrepreneurial

_____ Strong Leadership

_____ Clear Mission

_____ Team Spirit/Morale

_____ Training Available

_____ Caring Management

_____ Gives Recognition

_____ Physically Attractive

_____ Quiet

_____ Efficient

_____ Large Organization

_____ Equal Opportunity

_____ Time Flexibility

_____ Faster Pace

_____ Slower Pace

_____ Private Office

_____ Stability

_____ Gives Feedback

_____ Child Care

_____ Shows Respect

_____ Professional

____ Dress Code   ____ Safety/Security

____ Resources Available   ____ International

____ Other/Comments _____

The Work Itself

____ Utilizes Abilities   ____ More Management Contact

____ High Visibility   ____ More Contact with Peers

____ High Structure   ____ Theoretical

____ Loose Structure   ____ Line Job

____ Emphasis on Doing   ____ Competency Valued

____ Emphasis on Managing   ____ Precision Required

____ Emphasis on Thinking   ____ Expertise Valued

____ Emphasis on Quality   ____ Task Variety

____ Emphasis on Quantity   ____ Work Alone

____ Involves Travel   ____ Work in Groups

____ No Travel   ____ Headquarters Job

____ Meaningful Outcome   ____ Field/Plant Job

____ Work with People   ____ Generalist Role

____ Work with Data/Ideas   ____ Specialist Role

____ Work with Physical Things   ____ Reliability Valued

____ Regular Hours   ____ Staff Job

____ Irregular Hours

____ Other/Comments _____

Results and Rewards of the Work (Motivations)

____ To advance or be promoted   ____ To earn financial payoffs

____ To gain control or authority   ____ To create a product or process

____ To realize a vision   ____ To build an enterprise

____ To achieve measurable results   ____ To have an impact

____ To make specific   ____ To be a change agent
     improvements
                                             ____ To compete and win
____ To master a craft or process
                                             ____ To achieve distinction
____ To gain recognition
                                             ____ To exploit hidden
____ To gain and impart expertise   opportunities

____ To pioneer or discover   ____ To achieve elite status

____ To respond to a challenge   ____ To overcome adversity

____ To meet high expectations   ____ To contribute to society

____ Other/Comments _____

_____

Lifestyle and Personal Values

____ Live an Honest Life   ____ Retire Comfortably

____ Have Leisure Time   ____ Live in Beautiful Setting

____ Live a Spiritual Life   ____ Have Many Friends

____ Be Financially Secure   ____ Be a Good Parent

____ Take Care of Family   ____ Live a Healthy Life

____ Enjoy Vacations/Travel   ____ Live Where I Want

____ Community Involvement   ____ Loving Relationship

____ Have Respect of Others   ____ Own Material Goods

____ Have Balance and Harmony   ____ Help Less Fortunate

____ Other/Comments _____

_____

Now list the 20 items you circled, from most to least important:

1. _____   11. _____

2. _____   12. _____

3. _____   13. _____

4. _____   14. _____

5. _____   15. _____

6. _____   16. _____

7. _____   17. _____

8. _____   18. _____

9. _____   19. _____

10. _____   20. _____

Notes

Introduction

1. "Occupational Outlook Quarterly," Bureau of Labor Statistics, January 2000.

2. Kim Clark, "Why It Pays to Quit," *U.S. News and World Report*, Annual Career Guide 2000, November 1, 1999.

3. Frederick Reichheld, *The Loyalty Effect: The Hidden Force behind Growth, Profits, and Lasting Value* (Cambridge, Mass.: Harvard Business School Press, 1996).

4. Sibson & Company study, cited in HR Update column, "Worker Retention Presents Challenge to U.S. Employers," *HR* magazine, September 1998.

5. Clark, "Why It Pays to Quit."

6. Manchester Partners Retention and Staffing Report, based on a survey of 378 organizations, 1998.

7. Charles Fishman, "The War for Talent," *Fast Company,* August 1998.

Truths about Turnover

1. Kepner-Tregoe survey, "Turnover: Calculating Its True Impact," *Success in Recruiting and Retaining* newsletter, National Institute of Business Management, December 1999.

2. "Turnover Rate Rises to Highest Levels in Nearly a Decade," based on study by Hewitt Associates, cited in Work Week column, *The Wall Street Journal*, October 7, 1997.

3. "The Economic Value of Employee Retention," Recreational Industry, December 1999.

4. Marie Gendron, "Keys to Retaining Your Best Managers in a Tight Job Market," *Harvard Management Update,* June 1998.

5. Peter Block, *Stewardship: Choosing Service over Self-Interest* (San Francisco: Berrett-Koehler, 1996).

6. Joshua Hyatt, "Dear Cherished Employee: You May Have Already Won $1 Million," *Inc.*, November 1999.

7. Haidee E. Allerton, "News You Can Use: Survey Says," citing America @ Work study, Aon Consulting, *Training & Development* magazine, November 1998.

8. Marcus Buckingham and Curt Coffman, *First, Break All the Rules: What the World's Greatest Managers Do Differently* (New York: Simon & Schuster, 1999).

9. "Study of the Emerging Workforce," Saratoga Institute, Interim Services, Inc., 1995.

Why Good Performers Leave

1. Marti Smye and Lesley Wright, *Corporate Abuse: How "Lean and Mean" Robs People and Profit* (New York: Macmillan, 1996).

Who *Are* the People Who Keep You in Business?

1. Charles Fishman, "The War for Talent,"*Fast Company,* August 1998.

2. Dr. John Sullivan, quoted in "Building an Employment Brand," Paul Wesman, editor, *The Right Communiqué,* volume 4, issue 2, Second Quarter 2000.

The First Key—Be a Company That People Want to Work For

1. Mort Meyerson, "Everything I Thought I Knew about Leadership Is Wrong," *Fast Company,* April/May 1996.

2. Ibid.

3. Haidee E. Allerton, "News You Can Use: Survey Says," citing America @ Work study, Aon Consulting, *Training & Development* magazine, November 1998.

4. Ibid.

5. Diane Stafford, "Employers Lose Hold on Workers," *Kansas City Star*, February 3, 1998.

6. Frederick Reichheld, *The Loyalty Effect: The Hidden Force behind Growth, Profits, and Lasting Value* (Cambridge, Mass.: Harvard Business School Press, 1996).

Retention Practice #1: Adopt A "Give-and-Get-Back" Philosophy

1. "Turnover: Calculate Its True Impact," *Success in Recruiting and Retaining Newsletter,* National Institute of Business Management, McLean, Va., December 1999.

2. Diane Stafford, "A Hero in Hiring," *Kansas City Star,* March 9, 1999.

3. Charles Fishman, "Sanity, Inc.," *Fast Company,* January 1999.

4. Sarah Fister, "A Lure for Labor," *Training,* February 1999.

5. Andrea C. Poe, "Time, for a Change," *HR* magazine, August 1999.

6. Talent Alliance, "Learning by the Numbers," *Training & Development Extra,* May 13, 1999.

7. Shelly Branch, "The 100 Best Companies for Work for in America," *Fortune,* January 11, 1999.

8. "Goals 2000: Educate America Act," U.S. Chamber of Commerce, 1996.

9. Harvey A. Hornstein, *Brutal Bosses and Their Prey* (New York: Riverhead Books, 1996).

10. Ibid.

Retention Practice #2: Measure What Counts and Pay for It

1. Marshall Goldsmith, "Retain Your Top Performers," *Zoom!* magazine, January 1998.

2. Howard Risher and Charles Fay, eds., *The Performance Imperative: Enhancing Workforce Effectiveness* (San Francisco: Jossey-Bass, 1994).

3. Scott Adams, "Dilbert," United Feature Syndicate, July 22, 1996.

4. Kim Clark, "Why It Pays to Quit," *U.S. News and World Report,* Annual Career Guide 2000, November 1, 1999.

5. "Money Talks: Hourly Hotel Workers See More Incentive Plans," Work Week column, *The Wall Street Journal,* January 6, 1998.

6. Stephen Kerr, "Risky Business: The New Pay Game," *Fortune,* July 22, 1996.

7. Ibid.

8. Peter Block, *Stewardship: Choosing Service over Self-Interest* (San Francisco: Berret-Koehler, 1996).

Retention Practice #3: Inspire Commitment to a Clear Vision and Definite Objectives

1. James C. Collins and Jerry I. Porras, *Built to Last: Successful Habits of Visionary Companies* (New York: Harper Business, 1994).

2. Kelly Barron, "Logistics in Brown," *Fortune,* January 10, 2000.

3. Collins and Porras, *Built to Last*.

4. Marc Gunther, "Those Guys Want It All," *Fortune*, February 7, 2000.

5. Brent Schlender, "Steve Jobs' Apple Gets Way Cooler," *Fortune*, January 24, 2000.

6. Peter M. Senge, *The Fifth Discipline: The Art and Practice of the Learning Organization* (New York: Currency Doubleday, 1990).

7. Collins and Porras, *Built to Last*.

8. Geoffrey Colvin, "The Ultimate Manager," *Fortune*, November 22, 1999.

9. Senge, *Fifth Discipline*.

10. Ibid.

11. Ibid.

12. Ibid.

13. Collins and Porras, *Built to Last*.

14. Gina Imperato, "How to Play the Service Game," *Fast Company*, February–March 1999.

The Second Key—Select the Right People in the First Place

1. "The Checkoff," Work Week column, *The Wall Street Journal*, Frederick Rose, editor, January 20, 1998.

2. John Cowan, "Here's a Simple Trick to Help You Hire People with Follow-Through," *Employee Recruitment & Retention*, Newsletter from Lawrence Ragan Communications, Inc., Chicago, March 2000.

Retention Practice #4: Understand Why Some Leave and Why Others Stay

1. *Retention Management: Strategies, Practices, Trends*, Saratoga Institute report sponsored by The American Management Association, New York, 1999.

2. Ruth Baum Bigus, "American Century Program Aims to Retain Staff," *Kansas City Star*, June 29, 1999.

3. Ibid.

4. Ron Lieber, "Want to Get Ahead? Get Back," *Fast Company*, July–August 1999.

5. Ibid.

6. Ibid.

7. Ibid.

8. Jack Stack, "Measuring Morale," *Inc.*, January 1997.

Retention Practice #5: Redesign the Job Itself to Make It More Rewarding

1. J. Richard Hackman and Greg R. Oldham, *Work Redesign* (Reading, Mass.: Addison-Wesley, 1980).

Retention Practice #6: Define the Results You Expect and the Talent You Need

1. William Bridges, *JobShift: How to Prosper in a World without Jobs* (San Francisco: Jossey-Bass, 1994).
2. Peter Vogt, "Acing Behavioral Interviews," *National Employment Business Weekly.*

Retention Practice #7: Ask the Questions That Require Proof of Talent

1. Herbert M. Greenberg and Jeanne Greenberg, "Right Person in Right Job Is Key to Success," *Advertising Age,* January 8, 1979.

Retention Practice #8: Give A Realistic Job Preview

1. John Paul Kotter, "The Psychological Contract: Managing the Joining-Up Process," *California Management Review* 15, 1973.

Retention Practice #9: Use Multiple Interviewers and Reference Checking

1. Joshua Hyatt, "The Screen Machine," *Inc.,* November 1999.
2. Ibid.
3. John Farr, "Better Interviews, Better Employees," *Restaurant Hospitality,* May 1999.
4. Max Messmer, "The Delicate Art of Reference Checking," *Business Credit,* May 1999.
5. James P. Miller, "Liars Index Moves Up," Work Week column, *The Wall Street Journal,* February 1, 2000.
6. Pierre Mornell, *45 Effective Ways for Hiring Smart! How to Predict Winners & Losers in the Incredibly Expensive People-Reading Game,* Berkeley, Calif.: 10 Speed Press, 1998.
7. Carol Hymowitz, "How Amazon.com Staffs a Juggernaut: It's Not about Resumes," *The Wall Street Journal,* May 4, 1999.

Retention Practice #10: Reward Employee Referrals of Successful New Hires

1. Frederick Reichheld, *The Loyalty Effect: The Hidden Force behind Growth, Profits, and Lasting Value* (Cambridge, Mass.: Harvard Business School Press, 1996).

2. Diane Stafford, "Wanted: Employment Ambassadors," *Kansas City Star*, August 26, 1999.

3. Adrian Slywotsky, "How Digital Is Your Company?" *Fast Company*, February–March 1999.

Retention Practice #11: Hire and Promote Managers Who Have the Talent to Manage People

1. Gallup Organization report on study of 100,000 employees from 2,500 businesses linking employee attitudes with critical business outcomes, 1998.

2. "Study of the Emerging Workforce," Saratoga Institute, Interim Services, Inc., 1997.

3. Retention Management study, Saratoga Institute, 1999.

4. John Sullivan, "How to Hire the Next Michael Jordan," *Fast Company*, December 1998.

5. John Sullivan, "Getting Managers to Own Retention," *Employment Management Today*, Winter 2000.

6. Brian O'Reilly, "Secrets of America's Most Admired Corporations," *Fortune*, March 3, 1997.

7. Development Dimensions International research on succession planning, *Training & Development Extra*, April 14, 1999.

8. Work Week column, *The Wall Street Journal*, November 26, 1996.

9. "Hiring Good People, "Ideas @ Work on the Air, HBS Publishing, June 2, 1999.

10. Haidee E. Allerton, "News You Can Use," *Training & Development* magazine, February 1999.

11. Marcus Buckingham and Curt Coffman, *First, Break All the Rules: What the World's Greatest Managers Do Differently* (New York: Simon & Schuster, 1999).

12. Heath Row, "Is Management for Me?" *Fast Company*, February–March 1998.

Retention Practice #12: Hire from Within When Possible

1. "Tech Firms Want Talented Employees to Switch Jobs," Work Week column, *The Wall Street Journal*, August 3, 1999.

2. Ibid.

Retention Practice #13: Creatively Expand Your Talent Pool

1. Dana Milbank, "Hiring Welfare People, Hotel Chain Finds, Is Tough, but Rewarding," *The Wall Street Journal*, October 31, 1996.

2. Adam Cohen, "Dressed for Success," *Time* magazine, July 13, 1998.

3. Catherine Yang, Ann T. Palmer, Seanna Browder, and Alice Canco, "Low Wage Lessons," *Business Week*, November 11, 1996.

4. Margaret S. Rizzo, "Desperately Seeking Applicants," *The Kansas City Star*, September 13, 1999.

5. Cora Daniels, "To Hire a Lumber Expert, Click Here," *Fortune*, April 3, 2000.

The Third Key—Get Them Off to a Great Start

1. B. L. Brown, "Career Mobility: A Choice or Necessity?" *ERIC Digest* No. 191, ERIC Clearinghouse on Adult, Career and Vocational Education, Center on Education and Training for Employment, Ohio State University, Columbus, 1998.

2. Kelly Beamon, "Just Say 'No,' " Employment Briefs, *National Business Employment Weekly*, November 24, 1998.

3. John Paul Kotter, "Psychological Contract: Managing the Joining-Up Process,"*California Management Review* 15, 1973.

Retention Practice #14: Give New Hires the Red-Carpet Treatment

1. Anne Marie Borrega, "Clean My House, and I'm Yours Forever," *Inc.*, November 1999.

Retention Practice #15: Communicate How Their Work Is Vital to the Organization's Success

1. Patrick Houston, "The Smartest Ways to Build Loyalty," *Working Woman* April 1992.

2. Dennis Murray, "What Makes This Practice Everybody's Darling?" *Medical Economics*, October 9, 1995.

Retention Practice #16: Get Commitment to a Performance Agreement

1. Hal Lancaster, "Performance Reviews: Some Bosses Try a Fresh Approach," *The Wall Street Journal*, December 1, 1998.

2. Ibid.

3. Ibid.

Retention Practice #17: Challenge Early and Often

1. 1998–99 Hay Employee Attitudes Study, Hay Group, Philadelphia, 1998.
2. Ron Lieber, "How to Design a Great First Job," *Fast Company,* June 1999.
3. Chuck Salter, "Insanity, Inc.," *Fast Company,* January 1999.
4. Ron Lieber, "First Jobs Aren't Child's Play," *Fast Company,* June 1999.
5. Ibid.
6. Ibid.

Retention Practice #18: Give Autonomy and Reward Initiative

1. Nikhil Deogun, "Man Says Boss Kept Him Chained to Desk by Chaining Him to Desk," *The Wall Street Journal,* April 2, 1996.
2. Eric Matson, "Congratulations, You're Promoted (Now What?)," *Fast Company,* June–July 1997.
3. Mark G. Becker, "Lessons in Empowerment," *Training,* September 1996.
4. 1998–99 Hay Employee Attitudes study, Hay Group, Philadelphia, 1998.
5. "We Know What to Do, but We Need Skills and Authority to Do It," Work Week column, *The Wall Street Journal,* August 26, 1997.
6. "Harrumph!" Work Week column, Frederick Rose, editor, *The Wall Street Journal,* September 2, 1997.
7. Jan Norman, "Employees Can Be Rich Source of Advice to Bosses," *Kansas City Star,* September 17, 1995.
8. Curtis Sittenfeld, "Powered by the People," *Fast Company,* July–August 1999.
9. Norman, "Employees Can Be Rich Source of Advice to Bosses," *The Kansas City Star,* September 17, 1995.
10. R. A. Heifetz and D. L. Laurie, "The Work of Leadership," *Harvard Business Review,* January–February 1997.
11. Diane Stafford, "Hotel Lets Its Workers Own Their Duties," *The Kansas City Star,* February 6, 1996.
12. Dennis T. Jaffe, Cynthia D. Scott, and Glenn R. Tobe, *Rekindling Commitment: How to Revitalize Yourself, Your Work, and Your Organization* (San Francisco: Jossey-Bass Publishers, 1993).
13. Marion E. Haynes, "Delegation: Key to Involvement," *Personnel Journal,* June 1974.

The Fourth Key—Coach and Reward to Sustain Commitment

Retention Practice #19: Proactively Manage the Performance Agreement

1. Ron Zemke, "The Corporate Coach," *Training*, December 1996.
2. Ibid.
3. Ibid.
4. Ibid.
5. Editorial, "A Little Praise Goes a Long Way in Keeping Employees on the Job," *Nation's Restaurant News*, September 26, 1994.
6. Kenneth Blanchard and Spencer Johnson, *The One-Minute Manager* (New York: William Morrow, New York, 1982).
7. Vincent Alonzo, "Employee Motivation: Talk to Me, Coach," *Incentive*, November 1996.
8. Micki Kacmar, "Faulty Evaluations," *The Kansas City Star*, March 24, 1997.
9. Michael Higgins, "Job Reviews Contain Flaws," *Kansas City Star*, March 24, 1997.
10. Zemke, "The Corporate Coach."

Retention Practice #20: Recognize Results

1. Kathy Simmons, "Mutual Benefits of Praise," *Kansas City Star*, August 29, 1999.
2. Ibid.
3. Frederick Herzberg, "One More Time: How Do You Motivate Employees?" *Harvard Business Review*, January–February 1968.
4. Bob Nelson, *1001 Ways to Reward Employees* (New York: Workman, 1994).
5. Ibid.
6. Phillip C. Grant, "How to Make a Formal Rewards Program Work," from *Personnel* journal, as cited in Bob Nelson, *1001 Ways to Reward Employees* (New York: Workman Publishing, 1994).
7. "Thanks a Bunch," Work Week column, Glenn Burkins, editor, *The Wall Street Journal*, September 7, 1999.
8. Michael LeBoeuf, *The Greatest Management Principle in the World* (New York: Putnam, 1985).
9. Jan Norman, "Recognition of Peers Can Be Great Compensation," *Orange County Register*, January 27, 1997.

10. Cora Daniels, "Thank-You Is Nice, But This Is Better," *Inc.,* November 1999.

11. Phaedra Hise, "Avoid the Stuff That Sucks," *Inc.,* November 1999.

12. Tom Terez, "Acknowledgement," *MeaningfulWork.Com,* September 13, 1999.

Retention Practice #21: Train Managers in Career Coaching and Expect Them to Do It

1. Adapted from *Special Report: Retooling Corporate Recruitment and Retention Strategies* by BDO Seidman LLP, Accountants and Consultants, Milwaukee, 1999.

2. Isabel Briggs Myers, Mary H. McCaulley, Naomi L. Quenk, and Allen L. Hammer, *The Myers-Briggs Type Indicator Manual, Third Edition* (Palo Alto: Consulting Psychologists Press, 1998).

Retention Practice #22: Give Employees the Tools for Taking Charge of Their Careers

1. Adapted from: David Noer, *Healing the Wounds: Overcoming the Trauma of Layoffs and Revitalizing Downsized Organizations* (San Francisco: Jossey-Bass, 1993).

2. William Bridges, *JobShift: How to Prosper in a World without Jobs* (San Francisco: Jossey-Bass, 1996).

3. Hal Lancaster, "That Next Promotion Could Be a Position of Your Own Design," *The Wall Street Journal,* November 26, 1996.

4. Ibid.

5. Ibid.

6. William Bridges, "Job Shift" Seminar Guide, William Bridges & Associates, 1996.

7. James E. Swails, "When Bottom Up Doesn't Work," *HR* magazine, August 1995.

8. Peter Ducker, "Managing Oneself," *Harvard Business Review,* March–April 1999.

9. Pamela Leigh, "The New Spirit at Work," *Training & Development,* March 1997.

10. Hal Lancaster, "You and Only You Must Stay in Charge of Your Employability," *The Wall Street Journal,* 1999.

11. Jodi Davis, "Leadership: The Role of Mentoring," Presentation, Kansas City, Missouri, October 14, 1999.

12. Christopher A. Bartlett and Sumatra Goshal, "Changing the Role of Top Management: Beyond Systems to People," *Harvard Business Review,* May–June 1995.

Retention Practice #23: Know When to Keep and When to Let Go

1. Stanley Herz, "Knowing When to Fire Key to Maintaining Control," *National Business Employment Weekly*, August 21, 1983.

2. Marcus Buckingham and Curt Coffman, *First, Break All the Rules: What the World's Greatest Managers Do Differently* (New York: Simon & Schuster, 1999).

3. "Hate to See You Go . . . ," *Training*, February 1999.

4. P. J. Adam, "Downsized Up," *Ingram's Magazine*, February 1997.

Retention Practice #24: Have More Fun!

1. Quoted in Phaedra Brotherton, "The Company That Plays Together . . . ," *HR* magazine, December 1996.

2. Erika Gerber, "Job Titles of the Future," *Fast Company,* July–August 1999.

3. Several examples from Bob Nelson, *1001 Ways to Reward Employees* (New York: Workman Publishing 1994), and from Brotherton, ibid.

Selective Retention: Planning to Keep the Right People

1. Patti L. Hanson, "Why Employees Leave: The Root Cause of Employee Departure," *Employment Management Today,* Winter 2000.

Keeping *All* the People Who Keep You in Business

1. Primary source for this section: Katherine Sty, Richard Griffin, and Marcie Schorr Hirsch, *Workplace Diversity* (Holbrook, Mass.: Adams Media Corporation, 1995).

2. Ibid.

3. Primary source for this section: Ron Zemke, Claire Raines, and Bob Filipczak, *Generations at Work* (New York: AMACOM, 2000).

4. Bruce Tulgan, *The Manager's Pocket Guide to Generation X* (Amherst, Mass.: HRD Press, 1997).

5. Zemke, Raines, and Filipczak, *Generations at Work.*

6. Tulgan, *The Manager's Pocket Guide to Generation X.*

7. "Lessons Learned from Mergers & Acquisitions: Best Practices in Workforce Integration," *Right Management Consultants Research Report,* Philadelphia, 1999.

8. "The Right Way to Deal with Downsizing," Right Associates Research Report in *Benefits* magazine, May 1993.

9. Mitchell Lee Marks and Philip Mirvis, "Merger Syndrome: Stress and Uncertainty," *Mergers & Acquisitions*, Summer 1985.

10. Diane Stafford, "Mergers Can Take Emotional Toll on Employees, Studies Show," *Kansas City Star*, October 7, 1999.

Index